The Politics of Law Enforcement

The Politics of Law Enforcement

Conflict and Power in Urban Communities

Alan Edward Bent
Memphis State University

Lexington Books
D.C. Heath and Company
Lexington, Massachusetts
Toronto   London

Library of Congress Cataloging in Publication Data

Bent, Alan Edward.
The politics of law enforcement.

1. Police—United States. 2. Public relations—Police. I. Title.
HV8138.B45   363.2'0973   73-18415
ISBN 0-669-92486-5

Published simultaneously in Canada.

Printed in the United States of America.

International Standard Book Number: 0-669-92486-5

Library of Congress Catalog Card Number: 73-18415

Contents

Contents

List of Tables

Preface

This book is about organizational power and conflict and focuses on the police as instruments for analysis. The police are studied for their political interest in obtaining power as individuals within the organization and collectively within the community. Collective police power is measured by the extent of their discretionary authority and freedom from external controls; individual power is perceived by the rational strategies on the part of police officials striving to attain or consolidate their personal power positions in the organization. Implicit in the police's struggle for power —both personal and collective—is the existence of conflict with challenging institutional and environmental forces and actors. The arena of conflict is wherever law enforcement takes place in urban America.

Public institutions exist to serve the needs and expectations of society. The police are one such institution—an arm of government whose creation and existence is necessitated by the imperfections of human behavior. The police are primarily an agency of social control, undoubtedly the "control agency of last resort" made obligatory by the inadequacies of the primary agents of social control: the family, the church, the school. and peer groups. It is the public agency charged with maintaining control over individuals and groups to insure their conformity with society's laws and norms.

The police task of control is more difficult the more the community is urbanized. The larger the community, the more heterogeneous and less stable it is, and the more likely that the primary group is weakened as an agent of social control. The diversities of urban society also promote disagreement about norms of behavior, compelling the imposition of norms on the population by the designated agency of social control—the police.

The demands upon police services in an urban society have been increased by the stresses existing within the communities. The tensions of an urban environment have led to a universal increase in crime and violence. This has created pressing requirements on the police by challenging law enforcement capabilities and effectiveness, while at the same time generating concern about the expanded role of the police in urban society. Law enforcement and police operations affect the democratic process more crucially than any other aspect of public policy. As the enforcement arm of the judicial system and as the designated agency of social control, the police possess far greater authority than almost any other public agency. If unrestrained, police activities have latent and manifest ways of affecting all citizens—lawbreakers and lawabiders alike—and this capability for antidemocratic behavior makes the police suspect.

Urban society, beset by increases in crime and violence and the growing irrelevancy of primary socializing agents, must look to the police, the institutionalized control agency, for the preservation of peace, order, and tranquillity in the community. The dilemma of a democratic society is how to give the police sufficient power to perform their role effectively, while at the same time maintaining restraints on the police in order to prevent abuses to democratic principles. Properly controlled, the police become a servant of the criminal justice system; unchecked, the potential abuse of police power could allow it to become master of the judicial system to the demise of liberty and justice.

This book looks at the discretionary conduct of policemen and whether adequate accountability measures exist—and, if not, whether they can be realized, while allowing for the necessary development of police capabilities in the performance of requisite functions. In its focus on the behavior of police officials and the relationship of the police bureaucracy to the urban political system, the work strives to be both descriptive and prescriptive.

The book first considers the police as a bureaucracy whose agents possess an extraordinary amount of discretionary authority. Evidence presented concerning the abuse of this authority and cases of police corruption argues for making the police accountable for their practices and behavior.

The character of law enforcement is determined by the attitudes and perceptions of individual policemen. The police officer's work-personality, which determines his choice of actions—to arrest or not to arrest, to use force or not to use force, and other job-related decisions—is seen as formed by institutional and environmental influences. These influences are examined in an analysis of the screening and selection process of police agencies, the occupational environment of law enforcement, conditions and attitudes toward law enforcement in the community, and police peer group socialization and reinforcement for their aggregated impact on the shaping of the policeman's work-personality. Cases and experiences of police practices serve to dramatize the effect of this relationship.

The interaction of the police and society is also viewed through police-community relations programs, which are explored in terms of "grass-roots" politics in hostile environments. Case studies of the programs existing in three cities are described and analyzed for their viability. Next, the political environment of the police bureaucracy receives in-depth attention. The analysis examines the accountability of law enforcement through internal and external controls over police practices and behavior. Also, the recent politicization of the police, with overt acts demonstrating their political "muscle," is examined for the countervailing attributes that these political activities may have in vitiating existing accountability measures and mechanisms. (The term *political* here is all-inclusive and embraces police union activities on behalf of occupational ends as these are pursued by traditionally political means.) Models of accountability and counteracting police political behavior are presented by case studies of real events and personalities.

The character of the police bureaucracy and its inclination toward bureaucratic reform are affected by the perceptions and expectations of citizens about the police. The degree to which the police perform their tasks in accordance with community values and needs, and the degree to which the police and the community share perceptions of values and law enforcement norms, is analyzed by identifying and measuring certain variables. Results were obtained by using an attitude survey that tested the correlation of sociopolitical attitudes of a sample of an urban police department and a sample of citizens in the community. The survey was conducted to measure the correlation of police-civilian attitudes concerning law enforcement requisites, and the demographic and political segment of the civilian population that the police best represent. Significant findings of this study are discussed in chapter 5.

To illustrate the relevance of the book's depictions and hypotheses, in-depth case studies are presented in chapters 6 and 7. The first of these chapters deals with the history of a police officer who ended up as the police chief of an urban department by skillfully manipulating the system of rewards and punishments existing in the agency and in the political environment. This was obtained from a series of personal interviews with the recently retired chief, and was substantiated by press accounts of the incidents mentioned.

The second illustrative chapter explores the most recent occupational practices and political involvement of the same police department since the departure of this police chief. These actual events expose the inadequacies of police accountability mechanisms and the virtually free hand that the police have in the interpretation and performance of their functions. The book concludes with an evaluation of contemporary conditions involving urban police and suggests alternatives to provide the maximum degree of democratic responsiveness and accountability consistent with the accepted societal responsibilities of the enforcement arm of the criminal justice system in a democracy.

Data for the book was obtained from a variety of sources: on-the-scene observation of police operations in several communities included many hours of riding in police patrol cars, witnessing a variety of police activities, and the interviewing of police personnel of different ranks in station houses, on the street, and in social settings. First-hand experience was complemented by an examination of existing research material and literature about police activities and personalities in a number of urban locations. Additionally, public officials, private citizens, and news media personnel were interviewed for their insights into local political practices and their perception of the role of the police in the local political system. Finally, computer analysis was applied to the attitude survey of police and civilian populations.

At the outset it must be admitted that it is difficult to do research of police departments. The prevailing atmosphere in the police is one of suspicion of outsiders, especially of academicians. The guardedness and occasional hostility of some police officials can be characterized by a conversation with a staff aide to the chief of police of the Memphis department. Before submitting to an interview, he wanted to know about the book's theme. When told about it, he responded: "That's useless muckraking. Why don't you just write about police professionalism?" This effectively terminated the interview.

Fortunately, many others—both within and outside the police—were extremely helpful in the development of this work. Because it would be impossible to name all the police officers from the several cities visited who contributed their thoughts and opinions—and because some of them would wish to remain anonymous—I wish to express my thanks to them in the aggregate.

I am especially indebted to Henry Lux, formerly chief of police of Memphis and presently assistant director of the Institute of Criminal Justice at Memphis State University. Mr. Lux submitted to a number of lengthy interviews about himself, and his refreshing candor and remarkable memory of events made chapter 6 possible. My thanks also go to Inspector Bill Wannamaker of the Memphis police, who saw to the distribution of the survey questionaire to a representative sample of the city's police officers. Without this help, chapter 5 could not have been written.

I am grateful to a number of other people whose insights, counsel, and skills helped me with the book. My former colleague at Memphis State University William R. ("Dick") Nelson read and edited the original manuscript and provided me with valuable advice about inclusions and exclusions of material. Other colleagues at Memphis State were also helpful: Yung Wei read chapter 5, giving me the benefit of his comments about its contents, and Ralph A. Rossum and Paul C. Peterson provided their thoughts about some of the book's conclusions.

My research assistant, Jeffrey S. Gross, contributed to every phase of the project that resulted in the writing of chapter 5, and his tireless efforts were invaluable. Martin Toma, Khalil Jahshan, and Hershel Lipow, graduate assistants in the Department of Political Science, Memphis State University, gave devoted service in support of the acquisition of background material for the work. Kathleen Mulligan and Jack Owens, students at Memphis State, did yeoman work in interviewing scores of respondents for the survey undertaken for chapter 5. The Memphis State University

Computer Center provided the use of their computers, and Kurt Kunzel assisted in the programming for the survey in chapter 5. The work leading to the writing of chapter 5 was supported by a grant from Memphis State University Research Fund.

I am indebted to Kenneth Crocker and Robert McCullough, former police officers, for contributing information about the "realities" of the police occupational environment and law enforcement practices. Dallas Gatewood, reporter for the Memphis *Commercial Appeal,* provided insights into the political culture in Memphis, and his recounted experiences of his days as a police reporter in this city were enlightening. My thanks go to Ed Ray, managing editor of the *Memphis Press-Scimitar,* for allowing me to use the data, tables, and findings from a series of articles published by the newspaper, done by staff writers Barney DuBois and Menno Duerksen, about the Memphis Police Department. Norman Brewer, former news director for WMC-TV in Memphis, was kind enough to furnish me with transcripts of his editorial telecasts, the "Norman Brewer Report," that dealt with the Memphis police. And Robert D. Gordon, executive director of the International Conference of Police Associations, helpfully forwarded me materials concerning his organization. Last, but not least, a special acknowledgment is owed my secretary, Mrs. Laura Ingram, who labored through several copies of the manuscript that finally resulted in the version at hand.

Each of these people, in his or her own way, improved the quality of the work, but none bears a responsibility for any errors of omission or commission that may have resulted. I am solely responsible for those.

Alan Edward Bent
Memphis, Tennessee
September 1973

1 Police: The Extraordinary Bureaucracy

If all men were perfect there would be no need for formal agencies to guard against human behavior detrimental to the lives, property, and well-being of society. But the human race is not made up of angels; it depends on the civilizing influences of the family, the church, schools, and other institutions to regulate behavior. And where these institutions prove inadequate or incapable of fulfilling their role, especially amid the socially dysfunctional stresses of an urban society, the maintenance of order and safety necessitates the creation of police agencies by the State.

The need for the police as an agency of social control exists in totalitarian and democratic societies alike. In a totalitarian state, the task of the police is relatively simple, because the maintenance of the social order takes priority over individual freedom and justice. In a democracy, however, the job of the police is regulated by the need to reconcile their objective of preserving order and safety with the democratic imperatives of personal freedom. Ultimately, the resolution of this dilemma is left up to the individual police officer, whose authority allows him to make on-the-spot decisions affecting the lives of citizens.

The license to deprive any citizen of his freedom and to use force—even deadly force—while acting in an official capacity gives every police officer an awesome authority. The improper use of these powers by law enforcement agents poses a threat to democratic order and safety. The enforcement of order and safety becomes meaningless if in the process the police violate the integrity of law and justice in the performance of their duties. In view of this, it is understandable that the conduct of police officers and their supervisors is of grave concern. The enforcement of order in democratic society, while an indispensable pursuit, must never be undertaken at the expense of liberty and personal freedom. Order enforced by police in a manner that abuses their responsibilities is, in effect, the legitimization of institutionalized disorder with dire consequences for democratic principles and ideals. To safeguard these values, it is essential that police officers be accountable for their actions.

Immediate significance must be attached to the role of the police because of their relationship to political authority. The police are the internal enforcement arm of the State, the domestic paramilitary counterpart of the armed forces, empowered with the responsibility for providing order so that the State can maintain the stability necessary for various social ac-

1

tivities. The enforcement of order is essential for the preservation of the State, and the police, as the agents charged with this responsibility, are intrinsic to this function at all levels of government.[1] The crucial importance of police functions to the maintenance of political authority results in an unusual amount of bureaucratic power for the police.

As a significant official bureaucracy, the police display a unique range of characteristics: symbolic personification of the political system, visibility, multiplicity of functions, discretion in performing these functions, and a monopoly on the legitimate use of force.[2] The extent and character of the mutual interaction between the police and the environment and their association with political authority make the police an extraordinary bureaucracy.

Their symbolic capacity exists because to the average citizen the beat patrolman represents the American political system, by being and acting as the most visible public official. It is at the street level that the role of the police in enforcing the official laws of the State becomes inextricably linked with the values that those laws embody. As with any formal institution of government, the police bureaucracy is a product of the cultural values of the society that produces it and within which it operates. However, the policeman at the street level not only symbolizes the authority of the State by allocating and distributing order in the community according to culturally and legally defined norms of "proper" behavior; he also possesses the capacity to decide which acts violate those norms.[3] This allows him the discretion to interpret behavior according to a personal set of definitions, with the prerogative to initiate the criminal justice process if the behavior, in his opinion, is illegal or immoral.

Related to the policeman's capacity as the omnipresent symbol of governmental authority is his visibility; he is the most conspicuous of all front-line bureaucrats. The working life of the beat patrolman as a street-level bureaucrat necessarily has always taken place in the "fishbowl of his environment."[4] Visibility is extended by the large numbers of police officials, with more than 300,000 men and women employed in the nation's 40,000 separate police agencies. In excess of 200,000 of these officers serve in 39,695 agencies of counties and smaller units of government; 110,000 work in the large departments of cities with populations over 250,000. The largest police department in the nation is New York City's with a complement of approximately 32,000 police officers.[5]

The symbolic capacity and visibility of the police are not only products of their large numbers and distinctive uniforms but also result from the multiplicity of the roles they perform in their extensive contact with the public. Conventional versions of the police role refer to the preservation of peace and the protection of life and property, the prevention of crime, the enforcement of laws, and the arresting of offenders.[6] However, urban social conditions and needs have led to a range of police services that go beyond the traditional role concepts of prevention and control cf crime. Depending on the political and social setting and the particular needs of the urban environment served, the police, in addition to their conventional concerns, may also be responsible for such activities as protection of public safety through the regulation of traffic and parking, inspection of buildings, issuance of permits, licensing and traffic control, guarding of public morals through censorship of books, movies, and plays, and myriad social welfare functions for lower socioeconomic groups.[7]

The wide variety of service functions performed by the police aid in the fulfillment of community life, for the police by their activities have gone beyond just being formal control agencies responsible for law enforcement and now also help fill the vacuum created by the breaking down of more specialized agencies of social control by acting as their surrogates. The ever expanding duties of the policeman that require a capacity for versatility justifies Ramsey Clark's description of skill essentials:

Law enforcer and lawyer, scientist in a whole range of physical sciences —chemistry, physics, electronics—medic, psychologist, social worker, human relations and race relations expert, marriage counselor, youth adviser, athlete, public servant—these are but a few of the many skills a major police department must exercise daily. Individual policemen must personally possess many of them—and perform them with excellence. Safety, life and property, equal justice, liberty, confidence in government and in the purpose of our laws will depend on it.[8]

The significance of the police looms even larger when the aspects of symbolic capacity, visibility, and multiplicity of functions are coupled with police discretionary power and the possession of a virtual monopoly on the use of legal force. In addition to their unique role of enforcing and reinforcing the norms of society at the street level, the police are allowed great latitude and discretion with the lives and welfare of citizens.[9] Unlike other complex organizations, which are based on principles of administrative efficiency and which utilize standardized rules and procedures to facilitate the tasks of acting officials, it is difficult, or even impossible, for the police to adhere to set rules or general principles. With upwards of 30,000 federal, state, and local statutes to uphold, the average policeman is faced with a monumental task of applying these laws evenly and performing his duties in a set standard of behavior. Theoretically, the multiplicity of laws may be construed as a traditional administrative device to define conditions of illegal or disorderly behavior that the policeman may encounter, thereby precluding any discretionary responsibility on the part of the individual police officer. In actuality, however, the overload of statutes has made impractical the mechanical application of law by the police. Instead, this overload invites the influence of prejudices of individual police officers or police behavior guided by special interests of an administrative or distinctly political nature, resulting in the law being administered unevenly and selectively.[10]

Policemen typically work alone or in pairs, and discretionary authority occurs because field supervision is made difficult by the wide dispersal of police officers at any given moment. They are generally left to their own devices because departmental rules and regulations are often unrealistic and there is a general absence of administrative rules and guidelines dealing with the complex human interrelationships faced daily by police officers.[11] Lacking supervision and adequate guidelines, each policeman is left to choose the standard of service and behavior for application in his area of responsibility. The patrolman on the beat thus becomes a policy-forming administrator in miniature, "who operates beyond the scope of the usual devices for control."[12] Furthermore, the police have employed "job action" tactics—strike, slowdown, overenforcement, or the "blue flu" —which serve to "ignore or fail to support the implementation of public policy or vitiate the law."[13]

The "nonmechanical," or nonbureaucratic, aspects of police behavior are not only reflected in street-level policy making but in discretionary decisions hidden from public view. The policeman is armed with the authority to perform such overt acts as shooting or arresting people, but in addition, the setting of the policeman's role offers the opportunity to make decisions that are often "hidden." Whether the criminal process is initiated or not—a suspect apprehended or not, a traffic citation issued or not, etc.—is up to the discretion of each patrolman. The discretion and autonomy of day-to-day police work allows for decisions, affected by direct interaction with the suspect, about whether to enforce or ignore particular violations and infractions.[14]

To complete the list of untypical powers and capabilities possessed by the police among public agencies it is necessary to consider that, as the internal enforcement arm of the State, the police maintain a monopoly on the legitimate means of violence. The police have the power to use coercion in the arrest process, and the use of violence in making arrests is within the discretionary authority of every police officer. The use of violence as a legitimate means of law enforcement has not only served the police in their function of crime prevention and control, but has also historically made police action the source of riots and crime.

The extraordinary panoply of powers and authority granted the police raise questions of compatibility with the democratic process. In a democracy it is imperative that a public organization so omnipotent as the police be thoroughly accountable to the political system it serves. Otherwise, the goals of law and order and the means to achieve them may easily come in conflict with concepts of justice and morality. The enshrinement of law enforcement at the expense of personal rights of citizens is inimical to a democratic political system. Other social agents, especially the political system, must safeguard the rights and liberties of citizens, and at times constraints must be placed on police activity and processes. To protect the rights of all citizens the police must be held accountable for their actions and behavior. To do otherwise is to allow a monolithic public bureaucracy to have its officials acting autonomously as judges, jury, and executioners, if they are so inclined.

The courts have been active in restraining the arbitrariness of the police, especially when their acts violate the personal freedom of individuals. A series of court decisions since *Weeks v. United States* in 1914 has stressed the need for impartiality in police action and the protection of individual rights through guarantees of fair play. *Mapp v. Ohio* in 1961 held that neither state nor federal courts can accept evidence obtained by law enforcement officers in violation of the constitutional protection against unreasonable search and seizure.

In 1963, *Gideon v. Wainwright* established that any indigent person accused of a felony is entitled to free legal counsel. In 1964 the Supreme Court held, in *Escobedo v. Illinois,* that it is the constitutional right of an indigent to be afforded legal counsel at the time of police interrogation. Finally, in 1966, *Miranda v. Arizona* combined and enlarged on the effects of the *Gideon* and *Escobedo* decisions by ruling that the police at the time of custodial interrogation must warn suspects that they need not make a statement, that if they do, it can be used against them, that they are entitled to legal counsel, and that a lawyer will be provided if they cannot afford to hire one.

There have been other landmark decisions influencing the integrity of law enforcement. *Rochin v. California* (1952) involved a narcotics arrest where police officers pumped a suspect's stomach to obtain the swallowed evidence. The court did not admit the evidence, ruling that it was gained through "conduct that shocks the conscience." *Katz v. United States* (1967) imposed a limitation on the use of electronic surveillance by law enforcement officials. The effect of the decision was to restrict the arbitrary use of these techniques by requiring court orders prior to their utilization. The use of court orders for permission to employ electronic surveillance or wire taps was seen as being much the same as needing court warrants for the search for material evidence. In 1969, *Chimel v. California* restricted the physical vicinity that can be searched without a warrant as incidental to an arrest to the area within the immediate control of the suspect.

An elemental obstacle to police openness and accountability is the bureaucratic nature of law enforcement. Bureaucracies create "symbols and myths'' to form a mystique about themselves and to enable a separation of the bureaucracy from the citizenry.[15] Mouzelis writes that according to Marx,

Bureaucracy becomes an autonomous and oppressive force which is felt by the majority of the people as a mysterious and distant entity—as something which, although regulating their lives, is beyond their control and comprehension, a sort of divinity in the face of which one feels helpless and bewildered. And, of course, this attitude is reinforced by the bureaucrats' creation of special myths and symbols which sanctify and mystify further his position. It is in this way that bureaucracy becomes a closed world. A sort of caste jealously guards its secrets and prerogatives, presenting to the outside world a united front of silence and hostility.[16]

The police have long practiced bureaucratic secrecy to the exacerbation of relations with the community. Tensions between citizens and the police have grown in recent years so that in city after city police are finding it difficult to maintain the barrier of bureaucratic secrecy as a way of neutralizing citizen demands.[17] Additionally, the unparalleled autonomy and authority possessed by police officials makes bureaucratic secrecy dangerous, as well as irrelevant, in view of the potential and actual hazards that this may cause the rights of citizens. Secrecy impedes accountability in a fundamental way by obscuring illegal and arbitrary acts from public scrutiny.

Law enforcement in a democracy requires the adherence of the police bureaucracy to a democratic value system. This means that the procedures and processes of the police should be circumscribed by such social values as procedural rights, civil liberties, freedom, justice, and human dignity. Unfortunately, the police, in order to facilitate their tasks, may forsake these values in favor of law enforcement efficiency. In a democracy, it should never be made "easy" for the police, for "easy" law enforcement does violence to the rule of law and allows the police to act as masters of the law rather than as its servants.

If power corrupts and absolute power corrupts absolutely, then the police, because of the extraordinary latitude allowed them, are in danger of this condition. The potential for self-aggrandizement is aided by the insulation of the police bureaucracy from the environment it serves. Despite the controls imposed by the judiciary, the peril exists that the police may be corrupted by a commitment to institutional or personal values over the value system of the community. The type of incestuous insularity bred by bureaucratic secrecy and "myths and symbols" loses touch with reality and confuses the loyalty of the organization. In the case of the police the loyalty affected may be that toward society and its norms, values, and laws. Most obviously the police must not be able to develop into an insular organization capable of prejudicing the law they were empowered to enforce, and steps must be taken to counteract this if they already have done so.

The avoidance of an undue concentration of power in the police bureaucracy needs the presence of access channels for inputs by the community so that citizens can play a part in shaping the character of law enforcement agencies. The interjection of outside interests reflecting the social values of the community into the police bureaucracy is useful in influencing the police to a more realistic awareness and observance of these values. For this access to be effective, however, it must be a legitimate form of activity for guiding and controlling police practices. The right of access by the community, essential as a check on bureaucratic behavior, counts for little unless there is a responsiveness on the part of the bureaucracy to the articulated needs of the public.

The availability of access is but one element of protection for those subject to police bureaucracy. Emmette Redford's list of essentials for protection from administrative abuse includes, in addition to the right of access, the right to know, the rule against bias, and the right to appeal.[18] It is up to the political system that created the formal institutions of law enforcement to insure the availability of adequate controls over police behavior and processes. To neglect this responsibility leads to the questioning of the system's commitment to democratic values.

The term *police state,* opprobriously ascribed to totalitarian regimes, is not applied simply because the police are nationally organized, for if this were the case, England, Denmark, Sweden, and Belgium would fit the description of police states. In totalitarian and free nations alike, police power is controlled by the government, but the crucial distinction is that in a totalitarian state the government acknowledges no accountability, whereas in a free country, the police are answerable to the law and to a democratically elected political body. The test of a free society, therefore, is not a question of whether a police bureaucracy, or any particular form of organization, is nationally or locally organized, but rather of whether the instruments of government—especially as crucial an instrument as the police—are accountable to the elected representatives of the people and to the community as a whole.[19]

Supporters of the present American police system are inclined to wave the red herring of a nationally organized police department as the sole indicator of the abuse of police powers. By contrast, the American example of the local organization of police departments is offered as a paradigm of democratic practice. Local police departments, the argument runs, assure community control over the police; a police department made up of friends and neighbors, protecting the lives and property of their fellow citizens, and subject to their control.[20] Unfortunately, the history of American police malpractice does not sustain the wisdom of local control over law enforcement, either in regard to improved law enforcement or to the viability of accountability measures over the police bureaucracy.

In 1931 a study performed by the National Commission on Law Observance and Enforcement, the Wickersham Commission, "found [police] practices so appalling and sadistic as to pose no intellectual issue for civilized men."[21] Jerome Skolnick writes that

> in reading about the American police, especially through the period of 1930's, one feels that constitutional issues of legality have been almost too remote to be of immediate concern. . . . For many municipal forces in the United States, the observer's question is, therefore, not whether the police operate under the constraints of due process of law, but whether they operated within the bounds of civilized conduct.[22]

Students of earlier police behavior and practices discovered these departments to be riddled with corruption and brutality and to be filled with political appointees.

Interestingly, the brutality of the old-fashioned police departments often went hand in hand with corruption. Pete Hamill's description of some of the exploits of an officer who operated during this era depicts the afflictions that beset the police department.

> [Johnny] Broderick was a cop who worked around Broadway during the 30's, after an earlier career beating up people during fur strikes. Often he served as arresting officer, jury, judge and punisher all in the same arrest. "Legalismo is a lot of bunk," Broderick once said, and there are some cops who still agree with him. . . . Broderick seemed to spend a lot of time in a macho contest with small-time hoodlums. It is interesting, but not crucial, to remember that when he left the force, there were rumors that he was too friendly with bigger fry. . . . and that at the height of his glory nobody could quite understand how Broderick could drive a Cadillac, wear monogrammed silk underwear and live lavishly on a salary that couldn't have been much more than $4,000 a year.[23]

It is not surprising that traditional reform concerns about the American police had stressed an improvement in the quality of personnel rather than any abstract philosophies of policing.[24]

Protracted criticism of the police by private persons, by the press, and by many groups occasioned by reported incidents of police malpractice suggests that many departments are still guilty of misconduct. The most common forms involve the abuse of police authority and police corruption. The arbitrary use of the "club, blackjack, and gun" found by the Wickersham Commission in 1931 is still endemic to the police. The use of excessive force is not only statistically routine but is often regarded by the police as legitimate.[25] The rationalization of the legitimacy of police violence is a function of the socialization of police officers to their bureaucratic myths and symbols, which stress the position of authority of policemen. Socially inculcated with a sense of self-importance by virtue of personifying the endowed authority of the bureaucracy, the police officer is apt to be confused about his personal relationship to his authority position. Possessing discretion over his behavior and without benefit of professional standards by which to guide this behavior, police officials may not always be capable of distinguishing between citizen attacks on their authority position from personal attacks on them as holders of that position. When this occurs, a perceived threat to authority may result in action that is more a fulfillment of personal needs than the disinterested enforcement of law. Excessive use of force may result when police officials overreact to citizen opposition to their invocation of authority. "Simply stated, the police believe that the key to law and order is considerable citizen respect for the individual policeman and that the way to instill such respect in those who lack it is with a night stick, a black jack or a squirt of MACE in the face."[26]

Exposures of corruption have been common historically. The Reverend Charles W. Parkhurst in the 1890s shocked his Victorian parishioners in New York with his accounts of the drinking, gambling, and sex that he uncovered through personal investigation. As was the case then, establishments catering to the indulgences of society continue to exist with the consent of the police. "'There is no harm in a little honest graft,' New York policemen have been saying for decades, arguing that when people want to gamble or drink when they shouldn't or party with a pretty girl for pay, it's their business, isn't it? What's the harm in it?"[27]

In New York City, graft paid to the police for the protection of illegal activities has been estimated by reliable experts to run into the millions of dollars annually.[28] The Knapp Commission's investigation of police corruption in that city uncovered widespread graft in the areas of "gambling, narcotics, prostitution, liquor, construction, hotels, tow trucking, and bodegas (small groceries in Spanish-language neighborhoods)."[29] Although narcotics is known to be the largest single source of graft in terms of total dollars, protection for gambling has been the most corrupting influence on police departments. Gambling graft has been exposed by former Congressman Adam Clayton Powell, Jr., as the source of the wholesale corruption of the police in Harlem. Powell read into the *Congressional Record* details of the typical payoffs resulting from the protection of illegal gambling: "Each numbers banker has to pay from $2,500 to $3,500 a month in protection ranging from the top of the division down to the lieutenants, sergeants, uniformed officers, two shifts of radio cars, all the detective squad including plainclothesmen, lieutenants and sergeants."[30] Graft payoffs in Harlem are so lucrative that police officers—black and white—are known to compete for appointments to that section of New York in order to cash in on these profits. Gambling and other activities that are loosely categorized as crimes involving morals—crimes that do not involve personal injury or theft—flourish because the public and the police wink at them. This attitude about "crimes without victims" has made the policing of these activities a waste of time and law enforcement manpower, causing some reformers to propose their legalization as a realistic observance of society's mores.

The thing to do is to bring all forms of gambling into the open, legalize everything, including casino gambling, Vegas style, and release those cops for more important duties. The average citizen does not feel that gambling is a crime; neither does the average cop, which is why gambling has been a source of more generalized police corruption than any other "crime."[31]

New York's police corruption is not peculiar to this city alone, and it is probably typical of police malpractice throughout the nation. The differences among corrupt police departments depends upon the extent of corruption and the degree of willingness of public and police officials to accept police corruption as a fact and to institute adequate accountability controls to minimize it. Michael Armstrong, an investigator for the Knapp Commission, stated: "It is not a question of a few rotten apples in the barrel. It is a question of finding a few good apples in the barrel."[32]

The exposure of police corruption is made difficult by the intensive inbredness of police departments and the reluctance of public officials to back investigatory efforts for various reasons. One of the strengths of the Knapp Commission, according to Whitman Knapp, who headed the commission, was that it had the support of Mayor John V. Lindsay and Police Commissioner Patrick V. Murphy. [33] However, knowledge about the corrupt practices found in police departments across the nation, as provided by other investigations and from the testimony of police officers, suggests the universality of this problem. In 1972, James C. Parsons, chief of police in Birmingham, Alabama, wrote about his personal observation of police corruption:

Recently I participated in a conference with several nationally noted police chiefs and during a dinner discussion the conversation turned to police corruption. As I expected, the chiefs were reluctant to even discuss the issue. One chief in a very large resort city stated that he would be surprised if 5 percent of his force was on the take. I do not believe that the chief was naive nor do I think he was unintelligent. In many private conversations with officers from lower ranks most will admit to a much higher percentage.

I personally can remember standing at roll call in a large room full of officers and knew that each and every one of them was on the take. I do not feel that it is unusual to make such statements, for I have heard other officers from other departments express the same sentiments.[34]

An officer with over three years service in the Memphis police department was interviewed in 1972 by two *Memphis Press-Scimitar* reporters.

Understandably preferring to remain anonymous, the officer "agreed to having his comments taped, giving names, dates and locations in connection with incidents he described as police bribe-taking, stealing and burglarizing by patrolmen, the rolling of drunks by officers and misconduct by higher officers."[35] The officer was quoted as saying that he was taking a big chance by talking.

"I've been told that I'd better not start my car in the morning. I've been told my kid was going to get killed going to school. Or that I might get shot on a prowler call.

"There's one thing I want to clear up. They're going to take these new policemen and put them with these crooked s.o.b.'s and they're going to ruin them. And that's got to stop."

"I love being a policeman. It's a good job, but I'm sick of the corruption. I want to see it stopped. I don't care if it puts 100 policemen in jail to do it.

"I want to be able to walk out of the house and when somebody sees me, rather than think 'Here comes a thief,' I want them to think, 'Here comes a policeman.'"

True to the bureaucratic practice of maintaining barriers between itself and the public, police officials have resisted investigations of their internal affairs and attempts to impose controls over their activities. Accordingly, policemen have mobilized their professional associations in behalf of personal prerogatives and in defense of institutional integrity. Edward J. Kiernan, when he was president of the Patrolmen's Benevolent Association in New York, attacked the Knapp findings as "still another package of hit and run charges designed to smear, in a mass indictment, every man of any rank who ever served in the New York Police Department."[36] Deputy Chief Inspector Eli Lazarus, president of the Captains' Endowment Association of New York, in advising members of his association not to respond to the Knapp Commissions's financial questionnaire, stated: "We simply cannot give in, passively, supinely, abjectly, to blanket insinuations of corruption and indecently be forced to bare private economic matters beyond the purview of legitimate inquiry."[37]

The uncooperative attitude of members of the New York police department and their professional organizations led the Knapp Commission to denounce the police department's code of silence as creating the climate that allows police malpractice to operate with impunity. By obstructing measures of accountability, police officials have only themselves to blame for the negative public opinion and for the continued existence of unsavory conditions in the police departments of the nation.

Improving the quality of the people who make up the police departments is an unquestionably valid objective of police reform. Having the "right" people as police officers means improvements in recruitment, civil service procedures, and training of police officers. But the solution to the "police problem" in the United States goes beyond that. The pervasive capabilities and authority of the police suggests that the conduct of the institution and the personnel who make it up may be tied directly to the character and goals of society itself. The duties that police officers are expected to perform and the manner in which they are performed relates in a fundamental way to how the institution perceives itself and its tasks. Whether police officers are good men or bad ones is linked to the values of the institution and the society that breeds it.

Organizational innovations can play a part in sensitizing the police to the public's social, substantive, and procedural needs. Fundamentally, these innovations can be described as applying to "what the police do, how they are organized to do it, and how they select and train their membership to operationalize democratic 'values.'"[38] The innovation in "what the police do" refers to the need for expanding their role in servicing communities and in reflecting and implementing social values. For this innovation to be legitimate, these activities should be appreciated as central to the police function and not as something to be relegated to a community-relations unit that bears little resemblance to the police department in which it operates. Instead of viewing these concerns as more within the domain of social workers, policemen should regard them as intrinsic to police responsibilities. Positive police-community interaction, emphasizing civility and informal rather than formal means of control, is a tangible effort at enforcing and reinforcing democratic values.

"How the police organize" is directed at introducing nonpolice inputs into police processes and operations. The issue here is how best to integrate civilians into police bureaucracies in order for democratic values to be better reflected. "The European experience, for example, provides a broader base of civilian control of the police than does the American counterpart. 'Civilians do not just oversee, but actually run most European police departments.'"[39] Innovation in the "selection and training of police," along with the improvements sought in organizational and community relationships, is aimed at furthering an openness of the police bureaucracy. Lateral entrance and the inclusion of human relations and social science content within a lengthier police education and training are ways of attaining the desired objective. In the United States the average policeman currently receives approximately two hundred hours of training. In contrast to this, his Italian counterpart averages two years, the Swedish policeman one year, the French six months, the German between three and four years, and the English four months.[40] This posits the need for a hard look at the length and requirements of American police training.

Recently the objective of broadening the democratic value perspective in the police bureaucracy has been seen in an increased focus on college education as a requirement for police officers in the United States. A growing number of small police departments in the western states and New

York state are requiring some college training as an entrance requirement. New York City was the first large police department to specify appropriate levels of college education as essential for entry into the department as well as for promotion to the various levels of police command. The realization, in recent times, that policemen are ill equipped to deal with many of the urban social, political, racial and domestic problems that they come in contact with daily has given impetus to the college emphasis.[41]

While these institutional innovations provide a means of democratizing the police bureaucracy and represent some of the best and most current thinking of police reformers, bureaucratic inertia and established practices make their widespread adoption doubtful. Law enforcement services compatible with the values of a free society are ultimately dependent upon accountability mechanisms that will allow recourse for the public to correct police malpractices. In view of the dubious practices of American police departments, the essential question is: Who will police the police? If, as George Bernard Shaw said, "All professions are conspiracies against the laity," then means must be found to preclude this tendency, especially as it concerns the police. The blue curtain of police secrecy must be parted to allow society to enter.

Perhaps, fundamental reform of the police bureaucracy and law enforcement can only occur if society itself is reformed. It may be cynical to assert that society deserves the police it gets, but after all, it is the values and the expectations of the community that color the type of law enforcement obtained. A hypocritical society can expect no more than hypocrisy in its law enforcement. The American penchant for responding to offensive behavior by passing laws against it persists even in cases when the behavior is regarded as innocuous by many in society. This approach is a simplistic reaction to the symptoms rather than a treatment of the causes of the behavior and ends up by making the task of law enforcement more difficult, the police more corruptible, and law enforcement more selective. It is indeed atavistic to prefer to fill our prisons rather than to address ourselves to the ills that cause deviant behavior. Finally, it is a test of our democratic commitment to see how long society will endure a street-level bureaucracy, with latent and manifest powers over all the citizens, so fecklessly held accountable to the society's democratic institutions. How long will it endure police officials possessing extraordinary discretionary authority without effective control safeguards to ensure wisdom and prudence in their actions?

Everything You Wanted to Ask About the Police But Were Afraid to Know

The police play the triggering role in the criminal justice process. The formal and informal interactions between the police and the public invariably include an interval for making the decision that initiates the criminal process: to arrest or not to arrest. In this regard the patrolman on the beat has considerable discretion. Although the discretion allowed the police officer in the arrest decision is supposedly circumscribed by statute law, common law, and departmental regulations, the personal characteristics of the police officer play an important part in how the discretion is used. Inevitably, the invocation or noninvocation of the criminal process depends on the behavior pattern and personal attitudes of the individual policeman.[1]

The nonmechanical nature of police work has made the application of routine bureaucratic standards and norms of conduct practically unattainable in the course of police-citizen interactions. The basis for the arrest decision and other occupational actions are essentially linked to the cognitive perceptions of the individual officer, and these perceptions define the officer's operational reality. Uniformity in the exercise of the arrest, along with other discretionary decisions depends upon the existence of common standards of perceptions among police officers. Law enforcement practices and processes approach standardization insofar as the range of experience of police officers are sufficiently alike so as to result in common responses. Whether these responses result in positive or negative behavior is conditioned by the character of the experiences.

The discretionary behavior of each officer is determined by his *gestalt*, a product of the sum total of the significant experiences that shape his attitudes. A policeman's actions and behavior are therefore more a product of his *gestalt* than of an observance of institutional and legal guidelines. The officer's *gestalt* is limited by the significant experiences derived from the police selection process, the occupational environment, the attitudes and conditions in the social environment, and his peer group socialization and reinforcement. It is these factors that determine the behavior pattern of the patrolman on the beat and the type of law enforcement that the community obtains.

Selection Process

The selection stage, a process that can signally affect the makeup of a police agency's working force, generally consists of written examinations, physical agility tests, oral interviews, and background investigations. Although the initial selection process is designed to provide an objective basis upon which to screen prospective applicants, the process incorporates a bias in favor of certain groups within society. Consciously or unconsciously, many police departments perpetuate existing mores, attitudes, and opinions within a department by screening for "compatible" applicants. The desired values and norms are discernible in the oral interview and attitudinal questionnaire stage. While these methods tend to eliminate unstable and undesirable personalities, they also have the effect of screening out applicants with "incompatible" values such as "liberalism" if the officials doing the screening feel this attitude is inconsistent with effective police work. Similarly, the physical requirements exclude still more potential applicants, and these requirements, especially the height requirements, usually end up by excluding many members of certain ethnic groups.[2]

In the police departments studied, preference was expressed for applicants who, having successfully passed all of the formal screening requirements, had prior law enforcement experience, some college and preferably a two-year college certificate or a baccalaureate degree, and for members of minority groups, especially blacks. The preferences notwithstanding, these departments, while having no difficulty in finding applicants with prior police experience, shared in common with many other police departments in the nation the problem of attracting members of minority groups and applicants with the desired college education. The difficulties encountered in attracting preferred applicants may be attributed to the stereotyped concepts of the police held by many segments of society and especially by members of minority groups and college men and women. Moreover, these stereotypes may have been validated by negative interactional experiences with police officials.

The homogeneity of personnel standardizes the conduct, biases, and norms found in police bureaucracies. When these attitudes are acted out in the community they provide the police with an occupational image. Individuals and groups that do not subscribe to these attitudes nor wish to be associated with the image that these attitudes produce are not likely to opt for an organization with which these conditions are associated. Thus, the homogeneity of police agencies tends to be self-perpetuating. A career in the police is attractive to those individuals whose norms and biases are consistent with those found in the police. Historically, police officials have been largely made up of working-class and lower-middle-class whites, and there is little evidence to show that this typology has changed recently. Even without the existence of screening criteria that bias in favor of applicants possessing the political attitudes and ethnic backgrounds that already predominate in police agencies, a law enforcement career con-

Occupational Environment

Once the applicant has successfully passed the screening process and is accepted into the police department, he begins to adjust his personality to the occupational environment. It is in the training phase, the recruit school, that he is exposed to an emphasis upon police values, standards of conduct, and norms. If the recruit does not already possess these value attributes, he will be indoctrinated with them, and the longer the training period, the deeper the imprint they make.

Initial formal training provides a sense of togetherness in becoming policemen. Recruits are taught that being a policeman means a steady job, job security, and pension benefits. The major theme of the early training is upon the authority characteristics of a police official, stressing that the police officer must make the public respect him. William Westley found that the neophyte policeman's personality is developed in three experiential phases: recruit school, contact with and instruction by his more experienced colleagues, and experience with the public.

The first phase functions to detach him from his previous life pattern and prepares him to accept a new one, and to provide him with a set of temporary definitions of behavior with which he can function until he becomes more thoroughly oriented. The second phase involves the interaction of the rookie with the more experienced men, and the communication, directly and indirectly, of the secrets and customs of the police. The third phase involves the rookie's taking responsibility for his own actions and learning that the public is everything that the older men said it would be. In the third phase the rookie becomes emotionally involved in upholding the values of the group because he comes to recognize them as involving his own self-esteem. At this point the rookie becomes a policeman.[4]

In most police departments in the United States, much of the time spent in formal training is on technical subjects such as fingerprinting, report writing, traffic accident investigation, narcotics identification, and defense techniques. When attention is paid to the human aspects of the police job, the focus is usually on the potential dangers that these human encounters offer. The hazards of the job are impressed on the police recruits with lessons devoted to the handling of such volatile encounters as marital disputes, violent individuals, traffic offenders, and drunks. Statistics that most police casualties in the line of duty occur while handling disturbances of this nature are cited to emphasize the risks involved.

The most far-reaching conditioning exercise performed in formal training is the teaching of police rookies to be suspicious of anything "out of the ordinary." To be properly suspicious is to be alert to any deviation from the norm, for any such deviation may indicate criminal activity. Accordingly, the police recruit is taught to develop a perceptual shorthand that allows him to readily identify suspicious behavior. The importance of developing this characteristic of a policeman's working personality is that he not only be able to recognize actual and potential criminal behavior, but that he be prepared to anticipate and respond to indications of danger. The sensitivity of police officers to potential danger to themselves in their working environment lends itself to characterizing suspicion as a personality trait essential to a policeman's self-preservation and effective law enforcement.

While the arrest decision is a fundamental attribute of the police officer's discretionary power and the first step in the invocation of the criminal process, the decision to investigate is more important because it provides the basis for the arrest decision. An officer's suspicion of a given situation or persons is the catalyst to all ensuing discretionary decisions and behavior. Therefore, the policeman's perceptual shorthand of suspicious behavior is the key attitude that sets off the chain of law enforcement responses.

"Attention-getters" that arouse suspicion are deviations from the norm as defined by the police officer. While some "attention-getters" are obviously suspicious, such as juveniles loitering, persons running at night or dressed as burglars, other situations would be considered almost commonplace by most people, except that they arouse the suspicion of a police officer if they transgress upon his value system or arouse his individual prejudices. Members of the "counterculture" and minority groups are more likely to invite the interest of police officers if their behavior is in any way out of the ordinary. An interviewed police officer stated in this connection, "I'll always stop a black in a middle-class white neighborhood at night because I think it's suspicious for a black to be there. He sticks out like a sore thumb because he doesn't belong in that neighborhood late at night." Another officer said that he liked to stop and interrogate "hippies" at random, for chances were always high that he could make a narcotics case since he believed that many hippies either possessed or trafficked in drugs. Many of these biases practiced at the street level were acquired initially in rookie training.

Most instructors are police officers, sergeants and above, and, while well-versed in day-to-day street tactics and the technical aspects of the job, most were trained long ago, and may be reluctant to accept newer policies with regard to police-citizen interaction. While most instructors attempt to be objective, their biases are usually clear, either by virtue of their asides while instructing, their racial jokes, or their obvious contempt toward recent court rulings.[5]

The rookie, having successfully completed formal training, enters the world of law enforcement as a commissioned police officer. The occupational structure that he finds consists of the training division, from where he came as a recruit trainee, the records division, communications division, and the action branches of each department: patrol, detectives, and traffic. Records, or the bureau of identification, concerns the application of scientific police work, specifically, fingerprint identification; it is known as one of the quietest places in the police station. The communications division is highly active and is the center of radio activity and station information. Most officers, however, are assigned as patrolmen on a beat, usually to a patrol car, for much police activity takes place through these patrol cars. The radio is the patrol car's link to the police department, "both from a physical or action perspective and in a personal, psychological sense."[6] Isolated from the community they patrol, the men in the police cars look forward to activity that breaks the monotony of a routine patrol. They listen to life as depicted over their radio, which is too often "cheap and sordid," since the view obtained through this source relates solely to criminal activity in the city.

The detective division is a highly desired prestige assignment, and it is commonly believed by most police officers that the "chief's friends are assigned there." Unlike beat patrolmen, the detectives do not perform service activities nor do they normally observe an established routine. Instead, each detective is responsible for working on criminal cases which he can pursue at his own pace, and he derives personal prestige from solving important cases. Keen competition is known to exist among detectives for the good cases, for the "good pinch." A detective is dependent upon "stoolies" or "snitches", informants who provide him with the vital information that enables him to solve cases. The detective's "experience is one of violence, bargaining, and a drive toward prestige. His attitude is pure cynicism."[7] Nevertheless, the glamor of the detective division appeals to the young patrolmen who seek action and personal glory.

Most police organizations can be accurately described as closed systems. Recruitment and selection for entry are conducted for only the lowest level of the organization, and promotions are made from within, with only the members of the organization competing for these positions. The essentially inbred nature of the police bureaucracy lends itself to a commitment to the status quo throughout the hierarchy.[8] This accounts for the characterization of the police bureaucracy as a "closed fraternity," and the longer the men remain in the organization, the more tied they become to the hierarchy that nourishes and absorbs them. In this type of system little or no reform from within the organization can be expected, and this is especially true at the higher levels of the hierarchy, which is made up of men who owe so much to the system and have been thoroughly socialized by it.

The closed nature of the police bureaucracy has the effect of deadening personal initiative and improvement. James Ahern, formerly chief of police of the New Haven department, noted that in this kind of a bureaucratic environment, if a patrolman on a beat does not aspire to being a detective, then he is left with the desire for a steady indoor job, in the training division or in some desk job. His primary ambition, at this point, is to "survive." Promotion up the ranks is dependent on organizational politics, and no matter where he finds himself in the hierarchy, his most important duty "will be to do favors for people." In view of the highly politicized nature of internal advancement, he necessarily guards his own position by developing protective "political walls." In this police "system," he ultimately ends up performing innocuous paperwork and working less for slightly more pay.

If he is lucky, and he does not make too many enemies, he may become a chief inspector, an assistant chief, or even chief of police. If he does, he will have received little or no more training or education than the cop on the walking beat, and he will have gained no wider perspective on the police department and its role than a decade of street experience and another decade of "indoor" work have given him. Although there are some notable exceptions, especially in larger cities, most chiefs of police are no more than fifty year old patrolmen.[9]

The catchy notion of replacing the "system" with "professionalism" is the current vogue in many police departments in this country. Proponents of police professionalism understand this to mean the replacement of the system's traditional allocation of rewards and penalties, based on how well a police official conforms to the expectations and norms of the organizational hierarchy, with a bureaucratic rationality based on administrative efficiency. The introduction of the concept of managerial professionalism by police reformers is an effort to gain bureaucratic impersonality, merit, and fairness in an organization traditionally beset with corruption and political favoritism.[10]

As a low-status occupational group the police are not developing the same standards of expertise, moral values, certification, and internal controls that are consistent with the codes of the "true" professions such as those found in medicine or law. Rather, police professionalism involves more the careful selection and training of officers, pride in work, a career system based on merit, and the utilization of the best management skills in the deployment and assignment of officers. Efforts toward police "professionalism" have stressed occupational reinforcement and enhanced solidarity among police officers, and this has created the byproduct of promoting the police bureaucracy into a "self-regulating guild."[11] The effect of these efforts has been an increase in the growth of police "brotherhoods," which in many cities have the expressed intent of insulating their membership from control by civilians, and even by police management.

Beyond the conventional concepts of police professionalism, which relate to acquiring bureaucratic efficiency and increased technical abilities, is the call for the elevation of the police occupation to a "true profession."

Richard A. Compton, the director of the Law Enforcement Program at the University of Mississippi, argues that until police officers are universally required to be properly trained, examined, licensed, and continually held responsible for the manner of their practice, there will be little opportunity for the police to raise their status, either financially or socially. According to Compton, the promulgation of these requirements promises to result in higher pay for policemen by according them recognition as "professionals," and it would assure society of better law enforcement officials.

At the minimum, policemen should undergo longer periods of formal training and be examined and licensed before being allowed to practice their occupation. Compton notes that licensing is made mandatory for the professions and even for some occupations. Licensing is required for medicine, law, dentistry, aviation, and teaching, as well as for activities such as barbering, hair styling, embalming, plumbing, electrical repair, and even operating a motor vehicle. To Compton, the essential distinction between the status of vocations and "true" professions is that the professions have a compulsory requirement for a postgraduate degree for qualification. Aspiring candidates for the vocations, while not subject to the lengthy educational requirements of the professions, must still undergo extensive training to qualify for licensing requirements in most states. Physicians complete approximately 11,500 hours of preparation; attorneys 9500 hours of preparation; teachers of elementary schools 7400 hours; morticians, 5600 hours; barbers, 4300 hours; and beauticians, 1800 hours. Policemen, by contrast, average 200 hours of training! In addition, no licensing is required for the group that is occupationally charged with making decisions and performing functions that have direct consequences on life, liberty, and property of citizens. No one person or group in society possesses such awesome authority as do the police. The discretion of a policeman affects personal life and safety, and capricious behavior by a single officer can produce disastrous results. "It seems strange, then, that our legislatures have not as yet seen fit to enact into law similar licensing requirements which would provide a greater measure of control over the selection, training, and standards of police practices. What is even stranger, however, is that the police themselves have not actively pushed for such uniform standards."[12]

But Compton is not sanguine about the acceptability of more stringent educational and training requirements for police officers. He notes that although there has been a proliferation of law enforcement programs in many colleges and universities leading to degrees ranging from the Associate of Arts to the Ph.D., most of the students enrolled in these programs are young men and women without prior police service. In-service personnel still do not see the value of advanced education, and this is borne out by their low enrollment in these and related programs. This suggests that most police departments retain an anti-intellectual bias because they do not encourage career officials to further their education.

The police officer may work under either "system" conditions or bureaucratic efficiency standards, but he must nevertheless conform to the production criteria specified by his department. All police departments attempt to provide measurable standards of law enforcement activity, and since the essence of their responsibility is the prevention of criminal activity, police agencies rate their efficiency in accordance with how well they perform this essential task. Statistics maintained by law enforcement agencies generally consist of the reporting of crimes and the "clearance" of these crimes. A crime is "cleared" when an arrest is made for the crime. Since the priority is to combat crime efficiently and productively, emphasis is placed on apprehension as essential to a police officer's duties.[13] In effect, the individual policeman's efficiency is judged by his ability to "produce" apprehensions, and institutional pressure is applied on each policeman to be "productive."

The stress on productivity has curtailed severely the practice of using patrolmen on foot patrols, a form of personalized service that promoted a closer relationship between a patrolman and the citizens on his beat. Foot patrols have been eschewed by police administrators because they are considered to be far less efficient than radio police cars, which can cover larger areas and respond more quickly. Philadelphia's Mayor Frank Rizzo, formerly the city's police commissioner, is one such critic of foot patrols because of their perceived detraction from efficiency-productivity:

The day of preventing crime is over. We have to have the ability to apprehend and this is what we do in Philadelphia. Foot patrols are expensive and limited to a relatively small area even with communications. . . .

We've got more foot beat men than we had before now. Let's be practical. You put a policeman in a residential area and he walks around and says hello and shakes hands—and what good does he do? This is not policing.[14]

The emphasis on clearance rates shows the effect of productivity pressures. Policemen respond to the stress by either ignoring or deviating from formal rules in order to show high production. This behavior is similar to the practices of foremen and production-line workers who circumvent rules in order to meet production quotas.[15] In the case of the police, the low visibility of much of their behavior provides them with the opportunity to deviate from the rule of law, in order to maximize their production. A policeman often views measures that impede his productivity as unjustifiable obstacles. Hence, due process of law—a set of judicially enforced constitutional guarantees of fair treatment for the suspect—is not generally accepted in the police culture as the affirmation of democratic principles but is rather seen as the imposition of harsh "working conditions." Policemen are frustrated by the concept of legal guilt embodied in due process of law and prefer to rely on their "professional" judgment about "factual guilt," which allows them greater latitude in their discretionary behavior. The exclusionary rule, which guarantees freedom from unreasonable searches and seizures by prohibiting the introduction of evidence obtained in violation of the Constitution, has sometimes led to "creative" apprehension in order to meet production demands. Faced with the insistence on "production" by their administrative and political superiors, while at the same time restrained in their capacity to "produce" by their judicial superiors, policemen all too often resolve this dilemma in favor of productivity, which promises greater organizational rewards.

Police officers in several cities admitted privately that they either knew of, or were themselves party to, cases of the planting of evidence on defendants during the course of apprehension. They stated that this action was justified when the defendants were known to be criminals, known to be "guilty" by the police officers on the scene, but had thwarted arrest on numerous occasions by skillfully "losing" evidence of their criminality. Queried about whether this type of police behavior is either morally or legally justified, one policeman responded, "I hate to lie to the judge, and I especially hate it because the criminal knows that I am lying. It hurts the policeman's credibility with the criminal element. But, hell, if I didn't plant evidence sometimes I wouldn't be making very many cases against some bad characters."

Detective Eddie "Popeye" Egan of the New York Police Department, whose police work inspired the book and movie, *The French Connection,* was a police officer with an incredible instinct for making narcotics arrests. Shortly before Egan was fired from the police force, Robin Moore, who wrote *The French Connection,* followed up on the man he made famous for additional insights into his law enforcement procedures. Moore found that while neither he nor Egan's police partner, Sanchez, actually observed Egan planting narcotics on two suspects during the course of an arrest, he inferred that this actually took place.[16]

Tactical units of police departments perform intensified patrols in high-crime areas at high-crime times and are often pressed hard for arrest productivity. The New Orleans police department's tactical unit was formed thirteen years ago by the present chief of detectives, Henry "Hard Rock" Morris. It presently consists of two platoons with twenty patrolmen, two sergeants, and a commanding officer per platoon. The unit is commanded by Captain Harold Foster, an ex-Marine noncommissioned officer, with twenty-five years of service in the New Orleans police department. The unit's mission is to supplement regular police patrols in high-crime areas by seeking "targets of opportunity," by actively looking for crime. The unit is also prepared to provide crowd and riot control.

The tactical unit operates during the peak hours of crime: 9:00 A.M. to 5:00 P.M., and 6:00 P.M. to 2:00 A.M. Patrols are performed by two-man marked squad cars that only respond to radio calls describing felonies in progress, so that they may not be distracted from their designated purpose of "finding crime." A major portion of the unit's work consists of stopping vehicles and pedestrians in a search for illegal narcotics. To be qualified for an assignment with a tactical unit a police official must at least be a high school graduate and preferably be a veteran. The unit is all white and the average age of the patrolmen is twenty-five. A senior police official with the unit stated that he wanted "good, aggressive men right out of the academy" to "beat the bush for crime." He proudly pointed out that the tactical unit led all other units in the police department with 150 felony arrests a month, with a high month of 190 felony arrests. As a form of incentive, the unit encourages competition for the number of arrests among the platoons. The same official, however, was unable to provide data on the number of convictions obtained as a result of the unit's apprehensions. An official from another unit in the department stated that very few of the arrests made by the tactical unit resulted in convictions because many of the cases had been thrown out of court for violations of due process and for other suspect practices.

The experience of riding "third" in tactical unit cars during their patrols provided ample evidence of the eagerness of the men to go after crime. Normally, the patrols would be concentrated in New Orleans' French Quarter and in the black neighborhoods. Vehicles and pedestrians were halted, with a preference shown for stopping and questioning "characters" (individuals known to the police officers to be criminals) and blacks, adolescents, and persons whose dress singles them out as hippies or "oddballs."

During an "unsuccessful" tactical unit patrol—a quiet night free of criminal activity—the officers in the police car decided to "visit" a teenage dance. One of the men, a member of the squad car partnership whose monthly arrest rate had led the unit on numerous occasions, said: "There's not much chance of making an arrest at the dance because all of the TAC cars are going to be there, since this is a quiet night. But you never know, we may luck out and catch some kids smoking dope or maybe even shooting it up." The car circled a converted warehouse where the dance was being held for approximately a half hour. While cruising in the vicinity of the warehouse, the squad car stopped on several occasions and its occupants got out to question couples sitting in parked cars. However, this did not result in the uncovering of any illegal activity. There were approximately three other tactical unit cars doing the same thing. Finally, before leaving the area, the squad car drove up to where another tactical unit team was in process of searching four adolescent boys who were spreadeagled against their car. "Find anything?" asked the driver of our squad car, as he pulled up to the other police officers. "Yeah, a couple of joints," said the patrolman of the tactical unit team making the arrest. He grinned and added, "Making cases. Making cases." Our squad car drove off with the driver muttering, "Lucky bastards." The other partner turned to the back seat and said, "We'll make a case tonight. My partner has a nose for crime and his nose tells him that we'll make a case." The other man said, "Yeah, we'll nail someone before the night's over."

A little later, the policemen were asked, "How do you think the tactical unit can be improved?"

One of the men replied: "We ought to be allowed to vary our hours of patrol. Every pusher and junkie in town knows our hours of operation and they stay off the streets until we're gone. You ought to see the drug activity around here after two A.M. when the characters hit the streets again."

"One more thing," added his partner, "they should let us carry a shotgun in the car just like they do in the L.A.P.D. [Los Angeles Police Department]."

"How do you know that police cars in Los Angeles have shotguns?"

"I saw it on TV, on *Adam-12*."

A half block or so from the police station, as the car neared a bar, a crowd of black males standing outside the establishment spotted the police car and scattered inside. Before the police vehicle had even come to a complete stop the officer sitting on the right side of the vehicle jumped out and ran into the bar.

"What's going on?"

Before joining his partner the driver of the squad car turned to the back seat and said, "Didn't you see? One of the blacks threw a gun into the bar when he saw us coming."

In a few moments the patrolmen emerged from the bar, and one of them was pushing a black man toward the car with one hand and holding an old revolver in the other. The suspect was handcuffed and put in the back seat. The revolver was apparently the contraband that the police officer had seen earlier, and a subsequent call over the radio to police headquarters resulted in the response from the car radio that the arrested man was a parolee. Driving off, one of the patrolmen said, "Well, we made a case tonight."

"It's not much of a case," replied the other one.

"Yeah, but it's still a case. And the night's not over yet."

A consideration of the policeman's occupational environment would not be complete without discussing the type of public he most often encounters in the course of his duties. Although the policeman must be able to differentiate among the publics he serves, his working personality is largely determined by the public to whom the greatest part of his occupational energies are devoted. If the policeman is a hero and a servant of the public, he is also its disciplinarian and avenger, and it is the latter two roles that are stressed by the occupational norms by which the officer's efficiency is judged. It is as disciplinarian and avenger that the policeman concerns himself with the public that forms his image of the external environment.

His view of society is a sordid one, as provided by the radio in his squad car and as reinforced by his encounters with felons and drunks and social outcasts of various types. To catch a thief one must know a thief, and the successful police officer is the one with connections with the underworld. The best police informants are prostitutes, petty gamblers, and other hangers-on associated with the demi-monde of criminality. To maintain and protect his sources of information, without which effective law enforcement would be impossible, the police officer is forced to allow certain kinds of crime to go on in order to detect others. Hence, prostitutes will be protected in order to catch narcotics peddlers, narcotics violators will be protected in order to catch burglars, and so on.[17] Law enforcement can become chaotic if police officers do not subscribe to the inviolability of other police officers' informants. Under the stress of productivity, however, it is not uncommon for policemen to begin arresting each other's informants. It may be self-serving, but it contributes little to the practicalities of crime fighting.

Conditions and Attitudes Affecting Law Enforcement

Emphasis on bureaucratic efficiency and technical improvements in law enforcement has given the New York City police department under Commissioner Patrick V. Murphy, the finest management, and technical equipment in its history. "With few exceptions, every cop on a beat now has a two-way radio. There are now 600 scooters patrolling the city's streets. Two 350-40 computers worth $3 million handle some 6.7 million inquiries a year under the Sprint system, guiding the deployment of police, we are told, to the scenes of crimes or problems with greater speed than ever before."[18] Yet, despite these advantages, New York's police department faces severe problems of internal corruption, a crisis of police morale, energized resistance on the part of policemen to internal and external controls, a failure of public confidence, in addition to the failure of the system of criminal justice. The New York experience contradicts the commonly held belief that police problems are caused by a lack of money or a lack of personnel. New York's department, like many other police departments in the nation, is faced with a set of problems, some of which are susceptible to solution within the department, and some which are not. What is striking about these problems is that many of them overlap and interact.

The failure of the criminal justice system has had a serious impact on police morale. In New York City, for example, the police make approximately a quarter of a million arrests a year. There are fewer than 100 judges in Manhattan Criminal Court, and only 180 felony trials went to verdict in Manhattan in 1970. The average arraignment in New York City takes less than two minutes, and with a serious shortage of criminal court judges, overcrowded jails, and an apathetic general public, most of those arrested by the police do not even go to trial due to dropped charges, copped pleas, and the failure of witnesses to testify.

[The] whole criminal justice system, with its built-in revolving doors, turns even the best cops somewhat bitter and cynical. Hang around any courtroom and talk to cops and all have at least one common complaint: They arrest a man, often at great physical risk, they book him, have him arraigned, and go to court with him, and before they can take a sip of coffee from the cardboard container in the hall, the man is on the street again. After a while, the cop wonders why he should bother, why he should take the risks involved—why, in fact, he should try to be a good cop at all.[19]

The failures of the criminal justice system are not only reflected in the large numbers of individuals who are arrested and then for one reason or another are not brought to trial, but also in the growing number of recidivists that the prisons produce. The prisons, their avowed purpose notwithstanding, have too often served as "occasional schools for criminals." The combination of the prisons producing and expanding the force of criminals, now better trained than ever from their experience behind bars, and an overworked court system that can do no better than to rubberstamp justice, has created little respect for the criminal justice system or the police officer who is the most visible symbol of that system.

Some of the faults with the system can be attributed to the inadequacy of fiscal support for the varying, yet interdependent, components of the system. Much of the criminal justice dollar is allocated to police work with the scant remainder sliced up among courts, jails, and rehabilitation programs. The result is that the police are expected to bear the main burden of criminal justice, "to do what other components of the system cannot, or will not, do. A cop can arrest. He cannot—must not—convict, and he certainly cannot reform."[20]

Adding to the problems of an overburdened system of criminal justice are an excessive number of laws, many of which are either difficult or impossible to enforce. Crimes involving morals—but not personal injury or theft—serve to turn the police into the guardians of the morality of a society that seems to be more willing to purge its conscience by legislating than by reforming. The police are expected to enforce laws against gambling, marijuana, sexual acts between consenting adults, prostitution, and pornography, and yet these activities flourish because of the support they receive from many of the same citizens who piously endorse the statutes that forbid them. The effect of these morality laws is a resultant failure of public confidence in law enforcement because the laws are practicably unenforceable.

Police practices vis-à-vis these activities are the source of much of the loss of confidence by the public in the police. "Immoral" activities such as gambling have been a source of more police corruption than any other "crime," and the revelation of corruption associated with gambling has resulted in a great deal of unfavorable publicity for law enforcement. It is apparent that many of these activities could not exist without police approval. Some police officers are as ambiguous about the morality of these activities as are many citizens, and the lure of lucrative payoffs from the operators of illegal enterprises induces corruption. Additionally, the realities of "crime fighting" perpetuate the existence of some individuals who practice these illegal activities because they are sources of valuable information that enables the police to apprehend "bigger criminals."

On the other hand, a zealous effort at prosecuting offenses involving morals requires the utilization of a large number of police officers and the expenditure of a great deal of money and often produces considerable enmity towards the police from many segments of society. Many citizens resent the intrusion of a police agency into their personal lives, and the enforcement of laws involving private morals is considered a nuisance because numerous persons do not culturally subscribe to the legal definition of these activities as crimes. Moreover, the role of guardians of individual morals allows officers a great deal of discretion in determining which acts violate the norms of society. This occurs especially where the legal definitions are vague, as in the case of pornography, thus allowing a great deal of bureaucratic discretion in interpretation. In this instance the police officers serve as public censors. For example, in the 1960s, the late brilliant comedian Lenny Bruce who used to do a bit about how the ancient societies created the police in order to keep the people from defecating where they shouldn't, was arrested in a number of cities by police officials who took offense at his use of scatalogical imagery and other "obscenity" in his monologues. More recently, a contemporary comedian, George Carlin, was arrested in Milwaukee when a policeman objected to the "language" in Carlin's act. Interestingly, the police have been known to be quite active in enforcing laws against pornography and obscenity, where payoffs are not reported to occur, in contrast to their lesser efforts in combating large-scale crime.

Whitman Knapp, now a US district judge, but best known for heading an investigation exposing widespread corruption in the New York City police department, stated that the prime causes of police corruption are the laws that society demands be enforced against some of its members but not against others. "We have to stop being lazy and give realistic objectives to our police departments. There is no doubt those laws (such as gambling and prostitution laws) must be trimmed," Judge Knapp said.[21]

It was paradoxical to have Judge Knapp make these comments less than a year after his commission reported that corruption was rampant in every division of the New York police department. He went on to say: "Part of the problem [of police corruption] is breaking down the monolith. . . . The reason the policeman develops this intensive inbredness is that he is, in fact, living in a state of hostility. It wouldn't be necessary for him to feel that he couldn't talk about the problems of corruption if he would get corresponding support from the public."[22] Knapp urged the public to become actively involved with the police and to develop a realistic attitude toward police corruption. Finally, he noted that one of the major difficulties is trying to persuade the public and the authorities that there is corruption, for the attitude of disbelief concerning corruption in law enforcement is common in the United States.

The easy, and inaccurate, description of the police as being primarily concerned with crime fighting results in their being judged by a goal they cannot attain. The police cannot prevent crime; at best, they can keep order.[23] The police do not create the conditions that exist in society. Crime, violence, and disorder have their roots in social and economic conditions that are beyond the scope of the police. Poverty, racism, and social and psychological dislocations of an urban community are the major contributors to disorder. These are problems with which society as a whole and all levels of government must cope. The police bureaucracy is the agency empowered to deal with the symptoms of these conditions. Police are incapable of redressing the wrongs of society; they can only try to curtail the manifestations of these wrongs. The more difficult that society makes it for the police to keep order, by an indifference to the problems that cause disorder, the less likely are the police to perform their designated service adequately. However, this is not to say that the task of the police must be made easy at the expense of democratic values; rather, it is to suggest that conditions existing in society can only be improved by society itself.

An added difficulty for law enforcement is the existence of serious tensions between the police and the society they serve. Some of these tensions occur because of police malpractice, while others exist because the police, as omnipresent symbols of the political system, are singled out for hatred by groups that oppose the political system and the society that nurtures it. Individual officers, no matter what their personal disposition, are at times confronted by a blanket hostility, especially in neighborhoods where "off the pigs" is a prevalent slogan.

The law-abiding citizen is usually indifferent about the police except when he becomes the victim of a crime and needs a police officer. Other than that, the average citizen's most common interaction with a police officer occurs when he receives a traffic citation. Members of minority and counterculture groups and the young are often the target of police excesses and are thus loath to provide any support for the police. "The students, protesters, and blacks are filled with hatred of the police. The police are filled with hatred of students, protesters, and blacks. We mix them at our peril."[24] It is the avowed hostility toward the police by some segments of society and a hostility that is reciprocated by the police that provides the sort of tension that sometimes leads to violence.

Deadly violence, the symptom of the rage that some citizens hold for the police and vice versa, occurs with some frequency. Although the police are charged with maintaining social order, in the process of performing this task the police sometimes themselves become social problems. This occurs when either by their actions or by their presence in certain neighborhoods the police become catalysts to violence. According to the FBI, 96 law enforcement officers were killed in the first eleven months of 1972. Twelve of those officers slain were in ambush attacks. This figure compares with 112 police officers killed during the same period in 1971.[25]

The victims of deadly violence have not all been on one side. Civilian fatalities occurring during the course of a law enforcement activity show that the police have done their share of killing. For example, the Chicago Law Enforcement Study Group, a joint project of Northwestern University Center for Urban Affairs and twelve community organizations, scored the Chicago police for having killed more persons over an eight-month period than did the police in any of the four other largest cities examined. The group charged that Chicago has a "trigger-happy society of policemen," and that the high death rate "exists alongside of police misconduct and official laxity in punishing the police officers involved." The group, using statistics obtained by the International Association of Police Chiefs in a survey taken July 1970 to March 1971, showed that 32 persons were killed in Chicago during that period, a rate of 0.95 per 100,000 population, as compared with 21 civilian fatalities in New York, or 0.27 per 100,000 population, 13 in Philadelphia (0.67), 8 in Los Angeles (0.28), and 4 in Detroit (0.26). Additionally, the Chicago study group stated that its own survey found that 79 persons—59 of them black—were killed by the Chicago police in 1969 and 1970. The group attributed the fatalities to an "undisciplined" leadership that fostered a willingness on the part of the police to use guns.[26]

A phenomenon of the times has been the emergence of urban vigilante groups and the public support given to some of these citizen patrols. Although there does not exist a mandate for autonomous self-defense groups in replacement of the regular police, their emergence posits a dissatisfaction with present law enforcement capabilities and practices. One study of vigilante groups found them to be formed with many different objectives in mind. Some are created to protect their community from the police as well as from crime, and they principally serve in an adversarial relationship with the police, checking on police activities in order to combat what they perceive as disruptive and abusive behavior by police officials. Other vigilante groups are supportive of the police and regard themselves as an extension of the regular law enforcement establishment. These groups do not blame the police for the breakdown of law and order but rather attribute this condition to police manpower shortages, overly permissive courts, and the rampant spread of the "criminal element."[27]

In order to deal with the disaffection of some citizens with law enforcement, police departments have made structural innovations that are designed to be more responsive to community needs for law and order. One such approach was the New York City police department's "neighborhood police team" put into effect in January 1971. The team under the command of a single sergeant consists of a sixteen-man squad responsible for a twelve-block sector near the Bedford-Stuyvesant section, which contains 15,000 residents. The sergeant, who is hand-picked, is, in effect, a twenty-four-hour-a-day police chief of his sector, and the patrolmen in his team are all volunteers. New York City's response to community needs for personalized law enforcement is to provide for a "psychological decentralization" of the police department. While critics of the system suggest that it may not be practical on a citywide basis, neighborhood police teams have been created for additional sectors in the city.

The concept of the neighborhood police team was obtained by Commissioner Patrick V. Murphy from the London police department when he visited England to study British police tactics. The idea of the neighborhood team is to assign groups of men permanently to a precinct, thereby enabling them to develop links in the community and emerge as identifiable figures. Commenting on the use of the neighborhood teams in New York, Commissioner Murphy said, "We've started the teams on a small scale in New York in order to have the police become an identifiable part of a community. We're not sure it will work as well as in London—there are different problems. But, judging from the success in London, I want to try to expand it at home."[28]

Another English practice learned by Commissioner Murphy is the "unit beat" system that he introduced in New York with some fanfare early in 1972. The "unit beat" system involves the assignment of a policeman to a one-square-mile area around his home. This practice, begun in 1967 in London, now involves about one-third of London's 21,000-man metropolitan police force. Unfortunately, the "unit beat" system, called "resident policeman" in New York, did not fare well in its initial test. The city's first two "resident policemen", picked to test whether patrolmen assigned to their home neighborhoods could build a special trust with the public, quietly transferred out of their home precincts after becoming the targets of telephone harassment and other abuse and annoyances.[29]

The conditions and attitudes prevailing in the society at large have had an influence on the work-personality of police officials. On the one hand, held in low esteem or with indifference by much of the general public or, on the other hand, faced with active hostility on the part of certain groups—a hostility they reciprocate—the police see themselves as embattled and frustrated by an environment that is not of their making. Whether the feeling of profound isolation from the general public is attributable to antagonistic police practices or to a general lack of support for law enforcement, the resulting police attitudes are distinctly those of a minority subculture: the magnification of group solidarity. Police solidarity, the camaraderie and fellowship among police officers, is what makes wearing the blue uniform every day bearable and gives "the feeling that they are doing a job that is important to society despite working conditions to the contrary."[30] Evidence of low morale among police officers in the departments across the country notwithstanding, policemen are stimulated by the solidarity of their peer group.

The feeling of embattlement from without and the compensating need for solidarity and support from within provides the police with the classic syndrome of an oppressed minority. In their minds, the police are the "blue minority." A police officer in Memphis spoke to this point: "To a cop, human beings come in six colors: white, black, brown, red, yellow, and blue. And we cops are all blue." But recently the police have been experiencing fissures in the "blue solidarity" with incidents of black police officials emphasizing their blackness over their blueness. In several cities, black policemen have opted for the exclusiveness of guild organizations that represent them as a racial group rather than join organizations devoted to the cause of the "blue fraternity."

As a matter of fact, black police officers, through their groups, have actively opposed some of the policies of police organizations and have also aligned themselves with black citizen groups in criticizing police practices in respect to blacks. For example, in New York City, a spokesman for the Guardians Association, which represents about 1900 of the 2100 black members of the police department, joined with leaders of a citizens group, the Black Committee to Insure Justice for Black Police Officers and the Black Community, in denouncing the fatal shooting of a black detective by a uniformed patrolman who mistook him for a criminal. A resolution jointly adopted by the Guardians Association and the citizens group demanded that the white patrolman be dismissed from the force. Sergeant Howard L. Sheffey, president of the Guardians Association, took on the Patrolmen's Benevolent Association, an organization representing the police as an occupational group in New York City, by charging that Edward J. Kiernan, president at the time, and other leaders of the association had indirectly caused the shooting by fostering a policy among policemen of "shoot first and ask questions later." Sergeant Sheffey said:

We repeat that we will accept no less than a full-scale investigation and not the listless or languid in-house variety. We also feel that it is only through good luck that more of our members have not been shot in similar circumstances.

We take a very dim view of the theory that any black man in possession of a firearm is a criminal liability and, as such, he is subject to all the racist and possible biased action that could be stored in a lifetime.[31]

Informed of Sergeant Sheffey's statement, Mr. Kiernan replied with a formal statement of his own: "Every policeman is saddened when accidents like this occur, but they will occur so long as strong police action must be taken to protect the citizens of New York."

Referring to a somewhat parallel incident, a press report described how the Guardians Association in Detroit called for the disbanding of a special police unit, three of whose members were involved in the shooting that led to the death of a deputy sheriff and the wounding of three others.[32] This demand was seconded by the Detroit branch of the National Association for the Advancement of Colored People. Thomas Moss, the president of the Guardians in Detroit, representing approximately 325 black policemen out of a police force of 5000, asked all ten black members of the special unit to resign immediately. In an interview for the press, Mr. Moss said that the Guardians would put pressure on the black officers to resign. If that did not work, he was quoted as saying, the organization would then point out the undercover officers to members of the community where they operate. He then added that the special unit could not function in black neighborhoods if the black members resigned: "White policemen would find it difficult to act in the black community."

The special unit, called STRESS for "Stop the Robberies—Enjoy Safe Streets," operates in teams of three men in plainclothes. They patrol high-crime areas in unmarked cars with the objective of stopping street crimes. The shooting that brought on the reaction of the Guardians Association involved three black officers from STRESS and five black deputy sheriffs who were off duty playing cards. The STRESS units were organized in January 1971, in an effort to cut down Detroit's increasing street crime. From the time STRESS was set up, through March 1972, officers of the unit had killed fourteen people, of whom thirteen were black.

Despite the controversy surrounding STRESS, both Mayor Roman S. Gribbs and Police Commissioner John F. Nichols asserted that the program would be continued. The commissioner justified the decision by releasing figures that showed total crime in Detroit had decreased substantially. He said that the STRESS program was one of the principal reasons for the dramatic drop in robberies. However, the commissioner announced that the operations of STRESS units would be modified by assigning experienced sergeants to the teams of three to four men who go out in plainclothes. Additionally, decoy operations of the unit would be more thoroughly planned. Finally, the officers in the unit would undergo psychological testing.[33]

Peer Group Socialization and Reinforcement

Police training, such as it is, provides the recruit with the basic indoctrination in the job task requirements of the occupation. But it is when the recruit passes into the police department itself that his socialization process of acquiring the norms of the occupation and of the particular department begins to occur through interaction with veteran officers. Often told to discount everything he learned in formal training, which is termed too "idealistic" for the real world of police operations, the recruit becomes privy to the "tricks of the trade" of the older men. These "tricks" may include illegal or unethical practices found to be expedient in law enforcement. Police veterans are also likely to impart their operational definition of "criminality" to the younger men. The rookie is taught to pick out suspicious behavior according to peer group perceptions, and if these perceptions reflect the biases and prejudices of older officers who feel that certain racial groups incline toward criminality, then these attitudes are probably transferred to the rookie. If the rookie is socialized "properly," then he will acquire the attitudes of the veteran officer to whom he is assigned. What the veteran officer sees as suspicious, the rookie will see as suspicious; the way a veteran officer reacts to a given situation is the way the rookie officer will react.

Because police work is performed in pairs or in small groups, and because compatibility is deemed essential in view of the dependence that police officers have on their partners for their survival, the pressures to accept and adopt institutional norms are great. While police officers do not always get along with each other, "there is probably a higher degree of compatibility and agreement on the basic goals, and means to those goals, in police work than in any other similar organization, including the armed forces. Those who cannot accept the means and ends of the organization quickly find the job unbearable and either resign or are dismissed."[34] The police officers who stay on, performing their duties in pairs or small groups, operate in accordance with the acquired norms. Without benefit of much supervision, these police officials enforce the laws with broad discretion and influenced by the values and attitudes derived from their peer group.

Fraternalism or solidarity among police officers increases in proportion to an actual or perceived loss of respect and authority in the community. Already a closed social group, the police draw even closer together because of what they feel is a decline in their authority—an essential aspect of many police officers' self-esteem—caused by lenient courts, their low status in the community, and the dangers to which they are continually exposed. Feeling themselves challenged and abused by the outside world, the police close ranks for self-protection, which is manifested by the rule of silence and the emphasis on the maintenance of respect for the police. Police solidarity in our society is described by Rodney Stark as obsessive. "Its primary manifestation is a cult of secrecy and loyalty not unlike that attributed to the Mafia. The one overriding rule among the police seems to be: Never squeal on a brother officer no matter what he does."[35]

Interestingly, the code of silence is not only observed against external inquiries but also against internal investigations. The process of shutting out internal control mechanisms begins early in the policeman's career. A former patrolman in the department of a large eastern city stated that in his first week in recruit training he was warned to watch his tongue: "One of your classmates may be a plant from the internal investigation division." This officer recounted that the group norm he was taught to observe was that the strongest criticism that one can make of a fellow officer is not that he is brutal or that he is corrupt but that he is a "fink", willing to breach the code of silence. The police code of silence, so like the underworld *omerta*, solidifies the "blue brotherhood."

Brotherhood. It means a fraternity of legally frustrated men with clean-cut hair, large coffee-ridden stomachs and impaired social lives who show up in embarrassing numbers to give blood to their wounded and race to town to 10-13's (assist officers) with their .38's loosened and the adrenalin shifting extra blood to the stomach and other vital organs, making them breathe faster. Men who stand at massive cop funerals in stricken lines and socialize with each other and look at clocks that have 13, 14, 15, etc., written over the normal hours, men who are linked always to each other by $700 walkie-talkies and their Bad-News car radio; men who feel, despite societies for ethnic cops. "We are all blue." The department is the family; the precinct is "the House."[36]

The monolithic solidarity of the brotherhood is not always there. It has been troubled in some places by divisions in the ranks on racial lines and by the disclosures of the Knapp Commission and other unfavorable publicity about cases of police malpractice which have invited scrutiny into police practices. Wary of "undercover agents" and internal affairs types, a sense of paranoia has beset some departments so that ultimately the sanctity of the brotherhood has been violated to the extent that a police officer's partner "is all he can trust." A former New York City policeman told ABC

News: "Aside from your partner, there's no sense of brotherhood in the Police Department. You never know if the new guy on the job is reporting to the Commissioner's office."[37]

Police officers working in pairs develop a strong sense of partnership described as "a marriage without the tensions of sex." Engaged in a sometimes dangerous occupation, they come to depend on each other, often for their lives. With the "police couple," the common and most elemental unit in police operations, solidarity and secrecy is inviolable. A successful partnership is where the men behave as "blood brothers, good buddies" and "chums in crime."[38] To break up a successful police pair may drive a wedge in the elemental link of solidarity and secrecy, and it also affects the effectiveness of a police department by impairing the morale of policemen made unhappy by the separation from their partners.

A case in point is the debilitating effect that the breakup of possibly the most famous police partnership has had on their arrest productivity. David Greenberg and Bob Hantz, better known as Batman and Robin, are a legendary pair in New York City, "two partners baptized in blood and named in Bed-Stuy for their agility in ledge crawling, throwing grappling hooks, dropping from sky lights, scrambling over roofs and fire escapes, disguising themselves and materializing from nowhere."[39] The pair achieved fame when, as patrolmen, they accumulated a record of 660 arrests in four years. Promoted to detective simultaneously and assigned to the 13th Robbery Squad in Bedford-Stuyvesant in Brooklyn, they were put on separate teams with opposite shifts. Unhappiness over the breakup of their team led to an indifference about their arrest production and the two men bottomed out the rating list based on the number of arrests of the fifty-six detectives in their division.

The partners were no longer quite so magnificent as the time when they, two iconoclastic white cops, were making more arrests in Bed-Stuy than all the black detectives put together, when they got this incredible record of 93 percent convictions on their 600 narcotics and stolen weapons arrests, that time when they got their names. Of course they were still, in their superior's words, "Fledgling" dicks, but there was a problem and the problem was, they were not together.[40]

The significance of the total range of police experiences shapes the occupational behavior of policemen, thus affecting the way they enforce the law. The police officer internalizes the effects of these experiences so that they occupy an important part of his value system. The work-personality of the policeman is the result of the sum total of these experiences, and this may explain the nature of policing in urban society. What the officer becomes, or rather what his attitudes become as a result of his significant experiences, is what society can expect in the way of police behavior and practice in law enforcement.

The excessive commitment to solidarity and secrecy has allowed the police to become impervious to internal and external controls on their behavior. At times law and decency have been abused without reaction from departmental authority for the sake of morale. Utilizing solidarity and secrecy as a cloak to shield them from societal and organizational checks, the police have covered up illegal actions, abrogation of departmental rules, personal misdemeanors, and violations of the rule of law and justice. Not only have these exigencies of policing impaired the organizational capacity of the police, but they corrode the viability of the American police, as presently constituted, as enforcement agents of a democratic legal system.

3

Street-Level Politics: Police-Community Relations

An ideal of government under law is voluntary compliance with the law by the citizens, thereby making enforcement negligible or even unnecessary. Minimum law enforcement in a democracy is only obtainable with a high degree of public support. This requires the police to become sensitized to conditions that are conducive to voluntary citizen compliance and minimal enforcement. Improvements in the development of an understanding of public service needs and in the building of public confidence in the police contribute to voluntary compliance with the law.

Public confidence in a police department is directly related to the image that citizens have of their police, and these images are formed from the impressions people gain about law enforcement. People—good, bad, and indifferent—are the concern of police forces; constant interaction with the public provides for the high visibility of the police. Policemen are observed during the performance of their regular duties: making arrests, patrolling, and providing assistance. The public also views them through the communications media and hears about them from each other. Thus, impressions are formed about the police from these direct and indirect contacts, and these impressions constitute the police public image.

The building of public support and confidence is made difficult by the customary obscurity of police operations and administration. A positive openness about a police department's programs, problems, and goals can do much to improve relations with the public.

The development of mutual trust and confidence between police departments and the public is not accomplished through a police public relations program alone. Public relations, as part of an overall effective public support program, is a way for a police department to present factual information about itself to a community. It is a prepared, one-way channel of communication designed to influence community opinion favorably in behalf of a police department. However, public relations by itself is a limited expedient and can be unproductive or counterproductive if it is not backed by positive police activities and behavior.

A public support program includes a two-way exchange between the police and the public. Public relations, in this sense, is subsumed under a total community relations program that includes an exchange of ideas

41

between police officers and citizens. The purpose of a police-community relations program is for each group to educate the other on basic needs, to establish acceptable means for realizing these needs, and to eliminate conflicts rooted in erroneous perceptions.

Recently, mounting tensions between the police and some groups of citizens have stimulated efforts to improve community relations in departments across the land. The creation of community relations units is an organizational attempt to minimize the personal discretion of patrolmen on the street level in an effort to guarantee nondiscriminatory service for all residents in an urban area.[1] Additionally, the community relations concept is seen as a means of de-escalating the adversary role of police in society. The strategic placement of community relations units in neighborhoods seeks the integration of the police with the community. Integration is made possible insofar as citizens are able to interact with police officials on a basis of equality and are allowed to participate in the determination of policy affecting police practices in their community.

Municipal governments, especially in large cities, have seen the practicalities of police-community relations centers and have encouraged their formation. This has come about in response to neighborhood pressures for an increased popular participation in local affairs. Municipalities have become increasingly willing to provide institutional arrangements designed to improve communications between neighborhoods and the municipal government, and to improve the provision of public service by offering it on a decentralized basis. These institutional innovations generate a continuing dialogue with neighborhood residents which sensitizes administrators to neighborhood requirements and aspirations, and the administrative decentralization of services can enable neighborhood variations in the delivery of services. Police-community relations units both increase dialogue with the community and provide more particularized and sensitive police services.[2]

A prevailing emphasis on police-community relations comes none too soon at a time when the policeman is increasingly withdrawn from the community he serves.

The major urban centers of today are torn along the lines of black and white over the administration of the law and the enforcement of order. The beat patrolman reflects the white community; he is a product of it and enters the black and brown communities with increased fear, anger and confusion. He receives little support from the ghetto in exchange for dangerous service. His major source of support comes from his own community and as a result there he is prone to provide "service with a smile."[3]

However, even in the white civilian community, the police officer does not feel at home. The nature of his job and his occupational environment isolates him, and he is wary of politicians and judges and administrative superiors and even of the citizens in his own white community, who, he feels, do not always provide him with the support that he expects. Consequently, the police officer derives his support and satisfaction from his fellow officers, and this tightens the bond of the "fraternity of the station house" as he feels himself, either by choice or by circumstance, to be an outcast in the society that he has sworn to defend and protect.

Unquestionably, it is in the black community that tensions between police and citizens are greatest. The ghetto is the locale of much urban crime, and as a result the presence of law enforcement officers is intensified there. Yet despite their urgent need for police protection, ghetto residents are antagonistic to the police. To the blacks living in ghettos, the police officer becomes the symbol of frustration, the symbol of a society they feel has treated them harshly. James Baldwin wrote that relations between the police and black citizens is based on hostility and fear. "The policeman moves through Harlem . . . like an occupying soldier in a bitterly hostile country; which is precisely what, and where he is, and is the reason he walks in twos and threes."[4]

The tension that exists between white police officers and the black community has had an effect on the solidarity of the police. Black officers are becoming increasingly conscious of their blackness instead of being steadfastly committed to the "blue" fraternity. They also have become sensitive to police practices in minority neighborhoods and are beginning to protect the rights of citizens in those neighborhoods. Black officers, through their ethnic associations, have joined with black citizen groups on a number of occasions in confrontations with police departments in cases of alleged brutality against minority citizens. In Detroit, in April 1972, during a conference sponsored by the Michigan State University Center for Urban Affairs, the MSU School of Criminal Justice, the Guardians of Michigan, and the Detroit Police Department, Sergeant Harvey Adams, Jr., president of the Pittsburgh Guardians, a black police officers' association, stated a loyalty to the black community over an allegiance to his occupation. He said black police officers "can no longer afford the luxury of identifying as some type of group with particular or special kinds of problems. The problem is between the black community and the white police institution." Adams also referred to the use of tactical mobile units by many cities as "escalations on the part of police departments of suppressing blacks."[5] The conference ended by issuing a list of twenty-two recommendations that included ways to solidify the ties between black officers and the black community and to expand the numbers of black officers in police departments. One of the recommendations was that a permanent investigating committee should be established within the Guardians to deal with cases of brutality in black and poor communities, and that this committee make its findings public.

In view of the poor relations that exist between the police and black citizens, it is not surprising that a great deal of police-community relations activities are addressed to the black community.

Although police-community relations programs are varied, there is a consistent pattern in the approach employed by many departments.[6] Much police-community relations activity can be described as public relations, with police departments using the news media and personal contacts in order to reach the public and favorably influence public opinion. The media is the vehicle for news releases, radio and television promotional activities, and newspaper articles promoting good will. Public relations involving personal contact include police speaker bureaus and guided tours of police facilities. Programs that seek to provide the police with a positive visibility include the use of scooter patrols, bicycle patrols, rumor control centers, and alcohol and narcotics education projects. The rationale for scooter patrols is that they combine the advantage of wider territorial coverage of squad cars and the personalized community contact of foot patrolmen. Bicycle patrols have been used effectively by the Long Beach, California police department in order to curtail many downtown crimes, which have given the police a bad rating in public opinion polls. Rumor control centers primarily function to quell rumors and hearsay during crisis situations, but they have served to prevent trouble from occurring in the first place when they are operational prior to the development of a crisis. Rumor control centers are often manned by staff workers and volunteers and are established by an agency other than the police. In communities where racial problems are minimal or nonexistent, but large numbers of adolescents are experimenting with drugs, a police-community relations unit may be primarily concerned with drug education programs. This may involve having mobile narcotics education exhibits of programs encouraging parents and teachers to take the initiative in narcotics and alcohol education at home and in the schools.

Police-community relations units have sponsored numerous youth activities, including teenage traffic safety programs, teen clubs, athletic programs, and police "mod-squads." One of the oldest police-community relations programs in the country has been the Police Athletic Leagues (PAL), which existed in many northeastern and midwestern cities for years. The thrust of the PAL program has been to effect good public relations with youths while attempting to come to grips with juvenile delinquency and crime. Another program that has caught on is the "mod-squad" approach. Some of the mod-squad programs—called by several different names—are solely directed to minority youths; others cut across the socioeconomic spectrum. Most of the programs provide formal training in police basics. In addition to their training, mod-squad cadets may ride in patrol cars and, in general, receive a thorough understanding of police operations. The mod-squad programs provide teenagers with "constructive roaming" by assigning them to aid beat patrolmen in some cities or having them patrol playgrounds, parks, vacant recreational lots, and school grounds during the summer months in other communities. Ultimately, this approach hopes to increase the teenagers' knowledge of police services and policemen, and tries to encourage the cadets to make the police department a career in the future.

There are several programs promoting a positive police image at the elementary school level. These consist of policemen visiting the school and talking and showing films to the children about the role of police officers. A well-received program has been "Officer Friendly," financed by the Sears-Roebuck Corporation, which involves programmed and outlined visits to public and parochial elementary school classrooms by members of a police-community relations unit. Officer Friendly comes into a school, introduces himself, shows a short film, and tells the children about the police as a public helper. Before leaving, Officer Friendly may give each child a copy of the police department coloring book, which stresses the idea of the policeman as a friend and protector.

Several police-community relations units are helping unemployed minority group citizens find work or, in concert with federal antipoverty agencies, are making available civil service jobs and training. Other police departments employ minority young men and women from low-income neighborhoods and provide them with a career development potential within the department or with job training useful in other employment. The community service officer (CSO) is one such employment program.

CSOs are generally men and women between seventeen and twenty-one who do not meet all the educational or physical requirements for the police academy, but are interested in police work and have contact with minority groups in the city. CSOs are usually assigned to a police-community relations unit and serve as liaisons between the unit and the hard-to-reach minority citizens. CSOs wear a police uniform, or a reasonable facsimile, but do not have law enforcement powers nor do they carry weapons. The purpose of the CSOs is to bridge the gap between the police and the ghetto community, and therefore, they are often recruited from the neighborhood in which they will function.

Many police departments also have citizen crime prevention programs as ways of enlisting the public in cooperating with law enforcement officials in combatting alarming increases in the crime rate. These programs are designed to provide the police with extra eyes and ears that can alert them about suspicious persons or acts. The programs come under a variety of names: "Operation Crime Stop," "Crime Spot," "Operation Observer," "Operation Citizen Alert," "Community Radio Watch," "Citizens' Observer Corps," and "Project Alert." The police department establishes a special telephone number for incoming calls, briefs its personnel, prints wallet-sized cards with "Operation Crime Stop" instructions and distributes these to the citizens, and coordinates an advertising campaign to convey the program to the public. Citizen-participants report their observations of suspicious activities to the police department's special telephone number. There also are a number of programs involving the cooperation of a police department and residents of a low-income area for expanded patrols aided by citizen volunteers to deter lawlessness in the high-crime neighborhoods.

A significant community relations endeavor is the police "outreach to the community," through storefronts and mobile centers. These neighborhood police-community relations "outposts" provide the police with the opportunity to interact with citizens on a personal man-to-man basis. They fulfill the concept of administrative decentralization by providing public services on a more personal and specialized basis. The centers are manned by police-community relations officers or by patrolmen who are capable of responding to the problems brought to them by the residents of the neighborhood. Most centers are devoted entirely to a service orientation and, unlike police substations, generally avoid involvement in law enforcement activities.

The officers in the centers, or storefronts, primarily deal with community services such as driver education and training, English training for foreign residents, sponsorship of neighborhood citizen-police meetings, coaching athletic teams, speaking in schools, helping citizens find jobs, explaining laws to citizens who do not understand the laws or who do not speak English, teaching citizens how to fill out accident and insurance claims reports, and teaching patrol officers how to communicate with the residents of the neighborhood. Storefront centers may occupy space in a permanent structure or be mobile. Fixed centers may be found in shopping centers, office buildings, church basements, reconverted city buses, house trailers, toolsheds on construction sites, warehouses, and housing projects.

In order to foster better two-way communication between the public and the police, police-community relations units sponsor institutional channels for an improved dialogue. Generally there are five types of arrangements for this interaction: meetings with citywide advisory committees; meetings with neighborhood advisory committees; meetings with committees of minority group leaders; neighborhood surveys; and police-community workshops.

Citywide advisory committees bring together the higher officials of a police department (and possibly city government officials) and the city's leading citizens for exchanges about problems and policies for solutions to police-community frictions. In larger urban areas, citywide advisory committees serve to coordinate the functions of smaller-scale councils, such as neighborhood councils. These committees are *not* civilian review boards and operate solely as liaisons between the police and the community.

A paradigm of neighborhood advisory committees is offered in St. Louis, the first city to offer a police-community relations program, beginning in 1957. St. Louis has nine neighborhood councils, which are called district committees. The district committees are similar to citywide councils, but they operate in limited geographical areas, high-crime centers, or in sections of the city where police-community relations problems exist. The membership of the St. Louis neighborhood advisory councils is made up of the neighborhood residents who choose to belong. A general meeting for each council is held once a month at the district storefront community relations center or the district police station. The police district commander or his representative attends each meeting. Meetings are conducted by the council's district chairman, who is elected each year by the membership. The councils have four operating subcommittees: law enforcement, juvenile, sanitation, and business. Chairmen for the four subcommittees are appointed by the council chairman. Complaints to the police district representative are submitted in writing and are reported on at the next meeting.

The St. Louis police-community relations unit also recruits neighborhood leaders from each city's 109 patrol districts to serve on crime prevention committees. This program is called the patrol area leader plan (PAL). PALs are citizen volunteers who are already members of the police-community relations district committees. This relationship enhances the program because it insures the cooperation of established neighborhood organizations. All district sergeants are assigned to this program, and their task is to serve as the PALs' contacts and to form a closer alliance between the citizens of their district and the police patrolman assigned to the area.

Once a week each district's PALs meet with their district sergeant contact over coffee and discuss the district's problems and offer ways to eliminate them. These are deemed valuable contributions because PALs live or work in the involved districts and therefore know their neighborhoods well.

PAL committee members hold their own meetings as often as they wish. All of these meetings are attended by police officers selected by their supervising officer or by the chief of police. District sergeants are expected to attend at least three of these meetings a year. The rationale of the PAL committees is to deal with crime prevention matters. Specifically, PAL committees: discover and discuss crime problems in the neighborhood; determine areas where police patrol resources can most effectively be used; evaluate patrol capabilities in the neighborhood; and determine methods for citizen cooperation with the police in the neighborhood. A representative of the police-community relations unit is always present at the meetings, despite the crime problem orientation of the committees, in the event community relations questions are raised.

Meetings with committees of minority group leaders occur where community relations problems exist, primarily in high-crime, minority neighborhoods. The thrust of this approach is to have open lines of communication with minority and militant organizations covering the political spectrum. For example, the Baltimore police department's Civil Rights Unit, a section of the police-community relations unit, does not limit its contacts to the city's black militant groups. The unit has maintained contacts with such diverse groups as Students for a Democratic Society (SDS), Peace and Freedom Party, Ku Klux Klan (KKK), Black Panthers, Congress of Racial Equality (CORE), and National States' Rights Party (NSRP). San Antonio's police-community relations unit has had a continuing dialogue with leaders of militant white, black and Mexican-American organizations.

Police-neighborhood surveys have been utilized by the police-community relations unit of Greensboro, North Carolina. These surveys were designed to provide knowledge about public attitudes, grievances, and expectations of the police. The weakness of this approach, however, is that it could be classified as a one-way communication flow if the police department does not act upon the inputs derived from the surveys.

The fifth and final approach used for improving police-community dialogue are workshops. Police-community workshops may vary from informal exchanges to highly structured meetings and generally take the form of "controlled verbal confrontations"—sensitivity sessions. The purpose of these meetings is to bring groups of policemen and citizens together for a period of time so that each group can be made aware of the damaging stereotypes that they have of each other and see how these stereotypes influence their attitudes and behavior. The sessions are ultimately resolved with both groups striving to achieve a basis for cooperation so that future problem solving can be accomplished constructively. This form of "controlled verbal confrontation" is complex and delicate and requires the guidance of trained professionals.

Case Studies of Police-Community Relations Models

Atlanta has a police department of approximately 1300 officers; 27 percent of the officers are black.[7] Of the black officers, one is an assistant chief who commands the single largest line unit in the police department: the Uniformed Operations Bureau. In Atlanta, the police-community relations unit is named the Crime Prevention Bureau. The bureau was formed in January 1966 because of a rising number of civil disturbances that had been occurring in the black community. Most of these disturbances were precipitated by the shooting of black men and youths by white police officers or neighborhood white merchants. The incidents invariably resulted in some violence, looting, and vandalism on the part of neighborhood residents. The Crime Prevention Bureau was organized as the police department's "outreach" into these troubled areas to abate incipient tensions through the development of a dialogue with members of the community, and especially with the community leadership.

The Crime Prevention Bureau issued the following statement:

The purpose of the Police-Community Relations Program is to win the citizens' respect and concern for their own community, to provide public understanding of effective law enforcement, and to gain public support of police law enforcement and the functions of the police.

We hope that through the efforts of our police officers we can maintain a better relationship with the people and that through greater understanding on the part of the community, we will be able, to a degree, to decrease the number of crimes in these given areas.

The organizational structure of the Crime Prevention Bureau has its officers categorized by their tasks following the bureau's subdivision into functional program elements. Consistent with the Bureau's functional program activities, regular police officers are assigned as crime prevention officers, missing person officers, and "Officer Friendlies." Community service officers (CSOs) —limited-duty, part-time personnel—and the Police Action Line complete the bureau's organizational structure.

The bureau's director is a black superintendent, who reports directly to the chief of police. The other supervisors are an assistant director, watch supervisors for the day and evening shifts, both of whom hold the rank of sergeant, and office supervisors for the day and evening shifts. Fourteen of the bureau's complement of twenty-four are black officers.

There are eleven crime prevention officers performing activities considered to be the crux of the bureau's outreach program to the community. Their immediate supervisor is the watch sergeant on duty during their work shift. Officers assigned to crime prevention activities are responsible for a number of programs, including working with Equal Opportunity of Atlanta (EOA) centers; working with schools and social agencies; delivering speeches to churches and civic groups and associations; counseling delinquent youths and school dropouts; and obtaining lodging for homeless and stranded persons.

In addition, officers of this unit assist other police department personnel in handling demonstrations, disorders, and similar activities. They are also utilized by the Training Division to provide guidance and assistance to police recruits.

The Crime Prevention Bureau is sensitized to the importance of its community relations outreach programs. In an explanatory handout about these concerns, the bureau described its approach:

The duties of the Crime Prevention Bureau are concerned mainly with eleven poverty stricken areas within the city. The eleven seasoned officers assigned to these areas have proved themselves in both temperament and general knowledge of their areas. Each officer assigned permanently to the Crime Prevention Bureau is required to spend a month in each of these areas to acquaint himself with the problems and services offered in these areas. After a month's circulation in the [EOA] Centers they are assigned to a particular center and area to work.

Nine of the eleven crime prevention officers are black. Interviews with bureau personnel and other police officers indicate that it has been difficult to interest white officers in community relations work because much of the emphasis is directed toward the city's poor black neighborhoods. There has been a high turnover of white officers among crime prevention officers. Many of the white officers in the bureau are assigned to the missing person and Officer Friendly programs.

Crime prevention officers, "selected because of their attitudes, their interest, and their ability to understand the problems of [their clients]" are assigned to areas represented by EOA centers. EOA centers are strategically located in the city's low-income black neighborhoods and maintain close contact with the residents through their myriad social and economic programs. The EOA centers were originally funded by the Office of Economic Opportunity, but since this source has now been eliminated, the centers are now dependent on state and local funds for continuing operations. The close identification of the uniformed police officers with the centers allows for expanded interaction between the officers and the public, and involves the officers in the services of the centers such as counseling on employment opportunities and higher education.

The officers operating in, and from, the centers help to bring about a positive image of the police and are in a position to personally come into contact with large numbers of citizens in a service context. Using the EOA centers as bases of operation and in cooperation with the center personnel, crime prevention officers assist in organizing new neighborhood organizations at the adult and youth level, such as Junior Deputy Clubs, Teen Clubs, Junior Crime Fighters, Crime Prevention Committees, Good Neighbor Clubs, Good Guys Clubs, and Girls' Youth Clubs. Although the officers do not become officials in any of these groups, they cooperate closely with each organization. The bureau feels that the creation of these groups helps to improve the neighborhoods served and minimizes the incidents of disorder.

Crime prevention officers also provide recreational outlets for the residents of their areas. The unit has station wagons equipped with a turntable or tape deck and speakers. With the aid of this equipment, the officers sponsor street dances by blocking off a residential street and providing the music for the festivities. A similar format is employed in parking lots of shopping centers, after the stores have closed. Merchants in some of the shopping centers have been prompted by EOA personnel to provide soft drinks and hot dogs for the dances.

Other rapport-inducing activities performed by the officers have included using sprinklers for the fire hydrants in highly populated low-income areas during hot days and providing tours of police facilities. The tours have been directed to youths to acquaint them with the police department and its functions. At times, crime prevention officers are assigned to the Mobile Precinct, a mobile community relations service. The bureau uses a converted library bus that carries educational displays to the neighborhoods on topics such as police activities or the dangers of drug abuse.

The key link in the bureau's dialogue with the minority community has been provided by citizens' neighborhood advisory organizations. The staff of the EOA centers encouraged the formation of these organizations as a means of organizing and politicizing the citizens of minority neighborhoods in order to establish a two-way communication between the citizens and the institutions that affect their lives. The police department, through its Crime Prevention Bureau, cooperated with the EOA in the development of these neighborhood groups and has found them a useful means of access to the minority community leadership. By the same token, the organized and politically aware citizen groups have gained by the attention they now receive from public figures and institutions and the accommodations that are made in their behalf.

The neighborhood advisory groups have a two-level structure. The lower level, called a citizens' neighborhood advisory council, consists of block area organizations within a designated district. A neighborhood district, coinciding with an EOA center's area, is divided by block areas, and each block area within the district has its own elected council.

Meetings are held as often as the membership desires, generally twice a month, and are presided over by the chairman and other elected officers. The agenda for discussion at the meetings consists of the various problems facing the block area and may include questions about street lighting, traffic congestion, garbage collection, teenage gangs, and police operations. A member of the Crime Prevention Bureau will try to attend all of the block area council meetings and will address himself to all service problems, including those that do not relate to police matters, in order to manifest the police department's varied interests and concern for the residents' general welfare.

The higher-level minority citizens' organization is called the neighborhood advisory committee, and each EOA center's district has a districtwide committee. These committees are made up of the chairmen of the block councils and they meet once a month in their district EOA center. Problems discussed at these meetings are similar to the ones deliberated at the lower level except that they are presented within a districtwide perspective. In attendance at the committee meetings are a police officer from the Crime Prevention Bureau and the mayor's representative. The mayor's representative will often relay the complaints of the committee to the mayor and to the board of aldermen for correctives. An officer of the Crime Prevention Bureau defined this as "bringing City Hall to the neighborhood."

Occasionally, specific and individual grievances are aired to the community organizer who directs an EOA center. The community organizer may at his discretion call an ad hoc meeting of either the districtwide committee or the area block council. The community organizer will also invite the presence of the Crime Prevention Bureau and the mayor's representative.

Model Cities, another program funded by the federal government, also sponsors meetings of neighborhood groups. The structure of these groups is not necessarily analogous to the one employed under the auspices of the EOA centers, but Model Cities, too, attempts to mobilize the interests of the community in behalf of neighborhood concerns. Model Cities organizers will sometimes ask for the presence of an officer from the Crime Prevention Bureau, but the bureau has a closer relationship with the EOA, because the bureau's community programs and the operational structure of the citizens' organizations sponsored by EOA were developed in concert with the latter agency.

Through its contact with EOA centers, the bureau has been able to provide a variety of services. Officers who receive complaints of improper performance by a city government agency refer these complaints to the city service coordinator at City Hall for corrective action. Cases of hardship are discovered through the EOA and brought to the attention of the proper authorities. With the cooperation of the city public schools, crime prevention officers obtain listings of school dropouts. These are then counseled by the officers, who urge them to return to school.

The educational programs undertaken by the bureau are not only oriented to the citizens but also serve the police department, and especially police cadets. All new officers hired by the city are assigned to the Crime Prevention Bureau while waiting for police training school to begin. The period they spend in company with the officers of the bureau acquaints them with the problems of the lower-class and minority citizens. This experience prepares the cadet for the realities that an urban police officer faces and conditions him to practice human relations in his job.

This assignment of the cadets also enables superior officers of the Crime Prevention Bureau to evaluate the attitude and performance of new patrolmen in the community relations context. The police department has given the bureau the latitude to recommend a cadet's dismissal from the force in the event that the evaluation by the bureau points out a racial bias on the cadet's part.

The Crime Prevention Bureau employs seventy-five community service officers between the ages of seventeen and twenty-five, recruited primarily from lower-income neighborhoods to work for a fifteen-week period each summer. This program is designed to rehabilitate disadvantaged youths by instilling values and to prepare them for potential careers in the police department or for some other useful capacity. Community service officers assist regular officers and perform certain limited duties in city parks, recreation centers, and other locations where youths are apt to congregate. They are also supposed to be helpful in the establishment of rapport between the police department and minority youths.

Atlanta was the first city to adopt this program concept as part of its police service. Despite the program's past difficulties, the city and the police department appear to be committed to the program and, in fact, have sought to expand the community service officer complement. The police department hopes to overcome the program's previous liabilities by screening for youths with aptitude, integrity, and stability. Also, the department now plans to utilize the CSOs in useful and constructive tasks and to provide them with training and educational opportunities.

The contributions of the bureau are twofold: the bureau is a feedback link between the police department and the community, and vice versa; and, the bureau is instrumental in crime prevention in the areas it serves. Ultimately, the contributions are interdependent and fulfill the essential objective of an orderly society—the prevention of disorder. The communications and the rapport that the bureau has established with citizens have minimized the apprehension aspect of the police officer's role because the cooperation gained from citizens has reduced the crime rate in the areas policed by the bureau.

Unfortunately, Atlanta's crime rate does not substantiate great optimism about the program. However, bureau officers point out that although crime statistics in Atlanta show a continuing increase, the statistics are obscured by the increase in the population of the city. In effect, they suggest that crime statistics do not provide a true index of the bureau's effectiveness, but that the improved attitudes of the residents of the ghetto toward the police—an intangible index—are the measure of the bureau's contribution.

The bureau does not ignore the traditional police role of apprehension of criminals, but the main thrust of the unit is providing services for the citizens and developing a congenial image of the department in hard-to-reach areas. The bureau states that "at the same time the officers must realize that they are still policemen and if a problem comes up and an arrest becomes necessary, the officer must make the arrest."

This philosphy has not met with the approval of all the members of the bureau. Among the officers interviewed, two of them suggested that arrests by bureau personnel were encouraged by superior officers, and that little community relations work was performed by the evening shift. Instead, bureau patrols in the evening hours might contribute to energizing the apprehension of residents. These officers were concerned that the active involvement in the "cops and robbers" aspect was detrimental to the bureau's community relations image.

There also seems to be some doubt that the bureau, through its crime prevention officers, serves as the feedback link between the police department and the community. While there is evidence that the bureau has opened up a dialogue with the residents and leaders of some minority neighborhoods, there is also visible evidence to show that little rapport has been established in other areas, the public housing projects in particular.

The projects are populated mostly by poor blacks, and the myriad acts of vandalism perpetrated by the residents are easily apparent to the casual eye. The high crime rate of the projects is also cause for concern. Sergeant Ernest H. Lyons, a black officer who gained a splendid reputation improving the image of the police in the EOA center districts, stated that conditions in the projects are different from those of the EOA neighborhoods. The project residents are poor migrants from the rural areas and are extremely difficult to reach whereas the citizens in the traditionally black areas are old-line Atlantans and more easily dissuaded from their antipolice bigotry. He summarized his analysis of the bureau's predicament with the housing project communities: "We come here and try to reach these people. But, it's very hard; they have set feelings against the police. They come from the rural areas and move into new housing projects and destroy them. To do a good job we [the bureau] would have to be here twenty-four hours a day."

The most pessimistic estimate concerned the bureau's link with the officers of the police department. Interviews with personnel of the department brought out little sympathy with the functions of the bureau, with the exception of the missing person function, nor much knowledge about the bureau's activities. A young black officer assigned to the Crime Prevention Bureau, who is completing his college education in the evenings, expressed the prevailing condition: "The bureau is achieving rapport with the black community. But unless every police officer practices community relations, we [bureau officers] are the illusion and reality rides in the squad cars."

The New Orleans police department consists of 1406 officers, with 80 black policemen and three black policewomen. Rank levels of black officers include a deputy chief for administration, the third highest rank in the department, and eight sergeants.

The Community Relations Division of the New Orleans police department was initiated in 1966 when two black officers were assigned to the newly created unit and charged with the responsibility of establishing reciprocal lines of communication in ten "target areas" of the city. The early efforts of the unit concentrated on the formulation and implementation of programs aimed at bridging the communication gap existing with the "target areas" in the minority community. This emphasis has been retained by the division.

The division's initial programs were launched in 1966 at a cost of $12,000 obtained from police department funds. Subsequent racial tensions in the city led to a growth in the Community Relations Division and to the receipt of added funding. In 1968 former Police Superintendent Joseph Giarrusso was able to persuade business leaders to provide fiscal donations for the division's programs. These funds from private sources were seen as "business investments" in community tranquility to preclude far greater financial costs from racial outbreaks. Additional police department funds were also provided which, coupled with the private grants, amounted to $30,000 for the division to use for operational expenses. The financial contribution was placed in a bank and called a "Recreational Fund." This term accurately described the division's original concept, which was to organize and supervise recreational activities for youths with an emphasis on activities during the summer months. With the expanded financial support, the first and only time that private funding was obtained, the division was able to implement its full range of programs in 1968.

The division is staffed by three supervisors, fifteen police officers, four civilians, and two community service officers. Organizationally, the division is responsible to the superintendent of police. The head of the unit is a black policewoman, who has the title of director, although she retains her basic police rank for pay purposes. Other supervisors consist of an assistant director, a black officer, and a white desk sergeant whose duties involve office management. Seven of the fifteen officers are black, and one is a Mexican-American. The civilians who perform clerical duties for the division are all black. The community service officers assigned to the division are black women who perform clerical duties and assist the police officers on some service missions.

The community service officer concept has been a disappointment to the superior officers of the division. This program is funded by federal Emergency Employment Funds and a matching city contribution. Ninety-five percent of the CSOs working in the police department are women, although the intent of the program was to employ young men from eighteen through twenty-five years of age from the city's black ghettos and to train them for potential future police careers. The young men were to contribute to the department as CSOs by helping in the development of rapport between police officers and black neighborhood youths. However, few qualified young men have been attracted to the program, despite a $395 a month salary for unemployable or difficult-to-employ youths with deprived backgrounds. Consequently, the present CSOs have done little in the way of assisting in actual police work and have not received any formal police training. The personnel in the program have been termed "unpromising."

The division is housed in a community relations center, a renovated four-story building in a black neighborhood. There is a gymnasium on the first level, and general offices make up the second and fourth levels. The third floor is used as a community auditorium with a seating capacity of one hundred and is available to civic and social organizations. The division is a centralized unit and all assigned personnel work out of the center. The division operates recreational programs directed at underprivileged neighborhoods and educational programs designed primarily to improve the police department's image in the community.

A fundamental problem with the New Orleans community relations unit, as with many others, is that its functions can be better described as public relations rather than community relations, in that there is no program aimed at establishing a two-way dialogue with the public. Instead, the activities tend to emphasize police image-building with certain community groups, particularly with the youth in lower-income black neighborhoods, with no access for a reciprocal exchange of information.

Although the division has stressed police public relations with the minority community, it is noteworthy that there has been a lack of positive relations established with the rest of the police department. The International Association of Chiefs of Police conducted a survey of the New Orleans police department in July 1971, and noted that "one gets the impression that police-community relations is a specialized function performed by a specialized division. This should not be the case; until the programs are designed to involve all police officers, police-community relations will not show any significant improvement." Interviews conducted for this study appear to confirm this earlier conclusion. Black officers assigned to the division have stated with pride: "The Community Relations Division is a unit run by black for blacks." White officers assigned to areas in the police department have concurred with this assertion—with some derision.

The Community Relations Division is mindful of the need to establish an outreach program to the neighborhoods in order to develop a two-way communication with citizens. Towards this end, superior officers of the division have proposed a program calling for each of the city's eight police districts to be assigned a "community relations advisor" to advise and assist the district commander "relative to developing programs to create an aura of mutual cooperation and understanding between the community inhabitants and the police." The proposal envisions the decentralization of the division to allow for the placement of community relations advisors in "strategic locations" in each district.

Each of these community service centers would be used as a meeting place where the residents of the district and the police district commander could discuss mutual problems involving police matters in the community. The centers would also be equipped to serve as limited recreation facilities for youths during the summer. The centers also would be used as information facilities to provide assistance regarding employment opportunities, police recruitment, other government agencies, and similar matters.

The concept of the proposed program is to have the Community Relations Division, through its community relations advisors, serve as the intermediary between the district policemen and the citizen. The objective is to bring the police and the public together through the centers and to facilitate communication between them. Community relations advisors would hold classes and informal gatherings to educate the patrol officers of the district about the needs and opinions of the public in the district.

Despite funding problems, the police department approved a pilot project for the proposed program. A community service center went into operation in the summer of 1972 in the "Desire" housing project area. The center served the housing project and the entire fifth Police District, a predominantly poor, black area. The Housing Authority donated office space in Desire for the center. The center provided home economics training, information referrals, and recreational opportunities to the residents of the housing project. The program ended at the end of the summer, and although there was a determination to expand the center's service activities to the entire Fifth Police District, funds were not allotted to a continuation or expansion of the concept.

The New Orleans "Urban Squad" is not a part of the Community Relations Division; it is in the Patrol Bureau under the deputy superintendent for operations. But, it works closely with the Community Relations Division and is a team-policing program that has gained the respect of other police officers in the department and the appreciation of the citizens they police.

The Urban Squad was formed in February 1971 and is the brainchild of its founder and commander, Sergeant Rinal L. Martin, a black officer with eighteen years of service in the New Orleans police department. Martin conceived of the idea of having specially selected, racially integrated two-man teams patrol the Desire Project, an area with the highest crime rate in the city, and work in close harmony with the residents in the curtailment of crime. His proposal was approved and the pilot project was initiated in Desire. The concept has since proved so successful that it has been expanded to other housing project areas—at the request of the residents of the projects.

The Urban Squad is made up of two platoons, with seventeen patrolmen working on the day platoon and sixteen patrolmen on the night platoon; six sergeants are divided evenly among the platoons. Personnel of the Urban Squad work twelve hours a day, six days a week, for a twenty-four hour patrol. The work schedule is preferred by the men because it provides them with overtime pay and improves communication between officers of the shifts, without having the conventional middle shift to disrupt the flow of information.

Currently, the squad is assigned to patrol four housing projects, with a team responsible for each of two projects. Desire Project and Florida Project are the responsibilities of one team; the other team is responsible for St. Bernard Project and the Park Chester Apartments. There are approximately 40,000 residents in the four housing project areas. The patrol is handled by a "salt-and-pepper" team of a white and a black patrolman. The unmarked cars are "follow-up" cars driven by sergeants. Urban Squad officers usually wear casual civilian dress on duty as a rapport-developing device. They are armed and carry handcuffs and a police badge.

When the squad took over Desire Project, the area had a notorious reputation as the site of the nationally reported "battle" with the Black Panthers, along with the dubious distinction of having the highest crime rate in the city. Today, members of the squad proudly point out, the project has the lowest crime rate in New Orleans.

This remarkable achievement of the Urban Squad has been attributed by Sergeant Martin to careful screening of applicants to the squad, careful groundwork laid in an area before the squad assumes policing duties there, "quality investigation," and positive supervision. Martin personally screens every applicant to determine his suitability for the squad; the qualities he seeks in a man are an even temperament and an awareness of social problems. Before the squad begins to patrol a new area, Martin asks the Community Relations Division to introduce him and some of the squad's key personnel to the community leaders. The squad then explains its concepts to the leaders and solicits their support, and thus sets the stage for the assumption by the squad of its new responsibility.

"Quality investigation," to Martin, means not only going after hard crime but getting to the roots of crime as well. When the squad goes after narcotics, their emphasis is on the pusher, and not the user. Sergeant George A. Duke, a recent recruit to the squad and already infused with the contagious enthusiasm of the unit, said: "We're people oriented, not crime oriented. When arrests are made, the Urban Squad finds why the crime is committed." And the squad tries to provide the correctives to the causes of crime. An example given was the case of daylight burglaries committed by a group of teenagers in one of the project areas. It was discovered that the youths were free to roam the neighborhood because the New Orleans school system had a rule that suspended a student for the day if he was late to school. The Urban Squad persuaded the school board authorities to revoke this rule and allow students to remain in school despite their tardiness.

Additionally, the Urban Squad gained the good will of the community by stimulating needed city services, a task that goes beyond routine police activities. The Desire Project was overrun by rats, so the Urban Squad, in concert with the Community Relations Division, requested the Sanitation Department to clear the rats out. The solicitation of better public services for the residents of the projects is an undertaking considered routine by the Urban Squad.

Finally, positive supervision, as explained by Sergeant Martin, means that a diminishing arrest rate should be emphasized rather than the prevalent stress on arrest records as the criterion of police excellence. This entails a closer working relationship between first-line supervisors and patrolmen to insure that these values are continually imparted and that field police operations undergo constant observation by higher-ranking officers.

Ultimately, the Urban Squad's concept is that the policeman's primary function of protecting life and property can best be accomplished with the support and cooperation of the public. This is the way to insure a diminishing crime rate and hence a lower arrest rate. The squad emphasizes public relations and never loses an opportunity to remind the citizens it serves that the Urban Squad is at work to prevent crime in their neighborhood and that since the Urban Squad took over, crime has been appreciably reduced. Recently an Urban Squad officer was chatting with a young black girl in a housing project, and she recognized the squad's characteristic patch, a white and a black hand in a handshake, on the officer's arm. "Oh, you're with the Urban Squad," she said. "The Urban Squad . . . yes . . . you're just a little bit better."

Apparently, many housing project residents agree with the girl's evaluation of the squad. Shortly after the Urban Squad personnel began to patrol Desire Project, the residents of St. Bernard Project asked for this same type of police protection. They wanted an Urban Squad, "just like the one at Desire."

The Birmingham, Alabama, involvement in police-community relations is representative of the changes occurring in the South. Ten years ago, the

Birmingham police was personified by its commissioner, Eugene (Bull) Conner, and his "supporting cast of snapping police dogs" championing the cause of racism. This has all changed. Since thirty-nine-year-old James Parsons became chief of police in 1972 he has implemented a series of noteworthy administrative and recruitment reforms. He has employed a university psychology department to test police recruits to screen out the potential "bullies and misfits." He has instituted an extensive community relations program and has emphasized the recruiting of blacks for the police force. "Last year, the Birmingham police department had only 10 blacks on a force of 792. The new chief tripled that number of black officers in his first months and vows to add lots more. Six years ago, there were none."[8] In his spare time, Jim Parsons has a weekly radio program called "Buzz the Fuzz" in which he discusses police problems with callers.

In Birmingham, the police-community relations unit was renamed the Public Information Bureau in June 1970. A community relations unit has been in existence since 1966 when one was formed because of racial disturbances in the city. However, 1971 is considered by the "new" bureau to be its first full year of operation. The bureau reports directly to the chief of police.

The Public Information Bureau is divided into two sections, the Police-Community Relations Section and the Public Relations Section. Each section is responsible for a number of programs. Bureau programs are either youth-directed or educational in behalf of the development of a positive image of the police department.

On August 1, 1971, a year-round athletic program was organized, consisting of Police Athletic Teams for baseball, basketball, and boxing. The Police Athletic Team programs are considered to be one of the bureau's major activities. The bureau also participates in a citywide track program sponsored by the Mayor's Council on Youth Opportunity.

The Police Athletic Program has eight baseball teams of twenty boys per team. All of the youths in the baseball program are black, aged eleven through fourteen, with the majority of them residing in housing projects and high-crime areas. Two police officers from the department coordinate the baseball program, either on or off duty. The team's coaches are community volunteers drawn from the areas of the city where there is a Police Athletic Team program. It takes approximately $1200 to field each baseball team and to operate it for a year. This sum is spent on uniforms, insurance, equipment, umpires, and transportation. The players furnish their own shoes and gloves. Police department funds provide $4000 a year for all the baseball teams; the rest of the money is obtained through private donations from business firms and individuals.

During the three years that the baseball program has been in existence, the Police Athletic Team has been able to take the winning team on a trip outside the city of Birmingham. In the first year, the winning baseball team was given a one-day trip to Atlanta to attend an Atlanta Braves game. The following year the winning team was treated to a three-day tour of New York City. The highlight of this trip was the team's two-and-a-half inning game with the champion of New York's Police Athletic League in Yankee Stadium before the regularly scheduled major league baseball game. Funding for these trips is provided by private donations.

The basketball program is for black thirteen and fourteen-year-old boys. There are eight teams of ten players per team. The cost of operating each team is approximately $250. The Police Athletic Team program also sponsors five boxing teams in the city with an unlimited number of boys per team. Seventy percent of the boys participating in this program are white. The age bracket for the program adheres to Golden Gloves rules and ostensibly provides competition for ages ten through twenty-seven; the oldest participant in the program, however, is eighteen years old. The boxing program is considered to be the most expensive. It costs approximately $550 to operate a team, and there is also a fixed $3400 expenditure for a portable ring used by all the teams. Participants in the program furnish their own boxing shoes.

There is evidence that the bureau has made progress in bridging the communication gap with the city's black community and that the white and black leadership in Birmingham now work in closer harmony. An example of this progress is the formation of the city's Community Action Committee (CAC), a biracial group that includes the mayor, the chief of police, the president of the Fraternal Order of Police, outstanding attorneys, members of the Chamber of Commerce, professors from the University of Alabama, college professors from the area black schools, black ministers, representatives of the NAACP, prominent black citizens, the editors of the *Birmingham News,* and others. The committee meets weekly to discuss problems that are of concern to the black community and that could affect relations between the races in the city.

An effort has been made to involve the district officers—the beat officers, patrol sergeants, and shift commanders—in community affairs by having the bureau sponsor neighborhood "gripe" sessions at community centers in black neighborhoods. These sessions generally occur when black community groups request the presence of representatives from the police department. The bureau accedes to these requests by making every effort to bring some district officers to these encounters.

Captain Loyce A. Tate, commander of the Public Information Bureau, stated that no community relations endeavor is going to succeed unless it has the support of the police department's "rank and file" officers. His predecessor in the job, Captain Glen V. Evans, a veteran of thirty-four years in the Birmingham police department, expressed the opinion that he was removed from the position of the unit's commander because he was too outspoken in citing the police department's shortcomings and was accused of "using the department to cater to the blacks." Tate is sensitive to the prevailing ethos and strives to obtain the support of the department and the department's rank and file. He suggested that although the Public Information Bureau probably still emphasizes the black community, he has, since assuming command of the unit, tried to also involve the white community in bureau programs and has "taken the branch into the white community, too."

Finally, when asked about the bureau's present emphasis, he answered that the programs are more oriented toward children: "At this critical age, we either win them for law enforcement or we lose them." About the concept of police-community relations, Tate said: "We have eight hundred policemen. We need eight hundred community relations officers."

Police-community relations consists of a give-and-take communications program. It involves the presentation of policemen and their ideas to the citizens, and a receptivity towards a flow of ideas from citizens. This interaction, of necessity, requires the police to present factual information about their activities to the public. By the same token, it requires a sincere receptivity, on the part of policemen of all ranks, to the needs of the public. Ultimately, the success of a public-support program will depend on the conviction of policemen that the image of their department depends upon the integrity, efficiency, and courtesy of each police officer, and not on viewing police-community relations as a specialized function.

Police Accountability: Dilemmas of Democratic Control

Police accountability is critical to the democratic process. Without adequate accountability measures, the police may be used as an arm of oppression by the State, or they may behave antisocially and illegally for their own ends. Accountability consists of the availability of democratic and hierarchical controls. In this country, controls are afforded through civil, external, and internal influences. However, a true picture of accountability cannot be derived without regard for the formal relations of power of all actors involved in the political process. Large urban bureaucracies have the capability to mount a "mobilization of bias" in behalf of their interests, giving them a countervailing leverage on the quality of political actions that affect them. The political behavior of the police in support of maintaining their autonomy and authority position has a direct relationship to the effectiveness of available controls over them. The phenomenon of the politicization of the police is not only descriptive of bureaucratic performance in the political system but has also provided some noteworthy insights into the real nature of community power in large cities.

The emergence of their political power, as manifested by the activities of guild or fraternal organizations, has served to solidify the police "value consensus" against encroachments on their authority. This poses some fundamental problems for police accountability. Ultimately, the test of true police accountability must be viewed in the broader context of all participating actors and influences on police service, to include the various political power relationships of the police in respect to the available accountability channels.

Civil Accountability

The degree of control over the police by political authority varies with the level of government at which police functions take place. In this country, although cities and counties are legally creatures of the states under state constitutions, states have generally divested themselves of their control over these jurisdictions and have allowed them to operate with scant interference. The principle of local autonomy has been aided by the belief in the sanctity of home rule, which professes that "Main Street has the intelligence and resources to meet its problems, and that suggestions from the Capitol State or from either end of Pennsylvania Avenue are out of order."[1] Consequently, except for the ultimate sanction found in state law, authority over the police in both policy formation and administrative direction is placed with the city council and the city's executive.[2] Police administration in the United States is largely a matter of responsibility of local appointing authorities, despite the fact that police are, in the main, concerned with the enforcement of state laws rather than of city ordinances.

Except for those exceptional instances when states run the local police, the administrative leadership of local police agencies is appointed by the city executive and city council. Accordingly, the police chain of command begins with the patrolman on the beat, moves up through the command channels to the administrative leadership—a single executive or a board or commission—and ultimately ends with the mayor or city manager. The usual role of the city council in police administration consists of appointing or confirming the appointment of the department head, performing legislative investigation of police failures, and perhaps participating in the disciplining and removal of the administrative head of the police.[3]

The administrative head of a police department is either a chief of police, a director of public safety, or members of a police commission. The chief, traditionally the highest civil service rank in any department, has a well-developed hierarchy befitting the semimilitary nature of the organization, and he is entrusted with great disciplinary authority and responsibility over this hierarchy. He also is expected to fulfill a dual leadership role. "He must provide leadership within the department, and as the head of the force he must represent it in relations with the administrative head of the city and through him with the municipal council and the public—the community."[4]

The director of public safety is a position that is utilized both at the municipal and state levels. In municipalities a director of public safety is employed sometimes in order to provide supervision over a chief who is protected by civil service. Even in cases where the police chief is reasonably efficient, the appointment of a director of public safety allows a city government to employ the best possible man to be the administrative head of a police department outside of the available resources in the department and without being constrained by the civil service rules about seniority. At the state level, governors utilize a director of public safety to provide supervision over a department that may combine such related functions as the state police, alcoholic beverage control, motor vehicle inspection, state fire marshal, weights and measures, and civil defense.

There are several variations of the police commission. A commission may be a small group of part-time officials appointed by a city council or a city executive with duties similar to those of a civil service commission, including devising institutional rules and regulations and administering personnel matters. A more limited version of a police commission may have it serving only as an appeal body for disciplinary and personnel matters. Another version of the police commission has it granted broader responsibilities, possibly with direct statutory control over the entire operations of a department, or, as in the case of the New York City department, the commissioner may be the equivalent of a chief of police and the executive head of the organization.

A problem found in many communities is that city charters or ordinances are overspecific about details relating to police management but ambiguous about the question of control over the police. These ordinances describe the organizational structure of the department, including salaries and working conditions, rules and regulations applicable to departmental affairs, and the number of personnel to be allowed in each rank. Yet at the same time, management of a police department is made difficult by vagueness in city charters as to where control actually resides. In some cases control is simultaneously granted to a mayor, a city manager or administrator, a city council and/or police commission, a director of public safety, and a chief of police.[5]

The history of police administration in the United States is largely an account of the problems associated with the various forms of municipal government. In the mayor-council type of city government it has mattered little whether supervision of the police was undertaken by the members of a council or by the city's executive head. In either instance, police administration has been subordinated to political and personal interests. The practice of having the police supervised by a city council is not only a violation of a basic principle of organization by placing executive control in a plural agency, but it has also allowed the mingling of this responsibility with the councilmen's interests in other matters, thereby encouraging "corrupt political controls, favoritism, and extravagance."[6] The effectiveness of police service under such circumstances has suffered from the dubious motives of those in control as well as from their lack of familiarity with the management of modern police operations.

In most cities with a mayor-council type of government, the mayor is the political authority with control over the police. He is the official empowered to appoint and remove all heads of administrative departments. However, the mayor, as an elected official, must yield to various pressure groups for his political success and survival. Consequently, "his office too often becomes headquarters for the dispensing of patronage, favors and gratuities which undermine the administration of line departments."[7]

The priority afforded to political interests in the mayor-council form of government and the historic circumstance of graft and incompetence in local government gave rise to reforms in municipal governance, resulting in the commission plan and the city manager form of city government. The commission plan of local government has a small group of elected officials serving both as legislators and administrators. The commissioners are elected officials who serve as the legislature of the city with each commissioner, separately, also heading a public agency. Police administration has not fared well under the commission plan; Leonard and More's evaluation of this form of municipal government was that although it initially gave hope for new improvements in police administration, ultimately it proved susceptible to corrupt exploitation. "The dual role of the individual commissioner as both legislator and administrator opened wide the door for illegitimate influence and pressure, and made police administration more vulnerable than ever before to the sinister forces in the community whose interests are opposed to those of the public."[8]

The city manager form of government has been considered to be the most ideally suited to offer competent public service. The manager, a professional public administrator, selects the most capable individual available to be the chief of police and then delegates to this public executive the responsibilities and authority necessary for the proper exercise of his functions. "With the complete separation of the legislative and administrative functions of government provided by this pattern of municipal organization, political interference with police administration is reduced to a minimum."[9]

However, the city manager form of government is not widely practiced in large cities where problems associated with urban life are most critical. Indeed, it is in the communities where law enforcement needs are most urgent that police administration is forced to submit to political priorities, at the expense of public service. Consequently, inadequate and incompetent police services are often the fault of municipal political systems that are incapable of delivering the kind of leadership and control over law enforcement that is in the best interests of the public.

While legal control of the police is vested in the state governments, the law enforcement experience of the states has been limited. In many states, the only statewide police jurisdiction is the highway patrol, and almost two-thirds of all state expenditures for law enforcement is for traffic regulation. But the states have aided local law enforcement by providing model laws and systems of criminal justice, setting standards, training personnel, and providing state administrative aid to local police. Other than these functions, the major task of law enforcement in the United States is left to the local governments.[10]

In line with state government efforts to improve local law enforcement was a model bill sent to the New York legislature by Governor Nelson Rockefeller in 1972. The bill proposed to create a division of criminal justice in the executive department by merging three existing units engaged in criminal justice work. The proposed consolidation was described as a way to strengthen anticrime efforts by creating a single authority to oversee planning, analysis, training, standards, and information gathering and dissemination for local police units. The proposal called for the formation of an office of planning services that would combine the powers and functions of the Division for Local Police, the New York State Identification and Intelligence System, and the Division of Criminal Justice.[11]

Because of occasional graft and corruption in local government and the inefficiency of police organizations in these communities, state governments have, at times, either threatened to take over the policing responsibility or have actually done so. In 1939 the state of Missouri assumed control of the Kansas City police department to help drive the Pendergast machine out of the city and to rid the police department of its "hoodlum element." Similarly, the state of Illinois threatened to take over the police department in Chicago after the great police scandal there of 1960. "Only Mayor Richard Daley's political strength in the legislature and his willingness to take drastic steps toward reform enabled Chicago to keep control of her police."[12]

In earlier days, state legislatures were apt to interfere with local police adminstration for dubious reasons. Ostensibly because of alleged failures of city authorities to maintain proper standards of order, state governments took control of police departments in New York, Chicago, Boston, Cleveland, Detroit, Baltimore, Cincinnati, St. Louis, New Orleans, and Kansas City, among others. In each of these cases a police board, with its members either elected by the legislature or appointed by the governor, was given complete control of the municipal police force. When it became apparent that the reason for the takeover of these police departments was often an attempt by state politicians to extend the range of their patronage activities, urban disapproval and opposition mounted until state control was subsequently removed from the police establishments in all of these cities with the exception of Baltimore, Boston, Kansas City, and St. Louis. The unhappy experiences with state-controlled municipal police departments occurred during the nineteenth century, when distrust and hostility between rural-dominated state legislatures and the developing urban governments were at their height. However, the memory of these experiences has lingered, making local units of government protective of their dominion over line departments of government and especially of the police bureaucracy.[13]

In view of the uneven quality of civil accountability of the police in this country, the centralization of police administration is sometimes looked on as an attractive alternative. The English model, described as a system of local control coupled with national supervision, is considered the ideal of centralized police administration. The London metropolitan police are under the direct control of the Home Office, while the other police departments in the nation are administered locally. However, the Home Office enjoys a large measure of indirect control over local police departments "through its power to inspect these forces and formulate regulations prescribing their organization, equipment and discipline. The organizational pattern tends toward uniformity of administration throughout England."[14]

Furthermore, a symbiotic relationship exists throughout the entire English system of law enforcement. For example, county or borough police forces are free to call upon the highly specialized facilities of Scotland Yard in complex cases, and these services are given free of charge. Also, Metropolitan Police Headquarters in London maintains centralized records, and this permits an effective response to mobile criminal operations.

Of course, the unified pattern of police administration and other governmental functions in England is facilitated by a centralized pattern of government. Our federalism, by contrast, makes the application of the unification of governmental functions a highly improbable occurrence, especially in light of the supremacy of the principle of local autonomy. The federal government plays an important role in law enforcement although, admittedly, its role is restricted to carefully defined parameters. This role includes operations such as customs law enforcement, federal tax collection, and agricultural, postal, and drug inspection. Federal law enforcement agencies also are responsible for policing organized crime, interstate theft, and transportation of a kidnap victim across a state line, and this allocation of responsibility can be very helpful to local police agencies.

Until recently, the esteem for federal law enforcement as a model of excellence has probably been accepted on faith, to the extent that it almost has become folklore. But recent accusations of the involvement of federal agencies in questionable activity have served to diminish the credence of their paradigmatic attributes. The Federal Bureau of Investigation, for example, the most highly respected law enforcement agency in the nation, has suffered unfavorable publicity as a result of the disclosures by the news media that its acting director destroyed documents that may have been evidence in the Watergate investigation. *The New York Times* reported that a few days before the resignation of L. Patrick Gray III, morale at the "once proud Federal Bureau of Investigation had dropped to an all-time low . . . after a year of confusion and controversy since the death of J. Edgar Hoover."

The disclosure that Gray had destroyed documents given to him at a meeting in the White House following the arrest of Watergate suspects, had a disquieting effect on the FBI. One agent was quoted as saying: "Nobody ever destroys files; nobody has the authority to do that. The FBI is a fact-finding organization, a fact-gathering organization. That's what we have built our record on."

"Discouragement was prevalent even among veteran FBI officials of the Hoover generation, with the strongest desire to uphold the traditions and standards of the agency."[15]

The reputation that the FBI built up during the Hoover years was primarily gained as a result of the capture of notorious bank robbers in the 1930s and the apprehension of pro-Soviet atom spies in the 1950s. Since then, the most noteworthy accomplishment of the bureau appears to be in maintaining voluminous files on radicals of varying political persuasions. The most troublesome of the radicals, leaders of the Weatherman group, are still at large after perpetrating acts of violence that resulted in a number of deaths. Furthermore, organized crime in this country, a concern of the FBI, is known to be alive and well and prospering despite the attention it is supposed to be getting from the federal agency.

The news about the misconduct by federal agencies in the Pentagon papers affair resulted in the government's case being dismissed by the presiding judge. *Newsweek* quoted an angry explanation by the judge: "The conduct of the government has placed this case in such a posture that it precludes the fair and dispassionate resolution of . . . issues by the jury."[16] The disclosures leading to the dismissal showed that three of the nation's most highly sensitive agencies—the CIA, the FBI, and the State Department—were involved in highly irregular actions, at the request of the White House.

First, the CIA admitted to providing technical assistance, an "ill-advised act," to the "Ellsburglars." Then came the information from the Justice Department that the FBI had been wiretapping Daniel Ellsberg in late 1969 and early 1970, long prior to his publication of the Pentagon papers. However, the FBI was unable to explain the mysterious disappearance of documents related to those taps from bureau files.

Finally, a onetime White House staff member and Nixon campaign aide, E. Howard Hunt, Jr., testified to his involvement in the Ellsberg and Watergate affairs as well as in forging State Department documents. He revealed that he helped plan the burglaries of Ellsberg's psychiatrist's office and of Watergate. Additionally, Hunt said he gained access to 240 top-secret State Department cables, enabling him to create two forgeries showing that John F. Kennedy ordered the assassination of South Vietnamese President Ngo Dinh Diem in 1963.

Another federal agency, the Office for Drug Abuse Law Enforcement (DALE), has caught the interest of the news media because of an incident involving some of its agents. On April 30, 1973, *The New York Times* reported that two families living in Collinsville, Illinois, a suburb of St. Louis, experienced a "night of terror" when four bearded men, later identified as agents for DALE, broke into their homes in search of narcotics.

Their doors were kicked in; their houses damaged, their arms shackled. And the screaming bearded men told some they were to die.

The long-haired, unshaven, poorly dressed, armed men who burst into the homes shouting obscenities were federal narcotics agents hunting, with no known warrants, for something or someone.

They went, however, to the wrong houses. And when they realized their error, after some innocent residents had begged for their lives, the men disappeared with no apologies.[17]

Subsequently, four of the eleven agents who participated in the raids were suspended—with full pay—by the nation's chief enforcer of drug laws, Mylea J. Ambrose, who also said that he was seeking an immediate grand jury investigation of the incident. In describing the affair Ambrose said that it looked to be a case of "more stupidity than anything else."[18]

In a follow-up investigation, *The New York Times* revealed that despite government assertions to the contrary, similar incidents had occurred earlier in connection with government-sponsored drug raids. Furthermore, these incidents were reported to have resulted in at least four fatalities, including the slaying of one policeman when a frightened woman, a previous burglary victim, fired a revolver through her bedroom door when she heard someone—later identified as narcotics officers—breaking into her house. In California, a father was killed as he sat in a living room holding his infant son, when a narcotics officer accidentally discharged his weapon during a raid. Details of the raids generally have them involving heavily armed police officers arriving at night, often unshaven and dressed in "undercover" attire, breaking down the doors to a private residence, and holding the residents at gunpoint while they aggressively search the house or apartment.[19]

The "no-knock" narcotics raids were authorized for federal agents by Congress in the Comprehensive Drug Abuse Prevention and Control Act of 1970 (PL 91-513). Similar statutes exist in some states. These laws enable the police to obtain a special "no-knock" search warrant allowing them to enter homes unannounced if there is probable cause that the evidence sought could be disposed of or destroyed, or if providing notice of police presence endangers an officer or other persons. The intention of "no-knock" raids is to provide a "sudden and overwhelming display of police force" to discourage resistance and the disposal of criminal evidence.[20]

The abuse of civil liberties by federal agencies has cast doubt upon their ability to provide models of excellence. If anything, the political rhetoric that has emanated from Washington in praise of law and order seems to be more encouraging to the expansion of police power rather than to the accountability of this power. An example is a testimonial delivered by former Vice President Spiro Agnew at the New York City police department's annual Holy Name Society Communion breakfast. Mr. Agnew was quoted by *The New York Times* as saying:

When it comes to the point of whether this Nixon administration, and particularly myself as an individual, is going to prefer the kind of diligent, strict law enforcement that is necessary to protect this country of ours, or whether we're going to agonize over the root causes and conditions of crime that's used as an excuse for some people to commit crime, I'll stick to law enforcement every time.[21]

External Influences

Outside of the formal system of civil accountability there exist external influences that could play a part in controlling police behavior. The external influences on law enforcement include the judicial system, citizen groups, civilian review boards, the press, and public opinion. The courts could enforce the laws violated by policemen when they engage in improper practices, for legal penalties exist for such acts as unlawful use of deadly weapons, denial of civil rights, assault, battery, manslaughter, and murder. But the courts often do not enforce these statutes because of the interrelatedness of the criminal justice system requiring cooperation among the elements of the system. Neither the courts nor prosecutors have sufficient investigative resources of their own, and this means that when charges of police misconduct arise evidence supporting these charges is gathered by the police themselves. Consequently, decisions arrived at by prosecutors and the courts are based on information provided them by police internal investigatory units. Furthermore, public prosecutors depend entirely on the cooperation of the police in order to prepare and try cases. Given the intimate nature of this relationship, it is understandable that prosecutors would be timid about bringing charges against policemen, unless these charges were initiated by the department itself.

Another factor that minimizes the viability of the judicial system as an effective control over police practices is the political nature of the system. Most local judges and prosecutors are elected and, because of the political climate of the times, prosecutors and judges can ill afford to have an "antipolice" reputation if they hope to gain and retain office. Cases against the police that are brought before the courts often work to the disadvantage of complainants. The citizen bears his own legal expenses in such a proceeding while the city or some other governmental agency generally defends the police officer. The police officer, too, helps his own case because he generally makes a very credible witness. Finally, the plea bargaining system is sometimes used to the advantage of a policeman accused of misconduct. This consists of bringing excessive charges against the complainant, with the prospect, however, of these charges being reduced if he does not press his accusation.

Citizen groups are varied and they have differentiated interests in police service. Chambers of Commerce and service clubs generally promote police professionalism out of civic pride. Churches and church groups have historically campaigned against vice and corruption, and recently they have added an interest in civil liberty causes and police-community relations in minority neighborhoods. In Atlanta, in 1972, a general conference of the United Methodist Church issued a statement that was part of a wide-ranging resolution that, among other things, urged reform of laws controlling marijuana, and opposition to laws permitting the police to enter a dwelling without warning under certain conditions. The convention criticized the abuses of unrestrained police power and warned against repression, citing "dragnet arrests, police harassment of minority leaders, charges of conspiracy, support of preventive detention [and] heavy punitive actions against campus dissidents"[22] as acts of repression.

Militants and agitators have been extremely active in their opposition to the police. However, some of these individuals and groups have been the cause of law enforcement problems because their rhetoric has at times turned to destructive action such as the assassination of police officers and the bombing of public buildings. Minority groups have utilized very effective pressure tactics in many communities. They are usually in the forefront of demands for more citizen participation in local governance, especially for community control of the police and/or civilian review boards. The ability of citizen groups to influence controls over the police suffers from several handicaps. These groups represent a limited number of citizens, they are pluralistic in their interests, and they generally do not reflect public opinion as a whole.

Accountability through civilian review boards consists of having complaints about police malpractice channeled through a publicly constituted committee of citizens. The boards also are empowered to review the disposition by the police department of citizen complaints with the right to recommend remedial action. Civilian review is not a substitute for investigation and disciplining by the department. Instead, it is meant to add to the capability of the department in these matters by allowing the civilian members of a community to review in a nonpolice environment cases of police misconduct and the police department's disposition of these cases.[23]

The police are almost universally opposed to civilian review boards. In city after city the police have mustered sufficient political support to block attempts at establishing extradepartmental mechanisms for reviewing police operations. Police associations have waged intensive campaigns against the review boards, directing their efforts at the general public and city councilmen. Challenges have also been made through the courts.

These efforts by the associations have been greatly influenced by their trade-unionist concern with work rules and grievance machinery, in addition to their commitment to maintaining police autonomy.

In New York City a civilian review board lasted just four months. It was discontinued as a result of a campaign by the Patrolmen's Benevolent Association, representing the largest police force in the nation, that urged the public to vote out the board. In Boston, the Patrolmen's Association showed its influence in city politics by defeating a proposed Model Cities program in November, 1968. The program included a proposal to allow citizens to hear, but not to judge, complaints against the police. Also proposed was an elected citizens' advisory panel to "provide guidance" for police in the model neighborhood.

"According to press accounts, council members bowed to heavy pressure brought to bear by an intense campaign conducted by the Patrolmen's Association. John Harrington, national president of the Fraternal Order of Police, has inaugurated a nation-wide campaign to oppose police review boards."[24] Furthermore, civilian review boards have been major issues in political campaigns in several cities, with "law and order" candidates clearly opposing them. A free press, especially an investigatory press, is potentially capable of influencing police accountability by exposing incidents of malpractice to the public. Unfortunately, a press that is totally free is hard to find as various pressures are mounted to preclude the reporting of embarrassing accounts of malfeasance by public officals. Most police reporters are assigned permanently to cover the police, and even if they do not psychologically become policemen rather than reporters, they must still rely on policemen for their information in order to function effectively. Inevitably, this calls for them to maintain friendly relations with the police or else to be ostracized from the squad rooms and thereby from the sources of their news stories.

A serious problem to the press has been the disposition on the part of some politicians to attack the communications media when news accounts do not coincide with their biases. An ominous restraint on a free press has occurred with incidents of repression of newsmen who publish unfavorable stories about the police. Nat Hentoff, writing for *Playboy,* reported that Kent Pollock, an investigative reporter for the *Philadelphia Inquirer,* has complained of investigations into his private life since writing a story about police corruption. Greg Walter, who works for the same newspaper, has also written critically about the police department and Mayor Frank Rizzo. Because of this, Walter charged: "Persons who are close to me, persons who were contacts of mine in . . . Philadelphia have been questioned extensively about my sex life, my drinking habits and God knows what all. And this information is all filed away."[25]

It has been the opinion of the general public about law enforcement that has made it difficult for political authorities and external influences to exert control over the police. It is the public that provides jurors, supports "law and order" or pro-police candidates, and is suspicious of the objectivity and credibility of the news media. The reaction of the public to police behavior during the Democratic Convention in Chicago in 1968 indicates support for the use of force by the police that is beyond necessity and outside legal limits. These attitudes would bear out Stark's statement that "the average American has a taste for rough and ready 'justice.'"[26]

But why is the general public acquiescent when public officials encourage the police to use their powers without restraint?

Part of the answer is fear: a national fear, born in the late 60s, of demonstrators, of blacks, of students, of muggers. The national desire, an almost desperate desire—as Richard Nixon accurately reads it—is for order. In this kind of climate, the majority of the people are much more concerned with their safety than with civil liberties —not only those of others but of their own.[27]

Internal Controls

Police departments who are trying to reform the "system" and replace it with a professional code that would allow an improvement in internal police accountability attempt to accomplish this through organizational and management devices. Commissioner Patrick V. Murphy of New York City, one of the best known "reform" police executives, instituted numerous management innovations in the city's police department. These innovations included a decentralization of decision-making responsibilities, planning and budgeting, and improvements in the allocation of manpower and in personnel policies.[28]

The basis for the management innovation pertaining to command decentralization was to have commanders accountable not only for the efficiency of their operation but also for any corruption within their command. Local police commanders were empowered to discipline their men for any violations of department rules and regulations, in line with the established policy of local accountability. In a one-week period near the end of 1971, Murphy removed seven commanders. Some of the commanders were charged with incompetence or failure to exercise control over their men; one of them was discharged because a policeman in his command was caught growing marijuana behind the police station in Central Park; another was removed because a patrolman in his command had been caught sleeping on duty, "cooping" in police terms; and some were removed because of corruption in their command.[29]

Another management innovation concerned the updating of the department's planning, programming, budgeting (PPB) system. Innovations were applied to the central headquarters planning office, and a new decentralized technique for planning was introduced by the commissioner. A planning officer, assigned to every precinct and borough command, was responsible for the collection, organization, and analysis of crime data for the discernment of patterns in order that manpower might be allocated most efficiently.[30] Murphy's other proposals for improving the New York City police department involved hiring additional civilians and increasing the authority of the commissioner to evaluate and dismiss incompetent policemen, lengthening probationary periods for patrolmen, and the use of one-man instead of two-man patrol cars. The implementation of Murphy's innovations and proposals for increasing the authority of the commissioner's office produced an unfavorable reaction from police officers and their associations, challenging the commissioner's control of the department. Edward Kiernan, then head of the Patrolmen's Benevolent Association, called for Murphy's resignation, stating that "he was destroying the department." A number of patrolmen voiced the same opinion, claiming that Murphy "was just [Mayor John] Lindsay's stooge, and, that, anyway, he had never really worked as a cop, he had never walked a beat, he wasn't one of us."[31]

Among the difficulties that police reformers have is that they seem to be standing with the critics of the police when they propose reforms. This makes the reformer an outsider to the system, and his authority, in the minds of officers socialized by the system, is arbitrary authority because it is unchecked by the system's norms. The rank and file of the police fear that authority in a person outside of the system would have unpredictable effects on their own position of street-level authority, their careers, and their working habits.[32]

Policemen opposed to interference in their practices state that there are adequate controls, internal and external, on the behavior of police officers. They cite as internal controls the existence in most agencies of an internal review process, which consists of procedures established by police departments for the investigation of charges of misconduct initiated either by civilians or superior officers. In small departments, the function of review and discipline is primarily the responsibility of the chief executive of the force or his immediate subordinate. In large urban police forces, a special unit responsible for internal review may be established to receive and investigate citizen complaints and other allegations of misbehavior by policemen. When an investigation is completed, cases of police misconduct are referred to a higher authority, either the department's chief executive or a board, where a wide range of sanctions may be applied. The sanctions range from an oral reprimand to dismissal from the force, or referral to the public prosecutor for criminal action.

The internal review model used by many police forces is that of the Los

Angeles police department, which has an Internal Affairs Division and a quasi-military board of rights to investigate and apply disciplinary action for incidents of police malpractice. However, Ed Cray pointed out that while the Board of Rights has exercised "draconian" measures to "correct" violations of departmental rules, actions taken against officers charged with misconduct toward citizens are rare, and sanctions are light. An example of this condition was the issuance of reprimands to two policemen who fired their weapons at a suspect in violation of departmental policies; for a similar offense a civilian would at least have been charged with assault with a deadly weapon. On the other hand, a policeman who "during a five-month period cohabitated with a divorced woman" was suspended from the department for twenty-two days.[33]

Citizens who file complaints with the internal investigatory arm of some departments, do so at their own risk. In the nation's capital, police statistics showed that 40 percent of those who reported police misconduct were themselves charged with the misdemeanor of filing a false report.[34]

When cases of police malpractice are actually brought before trial boards for disposition, the process is not entirely objective. In most cities, evidence against officers charged is presented to the board by a public prosecutor. In addition to having to rely on the department's investigation for the presentation of his case of police malpractice, the prosecutor depends on the close cooperation and collaboration of the police department for the preparation of other cases. It is, therefore, unlikely that a public prosecutor, who depends on his intimate relationship with the police, will be overzealous in the prosecution of a police officer.

The unfavorable view that policemen hold of their internal investigatory agency generally contradicts their expressed support for internal control mechanisms. The most universally despised assignment for policemen is the "shoo-fly" detail—internal affairs division, the internal investigation division, or the special squad—the terms applied to describe the internal agency. Officers assigned to this type of unit often find themselves ostracized by the rest of the men, especially if they are committed to uprooting departmental corruption.

Politicization of the Police

Law enforcement has had an historic involvement with politics. Going back to the days when political machines and bosses ran the cities, the police cooperated with the politicians in power in permitting election irregularities and graft and corruption because they owed their jobs and promotions to City Hall. The police have a long-established role as maintainers of the political and social status quo. In this regard, there are numerous examples of their antilabor, antiminorities, and antidissent activity in behalf of the established policies of the time. Now the members of the police bureaucracy are embarking on a new phenomenon. No longer content with just being the enforcers of public policy, they are, instead, emerging "as a self-conscious, organized, and militant political constituency, bidding for far-reaching political power in their own right. . . . They now seek the power to determine these policies."[35]

The political power of the police has been expressed through the organizational framework of their union, guild, and social organizations. Although these organizations have been around a long time—for example, the Patrolmen's Benefit Association in New York City was created in 1894 during Theodore Roosevelt's tenure as commissioner of police—their rapid transformation into an effective channel for the political aspirations and sentiments of the police subculture came as a result of the lessons learned in a series of successful moves for improved economic benefits and, especially, to prevent the creation of civilian review boards. These victorious engagements, realized through political means, have encouraged the police occupational associations to aggregate the interests of the rank and file to affect public policy and influence political judgments, in addition to their traditional trade union objectives of improving employment benefits for their members.

Police organizations wield power on several different levels. As labor organizations they employ standard weapons of economic warfare such as strikes, threat of strikes, and slowdowns, or rather, modified and imaginative versions of these practices. The police version of economic pressure consists of "job actions": the "blue flu" or threat of the "blue flu," slowdown in ticket writing, overenforcement of the laws, or varying enforcement of the law. At another level, still as labor organizations, they act as vehicles for negotiating and presenting employee viewpoints to management. Finally, they operate as political organizations employing traditional political techniques for gaining their objectives. On this level they have been extremely active in lobbying, supporting political organizations friendly to their aims, overtly working for pro-police political candidates, as well as working against those whose policies and ideologies are rejected by the police rank and file.

Indicative of the emergence of the police as a powerful political force have been the cases of police officers moving into elective office. In Minneapolis and Philadelphia, cities with a tradition of liberal leaders such as Humphrey and Naftalin, and Clark and Dilworth, policemen successfully campaigned as candidates for mayor on "law and order" platforms. In 1969, John Lindsay, running as the Liberal party candidate for mayor, selected the chief inspector of the New York police department to run for city council president in order to provide some "law and order imagery to the Lindsey ticket."[36]

Police unionization efforts go back to 1897, when a group of special police in Cleveland attempted to form a union by petitioning the American Federation of Labor for a charter. The AFL did not grant the charter on the grounds that "it is not within the province of the trade union movement to especially organize policemen, no more than to organize militiamen, as both police and militiamen are often controlled by forces inimical to the labor movement."[37] In 1919, at a time of general labor unrest in the United States, the federation reversed its earlier stand against police unions and began admitting to membership all police officers. By September of 1919, thirty-seven police locals had been chartered by the AFL, and policemen in the departments of several cities were seriously considering the prospect of unionization.

Then, an event occurred that dealt a blow to police unionization for many years. The Boston Social Club, a newly affiliated police local with the AFL, went out on strike on September 9, 1919. Calvin Coolidge, the governor of Massachusetts, ordered in the state militia to patrol the city left unattended by the 1200 striking policemen. Order was restored the following day, but not before riots in downtown Boston had killed seven people. The striking policemen were summarily discharged, and none were ever rehired or collected past benefits despite litigation in their behalf. Coolidge later said: "There is no right to strike against the public safety by anybody, anytime, anywhere."[38] As a result of the Boston police strike, police unions across the nation were forced either by municipal officers or the impact of public opinion to give up their charters.

Twenty years after the Boston strike, police unionization made a comeback when the American Federation of State, County, and Municipal Employees (AFSCME) chartered a police local in Portsmouth, Virginia. This occurred at a time when both the AFL and CIO sought to recruit municipal workers into their national unions. The AFSCME made a concerted effort to organize police locals, and by the end of 1944 thirty-nine such locals were reported. By 1951 the AFSCME had successfully organized sixty-one police unions, although two years later the number had dropped to fifty-eight.

The high point in police unionization activity occurred between 1961 and 1966, a period during which the police sought to improve their lagging salaries through collective action. However, by 1968, it became clear that police union action was not solely directed at economic objectives but involved social issues as well. In this connection, Sylvan Fox described in *The New York Times* how the police in New York City in 1968 had turned down the best economic contract ever offered policemen. Police depart-

ment officials interviewed for the article expressed the feelings of dissatisfaction prevailing in the department. One official was quoted as saying,
"Policemen are feeling their muscle all over the country. They want to be
special. They want status." Another official stated, "I think it's really a
general frustration that the police are feeling toward the establishment.
They feel they're not getting the kind of recognition and respect they're
entitled to—from either the community or the administration."[39]

Police dissatisfaction with working conditions was also reported by
Albert J. Reiss in interviews with policemen in Boston, Washington, and
Chicago, and in a study performed by the Opinion Research Corporation on
police attitudes about their work. Reiss found that "the police believe their
conditions of work have . . . worsened. Eighty per cent state that 'Police
work is more hazardous today than five years ago.' Sixty per cent believe
that the way the public behaves towards the police has changed for the
worse since they joined the force."[40] The Opinion Research Corporation
revealed that patrolmen in the twelve metropolitan cities studied "have a
high level of dissatisfaction with their jobs, feel that they are misunderstood
by the public, and are convinced that they do not get sufficient backing
from the police department."[41]

The police have reacted to their perceived disadvantages by behaving
like a militant political movement. The basis for their transformation into
an active political force lies in their belief that their working conditions
have been made difficult by increasing permissiveness of society, a condition generally attributed to the predominance of liberal policies and politicians. Such attitudes are probably caused by the conservative views held
by most policemen, linked to their social origins, occupational experiences, and the history of political influences over police practices.[4] In
addition, the growth of police organizations represents the need for problem solving by collective bargaining. Civil service and merit systems, while
effective correctives of the earlier inefficiencies of municipalities, have not
brought about any real bureaucratic rationality in the police service. As a
result of the dissatisfaction with internal working conditions, policemen
have increasingly turned to collective bargaining as a means of redress
against practices and policies of the police hierarchy, and for conventional
trade union objectives.

The American Federation of State, County and Municipal Employees,
a public employee union affiliated with the AFL-CIO, has not captured a
contested representational election involving police since April of 1966
when Local 1195 of the Baltimore police was chartered. The AFSCME has
several handicaps in competing for police members. The union strictly
forbids police "to strike or take strong positions or demonstrate" and has
suspended striking police locals. Another obstacle to AFSCME's potential
as a police representative is the industrial nature of the union, which

organizes workers by employer rather than by occupation or craft. Police-men view this eclecticism with disfavor because they believe that an organization exclusively identified with the police suits them better than an organization representing a wide variety of workers. Finally, the liberal social viewpoint of AFSCME has proved to be its greatest handicap in police unionization.

AFSCME is probably the most politically liberal trade union, having been praised for its liberal stands on civil rights, and domestic and foreign policy. (AFSCME was the union involved in the Memphis sanitation strike in 1968.) If they joined the AFSCME, policemen would no doubt find themselves aligned against their union as well as their employer on political issues.[43]

The organizations that have experienced the greatest success in police unionization have been police professional associations: the Fraternal Order of Police (FOP) and the International Conference of Police Associa-tions (ICPA). The Fraternal Order of Police was founded in 1915 and claims a membership of about 100,000 policemen. The FOP is not affiliated with the AFL-CIO and does not see itself as a labor union, and the only full-time member of the national staff is its president, John Harrington. Its structure could best be described as a loose confederation of local lodges with the national organization encouraging local autonomy. The FOP, through its local organizations, is active in bettering the material benefits of the police such as higher wages, shorter hours, and improved working conditions. Additionally, the national organization and its local affiliates have been zealously engaged in efforts to defeat proposals for civilian review boards and in lobbying state legislatures to strengthen criminal statutes and crimi-nal procedures. Although the national association professes to be against police strikes, FOP locals have engaged in concerted job actions.

The largest police "union" is the International Conference of Police Associations, formed in 1954 and headed by Edward J. Kiernan, formerly president of the Patrolmen's Benevolent Association of New York City. The ICPA is an umbrella organization for a large number of autonomous locals and claims a police membership of approximately 165,000. Included among its member locals are the police associations of San Francisco, New York, Seattle, Pittsburgh, New Orleans, Washington, D.C., Chicago, Oak-land, and Memphis. The ICPA, like the FOP, maintain a substantially lower dues structure than AFL-CIO unions.

The national provides help to its affiliates in local contract negotiations and in efforts to improve pay and working conditions. It also represents the locals at the national level by lobbying for federal legislation favorable to law enforcement. The ICPA is actively opposed to civilian review boards and the use of lie detector tests for policemen charged with police malprac-tice. In regard to the lie detector tests, Robert Gordon, the executive director of the organization, states, "Why should policemen be subjected to a procedure that is illegal for the average citizen? All we ask is that the policemen have the same rights as any citizen."

The stand against lie detectors for police officials is part of a nationwide struggle on the part of police organizations such as the ICPA and FOP for a "Policeman's Bill of Rights." Much of the lobbying activities performed by these organizations concerns the passage by Congress of such a bill, which would provide policemen with procedural protections against disciplinary actions and would allow them to engage in off-duty political activities. In addition, the bill calls for police representation on complaint review boards and protection from having to disclose their finances to department authorities.

The philosophy of the ICPA was revealed by Edward Kiernan in his "President's Message," published in the organization's promotional brochure. He urges policemen, "one and all," to join the ICPA in order to "awaken this sleeping giant, 'The law enforcement officer.'" Kiernan writes:

The ICPA began a program toward waking the "sleeping giant" and embarked on a campaign that would give every policeman throughout North America the same basic rights enjoyed by organized labor. Our goal is to see to it that every policeman is guaranteed the same rights or representation enjoyed by all workers, such as, the right to take part in good faith collective bargaining, the right to formal grievance procedures, the right to take part in the political process of our Country and above all, the right to organize.

Recently, Kiernan was quoted by the Memphis *Commercial Appeal* as saying, "The need for job actions or strikes is becoming extinct among police unions. But when you back them (policemen) into a corner, watch out."[44] Over the years, ICPA locals have engaged in a number of job actions. In 1971, 22,000 New York City policemen staged a wildcat strike. "For six days, policemen played cards at precinct stations, drank beer and shouted obscenities at other policemen who crossed picket lines." *Time* reported that during the strike the union (Patrolmen's Benevolent Association) violated state law, ignored court injunctions, and the strikers even rejected appeals from their own union leaders to return to work.[45] In that same year the ICPA local in Milwaukee staged a five-day "blue flu" with about half of the department phoning in sick. In Seattle, although the local did not resort to strikes or slowdowns, police pickets marched on City Hall during contract negotiations.

The most significant efforts of police organizations have been their political activities. The gaining of power through concerted police political activity has been noteworthy for some time. Their intrusion in the political process first received national attention when police membership in the

John Birch Society was discovered during the 1964 Boston mayoralty race when the city's patrolmen came out in support of an ultraconservative candidate. Since then, the police have been applying political techniques in defeating existing and proposed accountability mechanisms, especially civilian review boards.

The victory over the civilian review board in Philadelphia, the first such agency to be created in the nation, in October of 1958, is exemplary of the political power held by police at the local level. The police review board came into being by an executive order of Mayor Richardson Dilworth. It was empowered to receive citizen complaints of police misconduct and, after examining a case, to determine the innocence or guilt of the police officers involved and to make recommendations to the commissioner relative to disciplinary disposition. Right off, the Philadelphia lodge of the Fraternal Order of Police voiced its opposition to the idea of a civilian review board, and even before the board was established, during the course of deliberations in the city council about its creation, a spokesman of the lodge threatened a revolt in the department if the civilian review board became a reality.[46]

A revolt against the civilian review board did not occur, but thirteen months after the board's inception, the Fraternal Order of Police filed a complaint in equity in the Philadelphia courts on behalf of seven officers called before the board on complaints. The FOP contended that the board operated in violation of the city charter because it disciplined department personnel. The charter specified that each city agency had sole disciplinary authority over its employees, and civilian boards formed to oversee the agencies were to serve only in advisory capacity. The Philadelphia common pleas court upheld the FOP's contention and the city was prepared to appeal. However, an out-of-court compromise agreement was reached between the leadership of the police organization and the members of the civilian review board. The most noteworthy effects of the compromise was to change the name of the board from the Police Review Board to the Police Advisory Board, and for the FOP to receive acknowledgment of its right to represent policemen before the Police Advisory Board. The authorization granted to the FOP to act as counsel for policemen at board hearings helped solidify relations between the lodge and its members because, significantly, police officers were no longer liable for legal expenses incurred in appearances before the board. Other than for these changes, the board continued to function pretty much as it had previously.

In 1964 the Police Advisory Board once again emerged as an issue in Philadelphia politics. The fight against the advisory board became associated with the politics and career of John Harrington, a sergeant in Philadelphia's highway patrol unit, who led a victorious insurgent slate in the Philadelphia lodge elections in 1964. Harrington had previously been unsuccessful in his quest for the FOP lodge presidency in 1960 and 1962. In all of his campaigns he advocated the need for more militancy by the lodge because "respect for law and law enforcement officers was diminishing." He claimed that "a defensive and benign posture of the incumbent FOP leadership" was to blame for this situation in Philadelphia. Shortly after winning the election in 1964, Harrington began his attack on the Police Advisory Board. His criticism was that although the board had discovered little police misconduct, it had been instrumental in lowering the morale and efficiency of all police officers in the department. Furthermore, he charged that the board's primary function was "to pacify the people who live in the low-class areas with police records."

The campaign against the board gained intensity in August 1964. Rioting and looting, lasting three days, occurred in north-central Philadelphia. The disorders caused property damage estimated at approximately $3 million and injuries to over 200 civilians and 100 police officers. Harrington sought to capitalize on the extensive damages by linking the advisory board with the riot. "You saw the pictures of the cannibals coming out of the stores with TV sets on their heads," he said. "If it hadn't been for the PAB we would have grabbed them and if they resisted, hit them with our blackjacks."[47] The FOP leadership claimed that the riots lasted as long as they did because Philadelphia policemen were constrained from using a degree of force that was necessary in this situation for fear of being called before the Police Advisory Board on charges of misconduct. Later, in testimony under oath, Harrington stated that the city solicitor, apparently at the urging of the mayor, requested his presence in the riot area to inform the men to employ whatever force was necessary to quell the riot and to assure them that the city had pledged that no PAB actions would ensue from these actions.

In 1965, capitalizing on his highly publicized battle against the Philadelphia Police Advisory Board, Harrington was successful in his bid for the national FOP presidency. A month after winning the national election, Harrington was named as the principal plaintiff in an FOP lawsuit seeking the abolition of the PAB. The Philadelphia common pleas court in March of 1966 decided that the board was "created for purposes and functions not authorized by law," because it went beyond merely advising the police department by performing a review function.[48] For approximately two and a half years after the court's decision the board remained inactive, while Mayor James Tate and the city of Philadelphia decided about initiating an appeal. Finally, in the middle of 1968, urged by the threat of attorney members of the board to move on the case themselves, the city solicitor's office appealed the case. The next year the Supreme Court of Pennsylvania reversed the decision of the lower court and held that the Police Adisory Board had been lawfully constituted. However, by then, the obstacles of inadequate staffing, inactivity for nearly three years, and the absence of funding were too great to overcome. The board continued to languish. "On December 27, 1969, while attending a promotional ceremony at police headquarters, Mayor Tate announced that as a Christmas gift to the men of the department he was issuing an executive order formally disbanding the Board."[49]

The Police Advisory Board, during its eight years and three months of operation, heard 207 cases out of the 1004 complaints filed. This meant that only 20.6 percent of the complaints against police malpractice reached the hearing stage, the rest either being informally resolved or dismissed. Of the 207 cases before the board, punishment was recommended in 24.1 percent of the cases, with 30 instances of an oral or written reprimand advised and 20 recommendations of temporary suspension. On a yearly average, approximately six cases reaching the hearing stage were resolved with recommendations of punishment. The board never advised dismissal.

The formal police opposition to a civilian review board in Philadelphia was the first such occurrence and presaged similar confrontations that were to occur in other cities. The Philadelphia battle is instructive because it shows how union leadership exploited the issue of civilian review boards in order to gain control of the internal organization. This suggests the need for militancy in police organization as a way of attracting and retaining a constituency. Civilian review boards are an issue profitably utilized by police organizations to engage the interest of the rank-and-file members who are sensitive about threats to their authority and insecure about their role expectations. The dramatization of such issues as civilian review boards mobilizes members of police organizations to form a power bloc in city politics. This ends up by giving police organizations not only a reason for their existence, but also a capacity to influence law enforcement policy. The successful challenges to civil and external accountability measures illuminate the potency of the police bureaucracy, through its organizations, in any power relationships at the local community level.

The police have employed trade union techniques to challenge internal accountability and management controls. Just as police organizations learned to benefit from the fragmentation of the political system in order to attain their objectives, so also have they sought to exploit the fragmentation within police departments. In 1972 contract negotiations between the management of the New York police department and the Patrolmen's Benevolent Association underwent difficulties that included the breaking off of negotiations at one period and the threat of job actions because of the union's disagreement about management policies. Among the issues in contention were proposed work schedules and a master plan initiated by Commissioner Murphy that outlined management controls to improve the operations of the department.

Claiming management prerogative, the commissioner announced that he would shift the work schedules of patrolmen despite the criticism of the Patrolmen's Benevolent Association that he was trying "to implement unilaterally certain matters that were the subject of negotiations."[50] Commissioner Murphy replied, "This department needs further reform and more modern management. That's my job and I'm charged with that responsibility."[51] The proposed change in work schedules involved increasing the number of patrolmen on the streets of New York by 1000 men during the high-crime evening hours.

Citing another prerogative of management, Commissioner Murphy announced the institution of one-man patrol cars as part of his blueprint of a new management analysis system aimed at impioving the quality of police service. The Patrolmen's Association voiced its opposition to the proposed use of one-man patrol cars, stating that this, along with the other initiatives in Murphy's master plan, was subject to negotiation. The commissioner replied that he would go ahead with his proposals despite the disapproval of the Patrolmen's Benevolent Association.[52] Among the key suggestions contained in the seventeen-page master plan were the elimination of some precincts, the dismissal of unproductive policemen, the development of a police "West Point" for training commanders, and the elimination of the policy of punishing "problem" policemen by assigning them to the busiest precincts.[53]

Contract negotiations in New York were also hampered by sharp opposition by the PBA to the proposal of a policy under which a patrolman suspected of corruption would be required to take a lie detector test. Edward J. Kiernan, president of the group at the time, stated that he was adamant in opposition to the use of lie detector tests. He maintained the tests would reduce policemen to the status of second-class citizens and represent another aspect of Police Commissioner Patrick V. Murphy's "continuing effort to break the union and destroy the merit system."[54]

Opposition to the use of lie detector tests came from not only the patrolmen's group but also from the Sergeants' Benevolent Association, the Lieutenants' Association, and the Captains' Endowment Association. The use of lie detectors was defended by Commissioner Murphy, who cited their extensive use by the Los Angeles and Chicago departments, where refusal to submit to the lie detector tests led to dismissal. On the issue of the tests, a spokesman in the Los Angeles police department said, "While there may be some constitutional questions involved, being a member of our department is not a constitutional right. The lie detector is a condition of employment here."[55]

The trade union efforts of police organizations are posing a challenge to internal management controls. Police unions are vying seriously for control of the police bureaucracy. Detroit police commissioner John Nichols once quoted a police union leader at a symposium: "'Chiefs, Superintendents, and Commissioners are temporal. They'll change. The union is the only permanency of the Department. It is we with whom you'll deal, we will make the policy.'"[56]

Rodney Stark's thesis is that the police enjoy their own version of the four freedoms: "Freedom from civil authorities, from the courts, from the press, and from public opinion."[57] From the evidence of union militancy, it can be added that, in some cases, the police enjoy a fifth freedom: freedom from internal controls. The development of autonomy for the police has been aided by the influences of a subculture of career officials that defines organizational norms and insures conformance to them by a system of rewards and punishments. In addition, police organizations possessing considerable political power have the ability to "negotiate" autonomy with civil authorities in the political system and with the administrators of police departments. Ominously, countervailing deterrents to the growth of police power are made impotent by the failures of the political system and by the apathy, or encouragement of this tendency, of the general public.

The abuse of police power has moved beyond conditions of incompetence and corruption and into an area of police repression and violations of civil and constitutional liberties. The loss of integrity of law enforcement is now encouraged by public officials at the highest levels of government who are employing police agencies for their own personal and political benefit. Additionally, this phenomenon is enhanced by an acquiescent citizenry, which, despite knowledge about police malpractice, has opted for the maintenance of order at all costs.

The seeds of a police state are sown by a democracy that becomes indifferent to the accountability of its institutions, especially when this concerns an institution with the capabilities as extraordinary as those held by the police. In America, although the theory of the democratic process is universally upheld, it is not universally practiced. The history of American cities provides numerous examples of misgovernment and of autocratic boss rule. However, in the past, the effect of bossism usually was that police forces were held in control by publicly elected officials, no matter how despotic or how corrupt, for a variety of reasons. Assuredly, these controls were not democratic nor did they insure impartial law enforcement. What they did do was to provide a system of police accountability that saw to it that the police bureaucracy remained subordinate to City Hall. Unfortunately, all too often, corrupt officials used police forces as a praetorian guard protecting their positions of political power. There are far too many cases where the political system has used the police as instruments of repression, to intimidate citizens from exercising their democratic rights.

Now, the diffusion of political power in most cities has allowed monolithic public bureaucracies capable of aggregating a consensus of interest to play a sizable role in the local political process. These bureaucracies are able to mobilize the political cohesion of their members by enlarging and dwelling on issues of common interest to the rank and file.

Police unions have been able to instigate and nurture a common front of occupational bias by their militant posture in behalf of the interests of their constituency. These organizations have been able to mount effective campaigns for the maintenance of their autonomy on all levels of government: at the municipal level the local unions have participated actively in the political system, while at the federal and state levels the national unions have lobbied effectlvely in behalf of their membership. Unchecked police power invites destruction of the principles of democracy. It may be an overstatement to draw a parable with a police state from not long ago, but it should serve as a warning to those who are indifferent to unchecked police power to say:

> First they came for the Communists; I am not a Communist, so I didn't care.
>
> Next, they came for the trade unionists; I am not a trade unionist, so I didn't care.
>
> Then, they came for the Jews; I am not a Jew, so I didn't care.
>
> Then, they came for the Catholics; I am not a Catholic, so I didn't care.
>
> Today, they came for me. . . .

Police and Society: Reflections in a Silver Shield

Theoretically, complex organizations such as the police bureaucracy behave consistently with the needs and expectations of the community they serve when they reflect the dominant values of their environment. Because of their inextricable linkage to the values of society, organizations act as agents of socialization in addition to functioning in a bureaucratic capacity. Accordingly, the police are not only agents of law enforcement, but are also supporters of community norms.

In order to determine whether the police truly depict the dominant values in a community, and whether social values play a role in determining bureaucratic behavior as suggested by general theory, police-citizen attitudes were tested on a relatively small scale. Data was derived from a sample of officers in the Memphis police department, citizens living in both black and white neighborhoods in the city of Memphis, and students attending Memphis State University. The testing of the total sample (N=534) was done by means of a questionnaire administered during the months of December 1972 through February 1973. The sample was designed to cut across class and income lines so as to afford a broad spectrum of representation from the community.

Responses from the questionnaire were converted into two scales describing attitudes about law enforcement. Respondents were also asked to rate a variety of political, occupational, and ethnic groups by using a "cell thermometer." Finally, the questionnaire called for the allocation of a prestige value for a number of occupation groups, including the police.

The city of Memphis, which served as an urban laboratory for the study, has a total population of 623,530, of whom 38.9 percent are black. The Chamber of Commerce calls the city the "Place of Good Abode" and recalls that it is the only four-time winner of an award for the "cleanest city in the nation." The Chamber also describes Memphis as the birthplace of the Blues, the Memphis Sound, and the Cotton Carnival, and the home of the Liberty Bowl. Publicized, too, are the city's 153 parks and playgrounds, approximately 750 houses of religious worship, and the development of new office buildings and high-rise apartments downtown and in outlying sections of the city.

What the Chamber does not talk about is that for much of the first half of this century, the city's political life was ordered by one man: "Boss" Ed Crump, whose rule and authority in Memphis and, for a time, in the state of

Tennessee was absolute.[1] The past that did much to shape the political character of the community is forgotten. Today, the city's government is succinctly described as a mayor-council form, with an elected mayor and thirteen elected city councilmen. Unmentioned also are the urban problems besetting the "Place of Good Abode," which are typical of contemporary city life. The crime rate is rising. Many of the city's blacks and poor whites live in squalid dwellings and rundown neighborhoods. The downtown area, enclosed by black ghettos, faces extinction as shopping centers built throughout the outlying white residential areas draw the bulk of the retail trade. Few whites can be found along the practically deserted streets of downtown after 6:00 P.M. Commercial and industrial properties too are attracted to the outlying areas, so that, in actuality, much of the functional activities associated with "downtown" are no longer located there.

The population of the city is made up predominantly of people who are either themselves from the rural sections of Tennessee and the neighboring states of Arkansas and Mississippi, or whose forebears came from those areas. The community's relatively homogeneous population base—the major demographic division being along white-black racial lines—and the rural background of many of the residents provide the city with the cultural characteristics of parochialism, religious fundamentalism, and conservatism. Observers of the Memphis scene, from the communications media or the local academic institutions, have called the city the archetype of "middle America." They have employed such descriptive terms for Memphis as "Main-Street, USA, with a Southern accent," "apple-pie America," and "banal."[2]

Census data, (Table 5-1), profiling the economic structure of the population of Memphis reveals that almost 37 percent of the white population fit a middle-class description, by economic standards, with incomes in the $10,000 to $24,999 category. Despite the large concentrations of whites in the middle-class income bracket, a majority of white families fall below the $10,000 income level. Black families are heavily represented in the under $10,000 bracket, with but some 16 percent of their number belonging to the middle-class, according to the criterion used.

A description of Memphis residents by their education level indicates a discrepancy in education between white and black residents, which may account for the difference in incomes for the two races. Table 5-2 shows that almost 30 percent of the white population are high school graduates, while only 16.06 percent of the black population finished high school. Over 10 percent of the white population have had some college. The corresponding figure for the black population is 4.26 percent. The percentages for residents who have completed four or more years of college are almost 10 percent of the white population and slightly more than 4 percent for the black.

Table 5-1
Family Income of Memphis Residents

Income	White Population	Percent	Black Population	Percent
Less than $1,000	5,263	3.43	3,749	7.32
$1,000-$1,999	7,047	4.59	5,099	9.95
$2,000-$2,999	7,491	4.88	4,789	9.35
$3,000-$3,999	9,064	5.90	5,916	11.54
$4,000-$4,995	9,495	6.18	5,240	10.23
$5,000-$5,999	9,961	6.48	4,695	9.16
$6,000-$6,999	10,542	6.86	4,346	8.48
$7,000-$7,999	10,828	7.05	3,638	7.10
$8,000-$8,999	11,038	7.18	2,940	5.74
$9,000-$9,999	10,131	6.59	2,519	4.92
$10,000-$11,999	18,373	11.96	8,315[a]	16.21
$12,000-$14,999	19,058	12.4		
$15,000-$24,999	19,096	12.43		
$25,000-$49,999	4,933	3.21		
$50,000 or more	1,327	.56		
TOTAL	153,647		51,246	

[a]$10,000 or more

Source: 1970 Census of Population and Housing: Memphis, Tennessee-Arkansas Standard Metropolitan Statistical Area, U.S. Department of Commerce, Bureau of the Census.

Table 5-2
Level of Education of Memphis Residents

Completed Education	White Population	Percent	Black Population	Percent
No School	4,856	1.51	3,516	3.30
Elementary				
1-4 years	18,689	5.81	14,276	13.19
5-7 years	37,571	11.69	23,157	21.39
8 years	32,127	9.99	14,499	13.39
High School				
1-3 years	67,194	20.90	26,361	24.35
4 years	96,309	29.96	17,389	16.06
College				
1-3 years	32,844	10.22	4,611	4.26
4 or more years	31,873	9.91	4,399	4.06
TOTAL	321,463		108,268	

Source: 1970 Census of Population and Housing: Memphis, Tennessee-Arkansas Standard Metropolitan Statistical Area, U.S. Department of Commerce, Bureau of the Census.

The police department in Memphis has 1058 officers. Table 5-3, showing the education level for each rank, points to the scarcity of college graduates in the department, particularly in the higher ranks. The department has sought to correct this condition by offering college incentive pay of $7.50 a month for each year of college completed by an officer and $50 a month for a master's degree. The department now requires two years of college as a minimum entrance requirement. However, waivers are granted to individuals who do not meet the new education requirements if the applicants have had prior law enforcement experience or military service. The data also reveals a decline in the level of education in the hierarchy beginning above the rank of inspector, with the low point in the average number of years of education being in the highest ranks in the department.

Description of the Civilian and Police Sample

Table 5-4 is a comparison between the police and general population samples by age, marital status, ethnic origin, and sex. Over 92 percent of the police sampled were white. This is approximately the same racial distribution found in the entire police department. The civilian sample was about three-fourths white and one-fourth black. The sample has a higher representation of white citizens than the actual demographic breakdown of approximately a 61:39 ratio of whites to blacks in Memphis, according to the census. The city does not have a significant percentage of Puerto Ricans, Chicanos, Indians, or Orientals. The percentage of women in the police sample reflected fairly accurately the overall ratio of females in the department. The citizen sample of women was less than their population percentage in the city.

Table 5-5 presents a number of demographic variables used to describe the police and civilian population samples. Under the level of education of parents, the general population sample showed a much higher proportion of both fathers and mothers with some college, college degrees, or advanced degrees. However, the majority of responses for both parents were in the grade school through high school levels, with some 56 percent placing their fathers and over 74 percent their mothers in these categories. In the police sample, the educational level of fathers was heavily concentrated in the lower end of the scale showing grade school, some high school, and high school. For the mother's education category, the largest number of police responses fell in the "high school plus noncollege study" category. Under education completed, the civilian sample revealed a broad distribution in all categories, although about 73 percent of the respondents selected high school, some college, and a bachelor's degree as describing their level of education. The police sample was only represented in four categories: high school, high school plus noncollege study, some college, and bachelor's

Table 5-3
Memphis Police Department Commissioned Officer Educational Level by Rank

Rank	Total	High School or GED Only	College 1 year	College 2 years	College 3 years	Bachelor's Degree	Master's Degree	Average number years
Patrolwoman	25	24	1					12.04
Patrolman	532	465	19	23	16	9		12.28
Warrant Officer	72	55	6	4	4	2	1	12.54
Detective	210	177	14	13	4		2	12.30
Lieutenant	169	148	7	5	3	5	1	12.13
Captain	32	22	3	2	1	4		12.56
Inspector	10	8				2		12.80
Chief Inspector	5	4		1				12.40
Deputy Chief	2	2						12.00
Chief of Police	1	1						12.00
TOTAL	1,058	906	50	48	28	22	4	12.31

Source: Records and Evidence Bureau, Memphis Police Department, October, 1972. During the time that this data was accumulated, the Memphis Police Department did not use the rank of sergeant.

degree. Of these, approximately 91 percent of the sample indicated high school and some college as appropriate. Significantly, none of the police sampled indicated that they held an advanced degree, while out of the civilian population surveyed, more than 7 percent held a master's degree, and 4.36 percent claimed a Ph.D. or professional degree.

In the income category, the general population sample ran the entire spectrum of income levels. However, the modal figure for the sample is classifiable as economically middle-class, with over 44 percent indicating incomes of from $9000 to $19,999. The police sample revealed incomes of from $5000 to $24,000, with about 79 percent falling in the $8000 to $14,999 category.

Under religion, Baptists were represented in large numbers in both the police and civilian samples, and overall, Protestants of various denominations dominated this category. Interestingly, while Memphis is generally considered to be in the "Bible Belt," over 36 percent of the civilian population sample and nearly 53 percent of the police sample indicated that they seldom attended church.

The social class category was derived by having respondents freely identify themselves according to their own perceptions. None of the police sampled placed themselves in the lower class, and only 17.90 percent chose working class as their category. However, over 4 percent of the police indicated that they were in the upper class as opposed to 2.19 percent who picked this classification in the general population sample. The category chosen most often by both samples was middle-middle class, as indicated by nearly 52 percent of the police and over 43 percent of the civilians.

The remaining three categories—occupational status, political identification, and political ideology—were again free-choice items based on self-perceptions. Under the occupational category, 44.17 percent of the police, the modal percentage, indicated that they believed themselves to be professionals. The corresponding figure for the civilian sample in this category was 31.36 percent. In terms of political identification, the police sample largely selected Independent and Independent Republican with 34.36 percent and 29.45 percent showing for these categories. Strong Republican was next in favor, although far behind with 9.20 percent, while Strong Democrat and Other Minority Party showed weakest with 2.34 percent and 1.84 percent respectively. Almost 8 percent of the police respondents indicated membership in the American Party. The general population sample's choice of parties was more evenly distributed. Identification as Democrats—Strong, Independent, and Weak—led the field with 42.58 percent, followed closely by Independent, Strong, and Weak Republican as selected by 40.11 percent. In the civilian sample, the American Party and Other Minority Party bottomed out the choices, with 2.47 percent and .82 percent. Ideologically, over 50 percent of the police viewed

Table 5-4

Description of the Police and General Memphis Population Samples by Age, Marital Status, Race, and Sex

Descriptions	Police Sample	Percent	Civilian Sample	Percent
Age:				
Under 25	16	9.81	112	31.64
26-29	64	39.26	64	18.08
30-34	50	30.67	44	12.43
35-39	12	7.36	25	7.06
40-44	19	11.65	30	8.47
45-49	2	1.22	23	6.50
50-54	0	0	19	5.37
55-59	0	0	19	5.37
60 and over	0	0	18	5.08
Totals	163	100.00	354	100.00
Marital Status:				
Married	142	86.58	239	64.60
Divorced	9	5.48	12	3.24
Separated	4	2.43	13	3.51
Single	8	4.87	91	24.60
Common-law	1	.60	1	.27
Widow/widower	0	0	14	3.78
Totals	164	100.00	370	100.00
Race:				
White	150	92.59	272	74.52
Black	9	5.55	92	25.21
Puerto Rican	1	.61	0	0
Indian	2	1.23	0	0
Other	0	0	1	.27
Totals	162	100.00	365	100.00
Sex:				
Female	6	3.70	165	44.84
Male	156	96.30	203	55.16
Totals	162	100.00	368	100.00

themselves as conservative, while 33.97 percent was the corresponding figure for the general population. The modal percentage for the civilian sample was under political moderate with over 44 percent regarding themselves in this classification.

From the description obtained through the sample survey, a general profile of the police emerges. The sample shows the police to be in the middle-class income bracket, Protestant in religion—albeit not necessarily

Table 5-5
General Characteristics of Police and Civilian Samples

Descriptions	Police Sample	Percent	Civilian Sample	Percent
Father's Education:				
None	0	0	5	1.37
Grade school	50	31.49	73	19.95
Some high school	35	22.01	57	15.57
High school	43	27.04	76	20.77
High school plus noncollege study	10	6.28	29	7.92
Some college	14	8.80	56	15.30
Bachelor's	5	3.14	42	11.48
Master's	1	.62	9	2.46
Ph.D. (or professional degree)	1	.62	19	5.18
Total	159	100.00	366	100.00
Mother's Education:				
None	0	0	5	1.37
Grade school	1	.63	83	22.74
Some high school	40	25.00	68	18.63
High school	48	30.00	121	33.15
High school, plus noncollege study	54	33.75	10	2.74
Some college	9	5.62	46	12.60
Bachelor's	7	4.38	24	6.58
Master's	1	.62	8	2.19
Ph.D. (or professional degree)	0	0	0	0
Total	160	100.00	365	100.00
Education Completed (Sample)				
None	0	0	1	.27
Grade school	0	0	11	3.00
Some high school	0	0	28	7.63
High school	73	45.63	53	14.44
High school, plus noncollege study	10	8.12	16	4.36
Some college	74	46.25	120	32.70
Bachelor's	3	6.00	96	26.16
Master's	0	0	26	7.08
Ph.D. (or professional degree)	0	0	16	4.36
Total	160	100.00	367	100.00
Income:				
1,000-1,999	0	0	5	1.43
2,000-2,999	0	0	6	1.72
3,000-3,999	0	0	6	1.72
4,000-4,999	0	0	16	4.58

Table 5-5 (Continued)

Descriptions	Police Sample	Percent	Civilian Sample	Percent
5,000-5,999	3	1.85	13	3.72
6,000-6,999	2	1.23	20	5.73
7,000-7,999	7	4.32	18	5.16
8,000-8,999	25	15.43	16	4.58
9,000-9,999	31	19.13	22	6.30
10,000-11,999	32	19.75	40	11.47
12,000-14,999	38	23.45	52	14.90
15,000-19,999	17	10.49	41	11.75
20,000-24,999	7	4.32	41	11.75
25,000-49,999	0	0	43	12.32
Over 50,000	0	0	10	2.87
Total	162	100.00	349	100.00
Religion:				
Catholic	14	8.59	32	9.09
Jewish	1	.61	7	1.99
No organized church	4	2.45	11	3.13
No church	7	4.29	24	6.82
Baptist	76	46.63	139	39.49
Methodist	19	11.66	55	15.62
Presbyterian	8	4.91	34	9.66
Episcopalian	4	2.45	23	6.53
Church of Christ	13	7.98	16	4.55
Other Protestant	17	10.43	11	3.12
Total	163	100.00	352	100.00
Church Attendance:				
Regularly	29	18.01	141	39.17
Often	32	19.88	66	18.33
Seldom	85	52.80	131	36.39
Never	15	9.31	22	6.11
Total	161	100.00	360	100.00
Social Class:				
Upper	7	4.32	8	2.19
Upper-middle	18	11.11	104	28.49
Middle-middle	84	51.85	159	43.56
Lower-middle	24	14.81	43	11.78
Working	29	17.90	47	12.88
Lower	0	0	4	1.10
Total	162	100.00	365	100.00
Occupational Status:				
Professional	72	44.17	111	31.36
Manager	3	1.84	29	8.20
Clerical	1	.61	48	13.56
Craftsman	1	.61	12	3.39
Machinery Operator	1	.61	10	2.82

Table 5-5 (Continued)

Descriptions	Police Sample	Percent	Civilian Sample	Percent
Police, private household worker, service worker, military, etc.	74	45.40	42	11.86
Laborer	0	0	12	3.39
Farmer	0	0	1	.28
Other	11	6.75	89	25.14
Total	163	100.00	354	100.00
Political Identification:				
Strong Democrat	4	2.45	58	15.93
Weak Democrat	5	3.07	43	11.81
Independent Democrat	11	6.75	54	14.84
Independent	56	34.36	51	14.02
Independent Republican	48	29.45	68	18.68
Weak Republican	8	4.91	38	10.44
Strong Republican	15	9.20	40	10.99
American party	13	7.98	9	2.47
Other minority party	3	1.84	3	.82
Total	163	100.00	364	100.00
Political Ideology:				
Conservative	82	50.62	124	33.97
Liberal	18	11.11	74	20.27
Moderate	56	34.57	161	44.12
Other	6	3.70	6	1.64
Total	162	100.00	365	100.00

practicing their religion—and having either a high school education or some college. Since the level of education of the police sample appears to be higher than the level obtained by their parents, this indicates upward mobility, probably from the working or even lower class. Furthermore, policemen see themselves as professionals with a high regard for their present occupation. Politically, the police sample best represents a conservative ideology, and a liberal ideology is underrepresented.

The populations sampled were surveyed for their general attitudes. Specifically, respondents were asked to rate a number of categories, consisting of political, occupational, and ethnic groups by grading them using a "cell thermometer." In the cell thermometer, a grade of 1 was the lowest value, while a 9 was the highest. Grades nearest a 1 showed a cold or unfavorable feeling about a group and those closest to a 9 reflected warm or favorable feelings. Table 5-6 shows the "feelings" of the group surveyed in the total sample. Mean scores are used to illustrate the feelings or attitudes.

Of the groups surveyed, the police sample showed the "warmest feeling" for the following groups: American Legion, National Guard, conservatives, Republicans, John Birch Society, blue collar workers, policemen, Ku Klux Klan, whites, and the military. Conversely, they indicated the "coldest feeling" for: Black Panthers, Democrats, liberals, women's liberation, and blacks. All the mean scores for these groups fell below 5, with the Black Panthers achieving the low of 1.191, followed by liberals, women's liberation, and blacks with scores of 3.497, 3.694, and 3.758.

Some of the feelings revealed by the police were quite disparate from those indicated by the other groups surveyed, while other "high-low" scores closely paralleled the feelings of other sample groups. For example, the low score showing cold feelings for the Black Panthers was just slightly "colder" than the 1.911 score given this group by the whites of the general population surveyed. The "warm" score for Republicans was only a little "warmer" than the score of 6.158 accorded this group by the white citizens. However, the police high of 5.236 for the Ku Klux Klan is not closely

Table 5-6
Cell Thermometer By Sample Groups

Categories	Total Civilian Sample	Whites	Blacks	Students	Police
American Legion	5.536	5.792	5.526	5.321	7.338
Labor Unions	5.447	4.960	6.079	5.302	5.382
Black Panthers	3.244	1.911	5.038	2.792	1.191
College Professors	7.005	6.881	6.397	7.736	5.433
National Guard	6.244	6.713	6.077	5.943	7.726
Jews	6.172	6.668	5.038	6.811	5.822
Conservatives	5.732	6.163	4.872	6.160	6.815
Democrats	6.279	5.792	6.667	6.377	4.726
Republicans	5.401	6.158	4.026	6.019	6.166
Liberals	5.295	4.683	5.090	6.113	3.497
John Birch Society	3.409	3.277	3.705	3.245	5.586
Women's Liberation	4.954	4.515	5.385	4.962	3.694
Government Workers	6.345	6.114	6.354	6.566	6.567
Blue Collar Workers	6.430	6.381	6.231	6.679	7.115
Policemen	6.184	6.757	5.436	6.358	8.535
Blacks	6.839	6.000	8.064	6.453	3.758
School Teachers	7.393	7.168	7.077	7.415	6.962
Ku Klux Klan	1.888	1.876	1.769	2.019	5.236
Whites	6.683	7.564	5.051	7.434	8.121
Military	6.036	6.772	5.526	5.811	7.586
Totals	333	202	78	53	157

matched by a corresponding score from any other group. Nor is the police low score for blacks approximated by anyone else. Interestingly, scores by the police and black citizen samples were close only in regard to feelings about government workers and Jews. The blacks surveyed had the "coldest" feeling about Jews, with a mean of 5.038 and the police were next lowest with 5.822.

The "warm feelings" shown by the police sample for military organizations, conservatives, and right-wing extremist groups and the adverse attitudes about liberals, Democrats, and women's liberation validates their self-identification as conservative ideologues. Furthermore, their "cold" feelings for blacks and "warmth" for the Ku Klux Klan reveals an anti-black bias by the sample group.

The perception of the police as an occupation group is not viewed alike by the police and the other groups surveyed. Sampled groups were asked to rank fourteen occupations in ascending order. Table 5-7 shows that the police sample holds the police occupation in high esteem by ranking policemen second, after doctor. Interestingly, detectives were ranked seventh by the police, but this is probably attributable to the low number of detectives (eight) that participated in the police sample.[3] The total civilian sample, however, also placed detective behind policeman. The total sample chose policeman and detective only ahead of soldier, electrician, insurance salesman, sales clerk, and student, thereby challenging the police sample's claim to professional standing.

Table 5-7
Occupational Prestige Ranking By Sample Groups

Occupations	Total Civilian Sample	Whites	Blacks	Police	Students
Detective	9	8	9	7	8
Soldier	10[a]	9	10	8	12
Policeman	8	7	8	2	9
Minister	3	3	1	3	6
Student	14	14	14	12	13
Sales Clerk	13	12	13	13	14
Electrician	10[a]	10	11	10	10
Insurance Salesman	12	11	12	11	11
College Professor	5	5	6	6	3
Doctor	1	1	3	1	1
Lawyer	4	4	5	4	4
Judge	2	2	4	5	2
Politician	6[a]	13	2	14	5
Teacher	6[a]	6	7	9	7
Totals	335	200	79	160	56

[a]Ties

Values About Law Enforcement

In the course of daily activities and as a part of the organic relationship between the police bureaucracy and the social environment, the police and social values have a mutual interplay. Two social value systems, "order-stability" and "democratic-active," are especially significant for their influence on police behavior and innovation. These value systems, defined first by Silverman and Kim, pose conflicting social values giving off different social expectations about the nature of law enforcement.[4]

"Order-stability" values are concerned with law enforcement tasks that insure order and stability, crime control, and improved police efficiency and productivity. The value structure is basically opposed to any possible interference—such as civilian review boards and civilian or judicial control of the police—with the achievement of "order-stability" objectives. "Democratic-active" values favor, in addition to order and safety, a law enforcement tempered by considerations of justice, human dignity, procedural safeguards, and respect for a pluralistic value system. These values are also partial to a service-orientation in law enforcement, a more active and positive role for the police in providing service to the community. Essentially the conflict occurs over the "order-stability" expectations of the police to perform efficiently, while the "democratic-active" expectation is for them to do the "right" thing rather than just the "efficient" thing.[5]

While both value systems are supportive of innovations in the police bureaucracy for the realization of goal expectations, they deal with innovation from different perspectives. Order-stability values in quest of the police doing the "efficient thing," favor the introduction of new technical innovations, modern management systems, and effective allocation of police manpower to improve crime control and law enforcement responsibilities. The democratic-active values seek to sensitize the police bureaucracy to service-oriented responsibilities and to social and procedural needs, in addition to law enforcement and order maintenance functions.

To illustrate and analyze the order-stability value structure, the demographic variables identified from the survey—age, race, income, education, sex, political party identification, and political ideology—were isolated. Democratic-active values are found to be most active where order-stability is least indicated. The chi-square statistic was used to associate the demographic variables with an order-stability scale. Construction of the order-stability scale was done by inspecting data obtained from the survey and selecting items from the survey questionnaire that were a priori evaluated to be germane to the hypothesis.[6]

The hypothesis, briefly stated, is that significant social values that are

Table 5-8
Civilian Demographic Variables and Attitudes about Law Enforcement

AGE AND "ORDER-STABILITY"/"DEMOCRATIC-ACTIVE"

Age	Low	Medium	High	Number
25 and under	9	23	9	41
26-39	10	45	17	72
40-49	2	20	21	43
50 and over	1	18	23	42
Total	22	106	70	198

$X^2 = 23.331^{**}$, df = 6, p = .00105

INCOME AND "ORDER-STABILITY"/"DEMOCRATIC-ACTIVE"

Income	Low	Medium	High	Number
Under $2,999	4	1	2	6
3,000-5,999	2	3	6	11
6,000- 9,999	3	17	4	24
10,000-14,999	4	31	18	54
$15,000 and over	9	51	38	98
Total	22	103	68	193

$X^2 = 28.450^{**}$, df = 8, p = .00068

RACE AND "ORDER-STABILITY"/"DEMOCRATIC-ACTIVE"

Race	Low	Medium	High	Number
White	47	(0)[a]	92	139
Black	8	(0)[a]	1	9
Total	55	(0)[a]	93	148

[a]Chi Square computed with Low and High only.
$X^2 = 10.980^{**}$, df = 2, p = .0046

Table 5-8 (Continued)

EDUCATION LEVEL AND "ORDER-STABILITY"/"DEMOCRATIC-ACTIVE"

Completed Education	Low	Medium	High	Number
Some High School	1	6	11	18
High School	1	15	12	28
High School plus noncollege study	1	3	6	10
Some College	3	35	23	61
Bachelor's	10	29	10	49
Master's	4	14	1	19
Ph.D. (or professional degree)	2	4	7	13
Total	22	106	70	198

$X^2 = 32.697**$, df = 12, p = .00152

POLITICAL PARTY AND "ORDER-STABILITY"/"DEMOCRATIC-ACTIVE"

Political Party	Low	Medium	High	Number
Strong Democrat	5	8	4	17
Weak Democrat	4	9	6	19
Independent	10	57	30	97
Republican	1	29	25	55
Other	2	2	2	6
Total	22	105	67	194

$X^2 = 17.920*$, df = 8, p = .02247

POLITICAL IDEOLOGY AND "ORDER-STABILITY"/"DEMOCRATIC ACTIVE"

Political Ideology	Low	Medium	High	Number
Conservative	0	32	46	78
Liberal	11	15	1	27
Moderate	11	56	21	88
Total	22	103	68	193

$X^2 = 53.377**$, df = 4, p = .00000

* = α = .05   ** = α = .01

discoverable have a relationship to police bureaucratic practices and innovation. The significant results obtained from the civilian sample data was a positive association between order-stability and the demographic variables of age, income, race, education, political party identification and political ideology. In Table 5-8 a "high" classification indicates order-stability while "low" is equated to democratic-active attributes. Because of the low number of democratic-active responses, the sample representing this value is quite small, thereby obscuring a clear description of the group's demographic attributes. A clearer demographic profile of the "order-stability" group can be obtained from the survey.

Under the age category in the table, the modal group for order-stability was in the forty through age fifty-and-over categories. Democratic-active values were most present in respondents twenty-five and under through thirty-nine years of age. The income group that most depicted order-stability was in the $15,000 and over category. Democratic-actives were scattered throughout the income levels, although the largest number indicating this value was also in the $15,000 and over group. Race and the tested values were positively associated. Inspection of the table indicates that the largest response pattern was by whites in both order-stability and democratic-active values. Blacks, however, were almost totally absent from the order-stability category.

There was a significant association between the education level of the respondents and their attitudes toward law enforcement. Respondents indicating "some college" and "high school" as their educational level had the highest representation in the order-stability value group. Interestingly, Ph.D. or professional degree holders fell mostly within the order-stability classification also.[7] The table shows that those holding a bachelor's degree had the highest frequency of democratic-active responses.

The relationship between political party membership and values about law enforcement showed Independents and Republicans highest in order-stability, with Independents also highest in the democratic-active category.[8] Under political ideology, conservatives dominated in order-stability, while liberals and moderates were represented equally in democratic-active.

A general profile of the civilian group with order-stability values can be detected from the data. Order-stability values are most likely represented by whites, forty years old or older, with a high school education or some college study, earning $15,000 or more. Additionally, the group is made up of Republicans or political Independents with a conservative ideology. Order-stability values are found least in the black population surveyed.

Democratic-active values have some representation among white college graduates, thirty-nine years of age and younger, earning $15,000 or more, ideologically liberal or moderate, and politically Independent

—although the profile is not clear-cut. Since order-stability values are predominant over the democratic-active, many of the demographic variables descriptive of a democratic-active group, from the survey, are just as attributable to order-stability respondents.

From the data, it would seem that the police and a large number of the white civilians sampled share common attitudes about law enforcement practices and the expectation of police "efficiency" as a law enforcement value. This applies to the respondents who indicated an unqualified preference for a law enforcement value, and out of this group order-stability was the dominant value.

Further evidence of the approximation of police attitudes to dominant social attitudes was observed when the total civilian sample was classified by order-stability and democratic-active values.[9] The "cell thermometer" and "occupational prestige ranking" indices were reintroduced for attitudes by value groups. The cell thermometer, using modal figures, presented a clear distinction between responses by the two groups.

The order-stability group displayed extremely warm feelings for the National Guard, conservatives, policemen, schoolteachers, whites, and the military. Extremely unfavorable attitudes were felt by this group for liberals, women's liberation, and blacks. Although the Ku Klux Klan is also represented by a "cold" score of 1, response frequency for this category was almost evenly divided between 1 and 5 in the order-stability group, but the conservative frequency was used in the table for this and all other categories. The "warm" and "cold" feelings by this group closely resembled the police attitudes about related categories in the earlier cell thermometer (Table 5-6). There thus appears to be a correlation between having order-stability values and sharing other social attitudes with the police, in the population sample.

The categories in the thermometer that received the most unfavorable ratings by the order-stability group were ones usually associated with social innovation. This attitude, if carried through to a negative feeling for bureaucratic innovation—especially if it carries a social direction with the end of "humanizing" the police—predicts difficulties for changes in the manner and practice of law enforcement. This is a compelling factor, since when values were strongly indicated they were held in common by policemen and the majority of white citizens of the sample. The democratic-active group, on the other hand, displayed warmth for socially innovative categories, and cold feelings for many of the categories favored by the order-stability group, including policemen. However, democratic-active values were absent from the police sample, as well as not being reflective of the dominant social value of the total sample.

Another interesting dichotomy between the attitudes of the two groups was revealed by the revised prestige ranking of occupation groups. The

Table 5-9
Cell Thermometer by "Order-Stability"/"Democratic-Active" Value Groups

Categories	Order-Stability	Democratic-Active
National Guard	9	6
Jews	5	7
Conservatives	9	3
Democrats	5	7
Republicans	7	3
Liberals	1	8
John Birch Society	5	1
Women's Liberation	1	9
Government Workers	7	6
Policemen	9	1
Blacks	1	9
Schoolteachers	9	7
Ku Klux Klan	1	1
Whites	9	8
Military	9	1
Total	175	34

Note: Cell thermometer scores are modal figures. A very "warm" feeling is indicated by a score of 9 and a very "cold" feeling by a 1. A score of 5 shows a neutral attitude. Scores between 1 and 9 indicate either some positive or negative attitudes depending on their placement on the range of attitude scores.

order-stability group rated doctor, minister, and judge highest. Policeman was accorded seventh place and detective eighth. Politicians and students bottomed out the prestige list. The democratic-active group ranked doctor and college professor highest with judge third and minister seventh. Detectives were rated ninth and policemen twelfth.

Certain questions and their responses received discrete examination for their bearing on police bureaucratic practices and innovation. Some significant attitudes about law enforcement were observed. Order-stability respondents agreed strongly with "the trouble with psychology and sociology is that they are not related to the everyday realities of the policeman's job." This is detrimental to innovations for "intellectualizing" the police. The democratic-actives disagreed strongly with the statement.

Another question asked whether "the most effective measure of police professionalism is a reduction in the crime rate." The order-stability group was in agreement with the statement, while the democratic-actives strongly disagreed. The next question read: "Police operations should be the concern of police professionals and not be subject to pressure from politicians and citizens." The order-stability group responded in favor of the statement, while the response from the democratic-actives indicated a prefer-

Table 5-10

Prestige Ranking of Occupations by "Order-Stability"/"Democratic-Active" Value Groups[a]

Occupation Groups	"Order-Stability"	"Democratic-Active"
Detective	8	9
Soldier	9	13
Policeman	7	12
Minister	2	7
Student	14	8
Sales Clerk	12	14
Electrician	11	10
Insurance Salesman	10	11
College Professor	5	2
Doctor	1	1
Lawyer	4	4
Judge	3	3
Politician	13	5
Teacher	6	6
Totals	175	34

[a]Prestige rankings obtained by modal frequencies.

ence for civilian control, either directly or through their political representatives. Democratic-actives agreed that "civilian police boards are more effective than police internal affairs bureaus in controlling police malpractice." The order-stability group did not concur.

Order-stability respondents felt, "The most effective way to improve police professionalism is to introduce new technical innovations, modern management systems, and effective allocation of police manpower." Democratic-actives were evenly divided on this question. The question may be interpreted as assuming the paramountcy of technology ("hardware") over personal qualities as necessary for improvement of law enforcement. The response by both groups was predictable based on the adherence of the order-stability value on efficiency, especially by improvements in police "hardware," and the ambivalence of democratic-actives toward "hardware" and "humanism" in law enforcement. Both order-stability and democratic-active groups were in agreement that "because of the nature of his work, a policeman should have a better than average understanding of values such as justice, freedom, and dignity."

Other responses that have a negative association with either social or police innovation: "The people who say they are intellectuals would be better off using common sense," and "Being poor does not provide any sort of explanation for the high incidence of crimes committed by the poor." To the former statement, the socially dominant order-stability value group responded in agreement, whereas the democratic-actives disagreed. The response by the order-stability group indicates their disassociation from intellectuals and manifests a bias against intellectuals and intellectualism. The anti-intellectualism of the dominant group provides negative consequences for police bureaucratic innovations that would involve academia and academics. The response to the latter statement had the order-stability group agreeing and the democratic-actives disagreeing with it. This, too, has an impact on innovation concerning police practices, as well as showing an indifference or an ignorance about the social causes of criminal behavior.

The study revealed a dichotomy between citizens in the sample in their attitudes about law enforcement. The dominant value, order-stability, as represented by a majority of the respondents whose responses to associated questions were unqualified, favored police innovations that related to "hardware" and efficiency methods for improved crime control and order and stability. This group was favorably disposed toward the police and had no quarrel with their practices. Additionally, the group rejected civilian and political control over the police and rejected the need for improving the personal and intellectual qualifications of individual policemen. The policemen sampled closely paralleled these attitudes and, as tested in the survey, reflected the most "conservative" sociopolitical values about law enforcement in the community.

The democratic-active group sample, while not representing a dominant value, suggest discontent with the police and policemen, and law enforcement practices. And these values are held by a number of the younger and better-educated of the white citizen sample. However, these values were not upheld by *anyone* in the police sample, showing that the existence of democratic-active values is minimal in the police bureaucracy.

If the sample in the study is representative of the values in the city of Memphis, and if Memphis is sufficiently representative of many American cities, then the "humanizing" and "intellectualizing" of the police is a difficult and perhaps unwelcome task. One can hardly be optimistic about improving police practices—beyond improving technology and efficiency techniques—or, more importantly, about improving the individual policeman. These democratic-active values have been shown to be essentially excluded from the police bureaucracy and not supported by the majority of the population. Changes in the bureaucratic practices of the police, or in their individual or social *gestalt,* cannot reasonably be expected so long as the bureaucracy is inured to a different value structure, and so long as the prevalent value structure in the police and the environment is mutually reinforcing. The potential for innovation must lie with the significant number of those in the bureaucracy and in the social environment who are not committed to either extreme of the law enforcement value. The challenge is to mobilize the interest of the moderates, or indifferents, on behalf of change.

"Making It" in the Police System

In 1945, Henry Lux, the son of a Mississippi river boatman, thought that he would like to become a policeman in the city of Memphis. He had just been discharged from the Army Air Corps, and he was home again in the city where he had been born, raised, and educated. A job awaited him with the telephone company, but when he saw an advertisement in a local paper about vacancies in the police department he decided to try to be a cop.

Memphis, at that time, was run by Ed Crump, who had gained control of the city when he was elected mayor in 1909 and then built a machine that was to keep him in power, whether in or out of political office, almost uninterruptedly until his death in 1954.[1] Crump's machine won election after election with the help of a solid voting bloc of blacks and public employees. Blacks made up approximately 40 percent of the city's population, and the machine registered and voted them in large numbers by buying poll tax receipts for them. In addition to the blacks living in the city, Crump and his lieutenants, Will Hale and Frank Rice, were not averse to bringing in blacks from the neighboring counties to insure a sizable vote in their favor. Policemen in the black wards were used to shepherd the citizens in wagons and on foot to registration places to insure their vote.

City employees, the other bloc of voters controlled by Crump, performed as called for by the machine out of fear of losing their jobs. In election years city and county employees were required to kick back 10 percent of their salaries to the Crump machine, and a large portion of these accumulated funds went to the purchase of poll tax receipts. In addition, public employees were assessed for books of poll tax receipts which they were obliged to sell to their friends and neighbors on their own time. If they were not able to sell their quota, they were then made to "purchase" the unsold books for $2 apiece. Applicants for the police and fire departments had to sell large blocks of poll tax receipts as a prerequisite to getting hired. Business establishments—including brothels—took consignments of receipts and parceled them among their employees who, in some cases, paid for them out of regular deductions from their paychecks.

Edward Hull Crump, Jr., the boss of Memphis, was reputed to be genuinely interested in providing an efficient city administration free from graft. The city benefited from his regime's programs of school and hospital construction, extensive street paving, noise abatement, harbor development, and public park extension. However, Crump tolerated no political opposition, however minor, and no freedom of speech, to the extent that the Boss employed a public censor, a man with less than a high school education, who zealously guarded the morals of the community by banning many books, plays, and movies. Labor was kept under the control of the machine for the benefit of industry, and many a union organizer suffered from the "rough and ready" justice of Crump's police department.

Although Crump's last elective office was in 1936, when he was US representative for Shelby County, he continued to rule the city from his offices of E.H. Crump Co., a family-owned insurance, real estate, and mortgage firm. *The Chattanooga Times* judged Crump's iron hold over Memphis in this way: "Memphis seems to have a good government if one overlooks the fact that the very essence of good government is missing there—the right of the citizen to vote freely and without fear for any man he chooses, and the right of the citizens to choose their candidates."[2] Even after Crump's death, in 1954, the vestiges of his Memphis machine maintained power for another five years. It was not until 1959 when political reformers gained the mayor's office and the four other commissioners' seats that the hold of the Crump machine over Memphis was broken.

In the Crump days, getting a job in the police department was a matter of political patronage. But the war had caused manpower shortages, and the department was forced to advertise openly for applicants. Henry Lux, veteran, twenty-three years old, and a high school graduate, had no political connections when he went to City Hall to see about a job with the police. Commissioner of Fire and Police Joe Boyle felt the young applicant's biceps and then took him up to see the mayor. The mayor looked Lux over, remarked that he looked like a "pretty good physical specimen," and hired him. This was the extent of the screening and testing procedures for police department applicants that existed in Memphis in that era.

Lux was now a policeman. From a friend he borrowed an old revolver, which he later learned would not even fire. He purchased a pair of airline trousers and a navy peacoat and a hat and went to work. His first day as a police officer was called his day of "training." He was assigned to Main and Monroe, a street corner in downtown Memphis, to work with an older officer who was instructed to "show him the ropes." The training began with the older man walking Lux to the corner and saying, "You blow your whistle every time the red light changes, and I'll be back in a minute—I'm gonna get a cup of coffee." The veteran policeman returned shortly before noon and asked Lux if he wanted to go to lunch. The same routine was repeated in the afternoon, and upon completing this, his first day of duty, Lux graduated from training and was "unleashed on the public."

The next day he was assigned to his permanent street corner on Main and Gayoso. He had been there for a few hours when a citizen came up to him and said, "There's something wrong with a man down the street. He's wrapped around a parking meter."

Lux walked down to where the man was lying and determined that he was drunk, but he really did not know what to do at this point. Finally, he decided to call police headquarters. Headquarters sent a patrol wagon to pick up the drunk, and when it arrived one of the police officers in it asked Lux if he had made out an arrest ticket. Lux replied, "I don't know what you're talking about. . . . I've never seen an arrest ticket."

The older officer then helped Lux make out the ticket. Then, to Lux's consternation, he was advised by the officer to appear in court the next day. He had never been in a courtroom in his life. In fact, he did not even know the location of the court. The following day Lux was able to get through his first courtroom experience by observing a preceding case, which was also a drunk case. When it was his turn, he mimicked the performance of the policeman in the earlier case and successfully passed his initiation in courtroom procedure.

He stayed there on the street corner blowing his whistle and working traffic until after the Christmas holidays. He was then transferred to a patrol car, where he made "a lot of good catches"—arrested a number of burglars and armed robbers. After two years and eleven months in a patrol car he was promoted to lieutenant.

He was made a lieutenant without having to take a promotion exam because of his record. Upon assuming his new rank, the only instruction given him was that he was to meet each patrol car under his jurisdiction at least once a day to pick up traffic tickets and to smell the breaths of the police officers in the cars to see if they had been drinking. Drinking, according to Lux, was quite a problem with policemen back in those days. Lux was now twenty-five years old, and he had under his command men who had been in the police department before he was born. Bored with just picking up traffic tickets and smelling policemen's breaths, Lux went to the library and got a book on supervision to see what he could learn. He also read a number of other volumes on related subjects. But, most crucial to his subsequent rise in the hierarchy, Lux learned to become a "good system reader" during his period as a lieutenant.

"Reading the system" meant finding out who was dispensing the rewards and what was required in order to receive the gratuities. Lux knew that in the city the political system was run by Mr. Crump. In the police department Lux learned that the system was also political, and so he attached himself to Claude Armour, commissioner of fire and police. Armour, one of the four commissioners in the city's commission form of government, was an elected official and a member of the Crump machine. Rewards in the police department went to those who understood the political nature of bureaucracy, the "system," and were willing to accommodate to it. Lux made the decision to serve the system. He correctly understood that Claude Armour was the system in the police department. In an interview, recalling this period in his past, Lux said:

"If I meant votes to Armour then that meant that I climbed in the system. I understood what the system wanted so I was able to rise in it. If you conform with the system as it is, then it gives you its rewards; if you don't, then the rewards go to someone else. This is the price of success in any system that I'm aware of."

Most important, Lux did political work for Armour and for the Crump machine. He became active in a civic club and his wife participated in women's clubs. Both he and his wife became community leaders and campaigned for the Crump machine. Lux's wife manned the Claude Armour campaign headquarters in several campaign years. Lux opened a canteen in a school in his neighborhood and invited all the teenagers to participate in it. He became highly visible politically in his neighborhood and campaigned actively for Claude Armour. In addition, he did favors for people in the neighborhood because he was able to go to City Hall and "get things done." His positive image in the neighborhood meant votes for Claude Armour.

"People would vote for Claude Armour because of me," recalled Lux. "You know, if I'm a nice guy and I do a lot of things for the neighborhood, he must be a nice guy too."

During this period when Lux was actively "serving" the system, he handled a number of important homicides, burglaries, and robberies. In 1954 he was promoted to captain. He stayed in the investigative field and continued to handle big cases. He and his wife also continued their political work for Claude Armour, who, since Crump's death in 1954, now relied on a personal political machine that was heavily dependent on the use of police officers and firemen as precinct and ward workers. Meanwhile, Armour instituted several improvements in the police department. He increased the number of days off for policemen from two a month to one a week. A pension system and a two-week training school were also instituted in the department. But, Lux remembers, the system of rewards remained unchanged, as it was still tied to standards of political performance, to political work in behalf of Claude Armour. "A man's advancement in the department had little to do with his merit."

Four years after his promotion to captain, Lux was elevated to inspector and given a desk in Armour's private office. Armour was now vice-mayor in addition to being commissioner of fire and police. As a reward for years of delivering the vote, Lux was made Armour's personal assistant. For the next few years his duties consisted of public relations. He attended the meetings that Armour normally had on his agenda and was called on to greet visitors to the mayor's office from time to time and to welcome important visitors to the city by handing them a key to the city. Another of his duties was to serve as the police liaison with the black community. In this capacity, he relayed some of the grievances the black community had about police service, especially about police brutality in their neighborhoods, to Armour. Lux recalls that while Armour was considerate of the problems in the black community, he dared not accede too much to their requests because of the political atmosphere in the city of Memphis, which was unfavorable to politicians known to "give in" to the black community. This experience, Lux feels, gained him a lot of friendships in the black community and helped him a great deal in understanding their problems.

In 1961 a police burglary scandal broke out in Memphis and Armour assigned Lux to investigate the case. After the police burglary case was solved, resulting in several officers being dismissed or indicted, Lux was retained in his investigative duties. As a result of the publicity surrounding the police scandal, in 1962 the International Association of Chiefs of Police was asked to perform a study of the Memphis police department. The recommendations of the IACP study included an increase in pay and training for officers and a reduction in the number of top-level officials in the politically infested organization. But Armour did not pay heed to the recommendation about eliminating the top-heaviness of command in the department and, instead, added to the three existing assistant chiefs by promoting four other officers to that rank. Henry Lux was one of the officers promoted to assistant chief. He was made head of the Night Patrol Division. For the next six and a half years his most important duty was to issue news releases to the press.

"I used the free time to my advantage," Lux recalled. "I did a great deal of studying on my own in the area of management during this period."

In 1968 a referendum was held and the city's commission form of government was replaced by a mayor-council form. Claude Armour resigned his elected post of commissioner of fire and police a few months before the election and took no political interest in the referendum issue. The new mayor, Henry Loeb, appointed Frank Holloman director of fire and police. Holloman was a retired FBI agent with no previous connection with the local police department. The department had been under civil service for some time, and James C. MacDonald, chief of police under the previous regime, was retained and continued to hold the highest civil service rank in the department.

Despite the existence of a civil service system that had been in force as far back as when Lux took his promotion examination for captain, recruitment, selection, and promotion in the department was essentially political. Although an examination was required for each promotion, the administration controlled at least 60 percent of the test, according to Lux, because 30 percent of the grade was based on a written examination and another 30 percent was on a subjective evaluation of a candidate's qualifications, and in both these cases grades could be allocated according to administrative bias or preferential consideration. The remaining 40 percent of the grade only applied in cases of promotion and consisted of efficiency ratings by superiors. The entrance test for the police department was relatively simple. Lux recalls that he and Holloman, as an experiment, gave the test to Holloman's sixteen-year-old son when he was a sophomore in high school. "He passed it with flying colors."

About a month after the new administration had been in office, the Memphis sanitation workers went on strike over a dispute with City Hall about a pay raise. Since most of the sanitation workers were black, this caused a delicate racial confrontation in the city, especially in view of the strike's support by a large part of the city's black leadership. In the second day of demonstrations at City Hall, Lux was moved to the day shift to become the commander of the Day Patrol Division. Holloman assigned Lux to handle the demonstrations because he liked what Lux had to say about how he would manage this task. Among Lux's ideas that gained favor was on-the-scene management of police forces in the demonstration area and the maintenance of liaison with the strike leaders so that they might try to police the strikers themselves. Lux's contacts in the black community, which went back to 1958, were seen as helpful to the police department in this time of crisis and confrontation.

Lux had an early opportunity to try out the concepts he had articulated to Holloman. The very first demonstration he was called on to control involved approximately five hundred sanitation workers and supporters who were demonstrating in the city council chamber during a regular Tuesday afternoon council meeting. Lux had advance information that the demonstration was going to occur in the council chambers and that the demonstrators were going to stage a sit-in there. He kept the police forces out of sight during the council meeting. After the stormy council session was recessed, the demonstrators predictably refused to leave and Lux recalls that "by this time they were getting belligerent. They were screaming at the council, shouting all sorts of things from the audience." The chairman of the city council then requested Lux to clear the council chamber.

Alone, Lux walked to the front of the chamber and shook hands with all of the leaders of the demonstration. Police personnel were still being deployed out of sight. Lux remembers telling the strike leaders something like, "You know why I'm here. Eventually we're going to have to clear the council chamber, so let's get together and work this thing out together. We've got no fight, it's not a personal fight, this is a sanitation fight with the city government, but I'm a police officer and I work for the city government." Next, he made an announcement to all of the demonstrators in a calm voice, stating that the police would now have to clear the chamber, but they would appreciate it if the demonstrators would leave on their own. He then walked out of the council chamber and was surprised to see that quite a few of the demonstrators left with him.

By now, City Hall was closed off so that no one could come in, and the police were prepared to carry out the remaining demonstrators on stretchers if necessary. Lux returned to the chamber a second time and repeated his announcement and, walking out again, was gratified to see more demonstrators leaving with him. He estimated that the number of demonstrators had now dwindled to about 250. When Lux returned to the Chamber a third time, he went directly to the leaders and said, "Now, as I see this thing, we're faced with this kind of a situation: You have come down to your city fathers to voice a grievance. You have asked them to do something about your problem, and now, darn it, they're going to have you arrested. You want to dramatize your situation, you want to be arrested. I understand that. Why don't we just select about fifteen or twenty of your leaders and walk over to the police station and then everybody will be happy."

They replied that they were going to talk it over among themselves and asked Lux to return. When Lux returned again, the demonstrators were down to approximately 150, by his count.

The leaders told him: "Our decision is that if you lead us over there, we'll all march over to the police station to be arrested."

Lux replied, "Man, let's go!"

All of the demonstrators dropped in line behind Lux and marched to the door of the city council chamber. When Lux got to the door he saw that there were about 200 to 300 black teenagers massed outside who were jeering and howling at the police deployed in front of City Hall. Knowing that the procession would have to walk between the massed teenagers, Lux turned to one of the leaders closest to him, a white minister who was an assistant pastor of a black church, and asked, "We're going to have a problem with these teenagers?"

The minister replied, "Let me go out and talk to them. Wait for me."

The minister left and Lux recalls that one of the inspectors who was in the back of the line walked up to him and said, "What are we going to do when we're outside, if they run?"

Lux remembers thinking at that point, "We're going to stand aside and say 'Amen!' Our mission is to get them outside of City Hall. If they run, let them." But he said: "I don't think we're going to have a problem. I think they're all going to come over with us."

The minister returned shortly and stated that the throng would part to let them walk between them. They were going to jeer and they were going to holler, he said, but they weren't going to do anything physical.

Lux told the minister, "That's fine. They can yell and say whatever they want as long as they don't get physical."

The procession, headed by Lux and a few police officers and followed by 150 demonstrators, including sanitation strikers, sympathizers, and some of the leading black churchmen of the city, marched across the street from City Hall to the police station, where they were all booked.

After the incident at City Hall, Lux was made responsible for policing future demonstrations in the city. He marched in the front with the leaders in sanitation strike parades. He stayed there in the front in full uniform carrying a radio through which information was passed to him about problems occurring on the parade route. When he received this information he would turn to the leaders and ask them to instruct their monitors to straighten out the problem so that the police would not have to become involved, if, in his judgment, the disturbance could be handled in this manner. On March 28, 1968, Lux was in the front of a march led by Martin Luther King. He was walking with King and Ralph Abernathy and other leaders of the Southern Christian Leadership Conference and other black groups. The march had gone about three and a half blocks when a disturbance broke out along Beale Street which Lux assessed to be beyond the control of the march monitors. Lux had to use the police forces that were deployed in tactical units—the police deployment used during all marches—and they were called to stop what had become rioting and looting. On April 4, 1968, Lux had to call on the police again as well as the National Guard, for on that day Martin Luther King was assassinated and riots exploded in all the black areas of the city.

In the end, after the demonstrations and marches and King's assassination and the rioting and looting, the sanitation workers got their way with the city. They were allowed to organize, with the Association of State, County, and Municipal Employees (ASCME) as their legitimate bargaining unit, and they received a substantial pay raise.

The year began with civil strife and confrontation, and after twelve years as police chief, MacDonald chose to retire in 1968. For the first time, the position of chief of police required a competitive civil service examination. To make sure that the exam was above board, Director Frank Holloman invited the International Association of Chiefs of Police to give the examination. At the time, there were six assistant chiefs in the department, but a criterion for eligibility held that an assistant chief had to have held the rank for three years to be eligible to take the examination. Only three of the assistant chiefs were eligible for the examination. Of the two men who took the examination, Lux was the only one who passed it. He assumed the duties of chief of police on May 15, 1968, and became the chief officially on July 1.

Veterans of the police department remembered what the conditions had been in the organization in the ten or fifteen years prior to Lux's becoming chief of police. A police captain with over fifteen years service with the department said, "To get ahead in this organization, you had to engage in the internal politics of the department. You needed to know who counted, and it wasn't always your immediate superior, because so many supervisors were only figureheads." Continuing, he added that an officer had to be able "to read the system" in order to be promoted. "It used to be that only those persons who had adopted the philosophy of the chief and the commissioner were the ones who had the best chance of being promoted."

"I remember back in the sixties, Chief MacDonald made a lot of promotions, but they were only 'pay-me-backs.' You know, those guys who had done campaign work for the commissioner or whose wife used to play bridge with the chief's wife," said a twelve-year patrolman, "and if you didn't play ball their way, like arrest some people and let others go, your supervisor would tell his supervisor and he'd tell the chief, and well, you might just as well kiss your promotion goodbye."

A lieutenant in the department said that in those days, especially in the detective division and uniform patrol, almost all promotions were based on "whom you knew rather than what you knew." He added, "Of course, it didn't hurt to be a member of the right lodge or civic club."

Another officer, a detective in traffic investigation, volunteered, "You had to have a 'jockey,' you know, someone who knows someone else. If you didn't, then nobody was going to know that you are alive."

Still another patrolman said that when Director Frank Holloman came into the department, officers started "checking around to see what clubs he belonged to. When they found out that he was a Mason, everybody and his brother joined the Masons. But what everybody didn't know was that Holloman didn't care what you were as long as you were honest."[3]

The first confrontation that Lux had with the men of the Memphis police department happened on May 15, 1968, the day Chief MacDonald left office. About three hundred policemen gathered in Overton Park to talk about forming a union.

"There were three hundred of them in the park and they were talking about hiring a lawyer and setting up a charter and forming a union local in Memphis," Lux recalled. "So I got into a car and drove out where they were and talked them out of the park and out of the union, brought them back to the police station."

Lux was asked: "You don't believe in police unions, then?"

"No," Lux answered. "I don't any more than I think the Political Science Department in a university should have a union."

Lux continued: "I think being a policeman is being a professional—or at least, should be being a professional. The complete professionalization of the police is sorely needed and it's unfortunate that the public doesn't realize this. The police service today, in most police departments, is what I call a rigidly structured, nonparticipative, politically oriented, and often politically infested service organization. This has to be changed."

When Lux became chief of police, he held as a priority the reform of the "system" that had operated in the department, and that he had served and that, in turn, had served him well. He began systematically to try to cut off from the department all of the political and personal interests that characterize a police system. His goal was facilitated by Director Frank Holloman's commitment to police "professionalism" and Mayor Henry Loeb's promise to keep politics out of the police. Henry Loeb kept his promise to Holloman and Lux, and his administration stayed out of the internal affairs of the police department in Memphis during his term of office.

Lux embarked on a program to upgrade the quality of the police department under the motto "knowledge is not synonymous with rank." He encouraged the men of the department to seek a higher level of technical or academic education, overtly signaling that the new "system" rewarded the men of education rather than men of connections. The rank of warrant officer, equivalent to a corporal, was instituted and given to some officers with a college background who were then offered administrative staff appointments, enabling them to participate in planning and decision making at the highest levels of the police department. A planning and research section was established, and several police officers who either had a college education or were working toward a degree were assigned to this unit. The thrust of the thinking in the new regime was to upgrade the police service through higher education and better qualifications for policemen. The new system of rewards and punishments in the department addressed itself to these goals.

On October 1, 1970, the director of fire and police, Frank Holloman, retired. Lux, now alone at the top, moved toward fulfilling the goal of upgrading police service in Memphis. The first initiative was the effort to break the parity of police and firemen's pay and to separate the police department from the fire department. By separating the police and fire departments, Lux felt that he could obtain a higher wage scale for policemen, thereby attracting a better quality of applicants as well as retaining the better people in the department. His appeal to the city council was made on the basis that the policeman's task was more difficult than the fireman's because the policeman was faced with discretion in making daily decisions whereas firemen are continually under the supervision of superiors. But he feared that his arguments would not carry sufficient weight with the council.

"There was another element that I needed," Lux remembers. "While I was informally trained and, I don't say this in a bragging way, I think I know management as well as a great many people in this country. But who am I? I'm Henry Lux, the cop, you know? The cop who finally made it to the chief's office. . . . Then I met Dr. Roland Frye of the Psychology Department at Memphis State University. I was very honest with him about my goals about separating the police and the fire department and asked for his aid in the matter, which resulted in the Frye Report. His report showed that it required more intellect or more training to be a policeman than to be a fireman. . . . The outcome of the report was that the council supported breaking the parity between the police and the fire department. . . . Finally, there was a referendum in a subsequent election that legally separated the fire department from the police department and now the two agencies are completely apart."

Next, Lux and Frye teamed up to provide management efficiency for the department. Lux had all of the high-ranking officers of the department undergo an evaluation of their management capabilities by a group of industrial psychologists, headed by Roland Frye, from Memphis State University. Those evaluations created a major shakeup in the personnel holding key operating positions in the department. On the basis of these evaluations, two friends of Lux, Assistant Chief W.W. Wilkinson and Assistant Chief Ed Routt, were promoted to head the two most important functional divisions. Wilkinson received the command of the Staff Operations Division, which was expanded to include the operations of the Administrative Services Division and the Staff Services Division. The Uniformed Patrol, Traffic, and Criminal Investigations Divisions were organized under the new Field Operations Division, headed by Ed Routt, formerly in charge of Staff Services. Both Wilkinson and Routt were promoted to the administrative rank of deputy chief. The other two existing assistant chiefs, Bill Price, formerly chief of the Uniformed Patrol, and Bruns MacCarroll, formerly chief of Traffic, placed low in the evaluations and were assigned as heads of Administrative and Staff Services. These positions were known as "paper-clip details" by officers, and both men shared a single secretary and were confined to rubber-stamping routine administrative orders from Deputy Chief Wilkinson's office. Chief Inspector W.O. Crumby, who was later to figure prominently in organizational politics, also placed low in the evaluations by the management consultant experts and was put in charge of the Traffic Division and away from the main police operation.

The evaluations indicated that the most capable of the department's ranking officers were Ed Routt, Inspector Jack Wallace, and Inspector Graydon Tines. Both Tines and Wallace became key figures in the Lux administration, with Tines commanding the Uniform Division, the largest single command in the department, and Wallace placed in charge of Special Operations, including the Special Services Patrol. The new organizational structure under Lux had Deputy Chief Routt as the number-two man in charge of all operations, and Deputy Chief Wilkinson in the direct command position under Lux as head of the Staff Operations Division. Price and Crumby were placed directly subordinate to Deputy Chief Wilkinson. Inspector Joe Gagliano, chief of detectives, remained in charge of Criminal Investigations. Chief Inspector Jack Wallace, the youngest member of the hierarchy and reputed to be a protegé of Lux, was placed in charge of Special Operations, an elite patrol function that handled special assignments in civil disorders and was used to provide supplementary patrols in high-crime areas.

Wallace was designated by Lux to be a troubleshooter for the entire department, and it was generally assumed that he was being groomed as a future chief. Lux frequently said of Wallace: "He is the best operations commander in the United States." Wallace was responsible for security during two visits by Vice-President Agnew to Memphis and commanded the night tactical units during the racial unrest in 1968. Twice, while he was unarmed, Wallace faced down armed men barricaded in their homes, acts for which he received a national citation in 1969.[4]

The management evaluation that caused major changes in the department's command structure was hailed in some quarters in the department but was also a source of major discontent and consternation in others. When questioned by the press on the nature of the evaluations performed, Dr. Frye declined to discuss the evaluations beyond saying, "A functional organization was created under Lux, using the best men he had at hand for the most important jobs."[5]

To bypass the rigidity of the police hierarchy at the top administrative layer of what he called "fifty-year-old patrolmen," Lux brought in outsiders to the organization and also employed the talents of younger, lower-ranked officers who were either attending college or were already college graduates. Remarkably, he obtained the services of about ten professors from Memphis State University who accepted commissions in the police reserve and, in addition to being able to ride around in patrol cars, performed research for the department. The research, which was done at no cost to the department, consisted of feasibility studies on the use of horses for traffic or for parks and the use of dogs in police work, and an effort to develop a psychological test to be used at the entrance level that could accurately isolate antisocial characteristics of police applicants.

Although Lux never gave a single civil service promotion to any man in the department during his tenure as chief, because he felt that the department was top-heavy already, he obtained a sizable raise for the men when parity between the police and the fire department was broken. He also got a college incentive pay system started by persuading the city council that the department needed to attract college men to improve police services in the city. The encouragement of policemen to pursue advanced education as well as to attract college-educated applicants was seen by Lux as requiring a system of rewards—primarily financial incentives. To achieve these aims he had to persuade the political system—specifically, the city council—to provide the necessary budgetary support in the way of increased salary and education incentive payments for police officers. To do this, he learned to "read the political system" and to manipulate it for his purposes.

"To recruit and retain college people, I had to offer rewards such as an adequate salary and the fulfillment of their need to participate in administrative matters. So, I had to appeal to the bias of the individual councilman to get his support for these rewards. If he was a liberal, I bore heavily on the angle of having an improved quality of police officers which would lead to minimizing the complaints of police brutality and racism. If he was a conservative, I would stress that smarter cops would catch more crooks and put them in jail. Liberals and conservatives on the council are tremendously concerned about police services, if for different reasons, so I manipulated the issue of education to conform to their particular interest. In the end I got the rewards I was after from the council, and the police here were upgraded."

An added incentive for college-educated police officers and police officers who were attending college was the administrative promotion to the rank of warrant officer, which allowed these men to serve in administrative and planning capacities in the department, rather than as beat patrolmen. He utilized his "college whiz kids," as Lux called them, in his twelve-man Office of Planning and Research. One of the more noteworthy accomplishments of the Planning and Research Unit was the isolation of peak crime areas in the city, which enabled an effective deployment and use of police manpower. Meanwhile, police training in the police academy, whose facilities were built in 1961, was lengthened to twelve weeks.

Finally, Lux instituted the so-called "10-Plan," a management efficiency device in which officers worked four ten-hour shifts each week, with overlapping shifts during the 6:00 P.M. to midnight high-crime period. In addition to being a management technique for the deployment of maximum manpower during peak crime hours, the "10-Plan" facilitated college attendance because, under the plan, shifts were changed on a three-month basis instead of the former method of changing eight-hour shifts on a monthly basis.

In 1971 the city council gave Lux the choice of either using police funds to hire new men or giving pay raises to the men already employed by the department. He chose the pay raises, saying: "I'd rather have a few well-paid, satisfied men than many unhappy ones."[6] The status of internal security was upgraded, according to Lux, by putting "some competent people in there." Internal security's investigation of citizen complaints about police malpractice showed that a disproportionate number of grievances were directed at one particular contingent of the uniform patrol. Lux commented that this unit was having approximately "fifteen times the number of complaints that the other two contingents were having," and he said that he dealt with the situation by "identifying the group of people that caused most of the complaints and segregating them by putting them in nonsensitive positions. I took them out of the field and put them in the jail [policing the jail] . . . other places to kind of neutralize them."

Lux's reforms during his tenure as chief had admirers as well as critics in the department. Not least among the critics were those officers who had been moved to lesser positions during the Lux administration. "I'm sure I turned off some people because of the innovations and the hiring of the professors. The professors were rejected fantastically by the old-line cops and, of course, this reached all the way to the top."

The bringing in of outsiders, principally nonpolice professors from Memphis State University, to aid him in planning for the department, caused some dissension.

"He put an emphasis on education, which immediately made the uneducated men in the department feel threatened," said one of several officers.

"He went outside the department for management advice, and this made many of the authority-oriented officers dislike him because it threatened the old military concept at the department. It was no secret that Lux wanted his command officers to be good managers first and cops second; and this threatened the command officers who were good cops but poor managers."[7]

There was dissension among patrolmen who could not or would not take advantage of Lux's college incentive plan and resented the extra pay and scheduling priorities granted officers who were going to college. The resentment toward college men existed because some felt that in the department they received "special" treatment under Lux. Lux's frequently stated theme about "quality rather than quantity" on the force was opposed by the older officers who favored more police and more hardware as answers to a rising crime rate.

"He sold a lot of people and they're still sold," a high-ranking police officer was quoted. "But he couldn't sell that idea to some of his own high-ranking officers, who maintain to this day that the only way to fight crime is with more guns, more cops, and more cars and helicopters."

Lux's contact with the black community had a varied reaction in the department. There were some men who felt that Lux's approach was a positive effort to cool tensions and restore order.

"He personally marched along the front ranks of some of the protests downtown, right beside the leaders," said an officer close to Lux. "It had the double effect of showing the white citizens that the police were present and showing the Negro citizens that Henry Lux was personally there to make sure none of the young hotheads would get out of line and cause them trouble with their march."

There were those, however, who were indignant about Lux's policy toward the black community. They saw his open-door policy to black leaders as a sign of weakness. They believed that the police should have drawn a harder line and dealt with the protestors as lawbreakers.

"The transition from the old-school, tough-as-nails policy to Lux's new ideas may have been too fast," a high-ranking officer still in the department was quoted as saying. "There is no doubt that it helped to factionalize the department into different camps; basically one which was for Lux and another against him. The people who were against him became the 'outs' in the department. He told them that if they weren't willing to modernize they could go sit in the corner. Some of them did, but they didn't sit. They plotted instead."

With his innovations now well under way, Lux began to articulate a topic in his many civic club and public addresses. His theme was that the police were wrongly blamed for the increased crime rates, and that any real reduction in crime must be rooted in social and not police concerns.

"At what point will our society no longer be able to support, economically, more men and hardware?" he asked. "I submit that we have already reached that point." He then made the statement challenging all the members of the community, saying the "war on crime is lost" unless society moves to eradicate the causes of crime, the conditions that create the criminals who must be dealt with by the police forces. Lux argued that preventive policing is at least as important as reactive policing; the police have too long been burdened with problems caused by social illness and are powerless to cope with the problem without social corrections.

By now Henry Loeb's term as mayor was ending, and he chose not to run again. With this was ended, also, Loeb's policy of keeping politics out of the internal workings of the police department. In 1971 there was a mayoral election in Memphis, and Lux's public statements brought critical responses from the candidates. Most of them proclaimed that they believed Lux's attitude to be antipolice and his leadership to be the cause of the "breakdown of morale" in the department. At least two candidates pledged to rid the department of Lux if they were elected. Lux, who had earlier opposed a city-county unification proposal on the ballot in 1971 because it called for the election of a police chief, remained adamant about keeping the police department out of politics. On October 5, 1971, two days before the election, Lux announced his retirement as police chief. On that day a career that began twenty-six years ago at $150 a month and reached the highest civil service position in a police department at a salary of $22,000 a year was terminated.

During his career in the Memphis police department Lux adjusted from serving a political "machine" to administering a police organization with distinction. As chief of police, he either initiated or extended efforts aimed at improving the quality of police personnel, improving the management of police resources, and ridding the department of the vestiges of the "system" and the men who were still linked to it. Realistically, the change in his personal direction was facilitated by the transformation in the political environment. By the time he assumed the position of chief, the political machine, which he courted on his way up the career ladder, was no longer in existence. Earlier, he had learned to "read" the political system to his own advantage. Later, he was to apply his ability to "read" the system to the advantage of improved police servlce. That his innovative efforts were to be short-lived is attributable to the durability of the police "system" and its close association with local politics and political actors. Ultimately, the bureaucratic "system" weathered the brief storm of Lux's reforms.

In the aftermath of Lux's retirement as police chief a political struggle ensued in the department that culminated in the "outs" wresting control from the "ins" with the help of the newly elected mayor. The extent of the political involvement in the struggle for power in the department was revealed in May 1973 by Barney DuBois and Menno Duerksen, investigatory reporters for the *Memphis Press Scimitar,* in a five-article exposé. These revelations bared the fragility of civil service controls and the inoperability of bureaucratic rationality in the Memphis police department. Political power considerations in the Memphis police bureaucracy continued to be paramount, and politics at the local level were still exploited for personal as well as organizational gain.

A few months before the mayoral election in 1971, a faction of police officers, men whose careers in the department had been negatively affected by the Lux administration, approached Wyeth Chandler, the front-running mayoral candidate. They were able to persuade Chandler that they represented the majority of policemen in the department and offered him their support in the election, in exchange for his support of their group in gaining control of the police hierarchy. The titular head of the insurgent group of policemen was Inspector W.O. Crumby, boyhood pal of the mayoral candidate and then head of the Traffic Division. Chandler agreed to this arrangement and promised to appoint Assistant Chief Bill Price, a senior member of the group, as the police chief in his administration. After defeating Juvenile Court Judge Kenneth Turner in a run-off election, Chandler made good his pledge and in November of 1971 announced that Price was to be his chief of police. Chandler's friend, Inspector Crumby, was later appointed deputy chief and became the number-two man in the new administrative organization in the department.

A police officer who knew of Chandler's 1971 commitment to the Crumby-Price faction provided the background for the political arrangement in an interview to the press: "These men were among the 'outs' during the Lux administration; they were in charge of paper clips. They made no bones about being afraid that Ed Routt might become the new chief and continue their exiles. Routt was a Lux man and was hard as nails. I'd say the political deal was more anti-Routt than pro-Price. They were scared of the man and they knew they didn't have much of a future in the department with him as chief. So they went to Chandler."

However, Price's appointment as the new chief was still contingent upon his passing the civil service examination required by law. Price took the test given by the International Association of Chiefs of Police, but surprisingly, two other eligibles—Crumby and Inspector Jack Wallace, who served as acting chief after Lux's retirement and until the new chief became official—also took the test. The test results have never been revealed, but DuBois and Duerksen learned that all three men made failing grades, with Wallace receiving the best score. Price was next and Crumby last. However, department sources intimated that the test scores were adjusted and all three candidates were given a "technical" passing grade. Thus, despite failing his civil service examination for the post, Price was appointed chief of police. When the Price-Crumby takeover of the department became an accomplished fact, a high-ranking officer in the Lux faction said: "This is going to be a catastrophe."

Now that a new regime was in power in the police department, personnel changes at the top were predictable. The Lux faction was driven out and the men from the old "system" who had suffered in obscurity during the previous administration were given key positions again. Routt, who was the number-two man in the department under Lux and once a leading contender for the top position, was demoted to Price's old job as head of Administrative Services. Realizing that he was now "surplus," he stayed long enough to reach his twenty-five-year retirement and left the department. He presently has a private security business in Memphis. Gagliano, when learning that he would not be kept on as chief of detectives, also opted for an early retirement, and is now chief of police of Germantown, Tennessee, a Memphis suburb. Wallace, who was considered by Lux to be a brilliant police administrator and the most promising young man in his hierarchy, joined Routt in Administrative Services. In commenting about this assignment he was quoted as saying: "I'm in charge of the janitors and ash trays." He did not have enough service time to retire and languished in his new post until the appointment of a police director who "rediscovered" him. George Hutchinson, an inspector who had been removed from Uniform Patrol by Lux because, Lux said, his shift had received most of the complaints of police wrongdoing, was promoted to Graydon Tines' position as commander of the Uniform Division.

Meanwhile, Tines was demoted to head Internal Affairs, a position formerly held by a police lieutenant, and was given several other "surplus" officers from the Lux period for his new command. Victims, also, in the Price-Crumby regime were many of Lux's innovations, and especially the department's close association with Memphis State University. Included in the programs that fell were: the so-called "10-Plan"; research and planning; aptitude, emotional and ability tests used in the selection of officers and administered by Memphis State University; and all planning and study association with Memphis State University, including a study on the usage of dogs in police work. Price reportedly told a Memphis State professor: "Dogs can't smell."

"When Price and Crumby came in I knew it was over," Dr. Roland Frye said. "Suddenly, nobody would talk with me. There were desks out in the hall from all the moving. I didn't need anything in writing to know our association was over."

When Henry Loeb was mayor, Henry Lux and Fire and Police Director Frank Holloman had requested and received a "no interference" from City Hall in the operation of the department. This policy came to an end with Chandler in the mayor's office. The mayor had told reporters that, unlike his predecessor, he "personally was going to have a hand in running the police department." Chandler's promise has been kept, as witnessed by newsmen who, when questioning Chief Price about important police matters often have to wait for him to telephone the mayor at City Hall before they are provided with answers. At times, Price has dialed Chandler's office in the presence of reporters.

Finally, according to reports, it is unclear as to who is actually chief of police in Memphis. Many officers privately claim that Crumby is operating the department, in fact, and wants to be chief, while Price is merely awaiting retirement. This is denied by Crumby, who said that it may appear to some that he runs the department, but this is because, as the man in charge of operations, his work is the most visible in the police department. However, he did state that he hopes to become chief, adding: "I think anybody wants to go to the top in his profession. Ambition is just part of life, and I think it is necessary for a man to do his job."

7 A Year in the Political Life of a Police Department

"I can say without reservation that a year ago we had one of the best police departments in the nation," said the old policeman, shaking his head. "Today we may be headed toward being one of the worst. Something has to be done."[1]

In 1972 there arose a crisis of confidence in the Memphis police from within the department and from segments in the community. Trouble within the department first became apparent when a detective in the Internal Affairs Bureau who was investigating a petty larceny complaint against two police officers was subjected to harassment for doing his job. Then two other Internal Affairs officers were set upon by uniformed policemen while they were using a secret department surveillance van in an investigation of a police bribery case. Next, a former patrolman volunteered charges of bribe-taking and complicity with neighborhood rackets among policemen. Other policemen disclosed malpractices in the city jail. They complained of money being taken illegally from prisoners and of unnecessary force being used frequently.

The mood of the police force became one of dissatisfaction with the departmental leadership—or lack of leadership—and an antagonism grew between the Internal Affairs Division and the Uniformed Patrol Division. General expressions of discontent were everywhere. By August the press reported that "police in the field have stopped policing."[2] In one night there occurred a backlog of more than one hundred complaints for the police to answer with a number of patrol cars out of service, and traffic and accident officers were responding to crime calls. Citizens complained to the press that it was not uncommon for a routine call for the police to result in a forty-five minute to an hour delay.

City Councilman Philip Perel, chairman of the council's police committee, called for an investigation of the department. Other councilmen subsequently joined in his request. Councilman J.O. Patterson, Jr., a recent Democratic nominee in an unsuccessful bid for the Eighth Congressional District, charged, "Corruption, in fact, exists in the Memphis Police Department." The councilman, a black, supported his accusation by making reference to certain police practices in black neighborhoods in the city. "There are policemen that practically have a circuit they ride to pick up their weekly take in bribes," he said. "Often these bribes are from people operating illegal businesses, but they are also payments to avoid police

127

harassment in many cases. People who are close to the scene have reported that police are closely associated with prostitution in this town."

Patterson strongly favored an investigation of the department, and added: "There is something wrong, internally, in the Memphis Police Department and I would like to see a Director appointed with a directive from the mayor and council to get in there and clean up the problem."[3]

The leadership of the Memphis police department had emerged in a triumvirate. Chief Bill Price, by virtue of holding the highest civil service rank, was the nominal head of the group. From 1964 to 1966 he served as aide to former fire and police commissioner Claude A. Armour. In this capacity, his functions consisted of providing Armour with information about the department and answering citizens' questions. He also worked in Traffic and in Vice. On a wall in his office hung a certificate of his graduation from the FBI Academy in 1966. Also on display were photographs of Mayor Chandler and Claude Armour. He is a thirty-one-year veteran of the department.

Insiders in the department claimed that the real power in the triumvirate was with Deputy Chief W.O. Crumby, who derived his strength from his forceful personality and from his long-time friendship with Mayor Wyeth Chandler. The son of a fireman, Crumby spent many years working in Homicide, where he earned a reputation as a crack investigator. To those who know him, he epitomizes the description of a "top cop." On a number of occasions orders, ostensibly issued under Chief Price's name, had originated with Crumby. One such directive restricted newsmen's access to police reports. This was later eased by Chief Price. Crumby has had twenty-three years of service on the force.

The third man at the top of the police hierarchy was Chief Inspector George W. Hutchinson. Hutchinson, like Price, is well regarded by the rank and file. Like Price, too, he served as an aide to Mr. Armour. His career path, however, had been closely tied to that of Deputy Chief Crumby. He has had the least longevity in the department of the trio, with nineteen years service.

The three police executives are popular with the men in the department. They have outgoing and friendly personalities and are known to have a high regard and affection for each other. Chief Price said: "I've brought in people I think will be loyal to me. Certainly I have that privilege."

Despite a general disgruntlement with the leadership in the department, many of the men were more likely to blame lower-ranked officers while being charitable to the officials of the triumvirate. Nonetheless, one policeman was quoted as saying: "The men have lost confidence in their leadership, so they have just stopped policing. They are waiting to see which way things will go."[4]

Malpractice and Internal Controls

Investigations of alleged misconduct by the police were being conducted by the department's Internal Affairs Bureau. The bureau came into being in 1964 as a result of public pressure calling for reform and investigation of the department following the disclosure of a police burglary ring. The investigations of the burglary ring in 1961 resulted in eighteen officers being discharged from the force, with six of them indicted by the Shelby County grand jury on charges of burglary and larceny. In response to the public call for an outside agency to look into the Memphis police, in 1962 Commissioner Armour invited the International Association of Chiefs of Police to do a survey of the department. The IACP's report made recommendations for more men and more money for the department, and more internal checks against corrupt practices. After a few delays, an Internal Security Bureau was created on February 1, 1964. It was staffed by three men, including its commander.

At the outset, the bureau was not only responsible for investigating complaints of wrongdoing and misconduct, but also did background investigations of police applicants, performed efficiency and waste studies, served as the intelligence arm of the department, and, additionally, kept tabs on police equipment. Shortly after its creation, two other men were permanently assigned to the bureau, with more men being added, on a temporary basis, when circumstances required it. In 1968 the intelligence function was removed from Internal Affairs, following the civil disorders that accompanied the city sanitation workers' strike and the assassination of Dr. Martin Luther King. The Internal Affairs Bureau was ultimately left with the sole mission of investigating officers when a Planning and Research Bureau was formed within the department.

From time to time, certain segments of the community have demanded the formation of an independent agency to investigate complaints about police malpractice. In October 1971 a black youth was killed, allegedly as a result of a beating administered by police officers. At first, the department requested its Internal Affairs Bureau to investigate the slaying, but furor in the black community led to the removal of the case from the bureau and into the attorney general's office. The subsequent investigation resulted in grand jury indictments against nine police officers and sheriff's deputies, four of whom were charged with first-degree murder. In the aftermath of this case, a "civilian review board" became an issue in the "nonpartisan" mayoral election held in November of that year. In his campaign, Wyeth Chandler accused some of his opponents of favoring a civilian review board, a charge that was universally denied by his opponents. Chandler, who won by a narrow margin, received the backing of a majority of police officers because of his outspoken opposition to a police review board and his promise to leave the matter of investigating the police to the police.[5]

In the first six months of 1972, the bureau, composed of a commander, two inspectors, two captains, a lieutenant, and five detectives, conducted 116 investigations of fellow officers. During this period, the investigations resulted in nine men being forced to leave the department—either through firing or resignation—with seven of them being charged with crimes. One of the most notable cases involved a police captain, second in command of the document section, with thirty-one years of service. He was charged with accepting a $30.10 bribe. The accused officer resigned from the force and was subsequently indicted. Another well-publicized case involved three black turnkeys accused of beating a white prisoner in the city jail. The complainant in this case was another policeman—a white officer—because the victim was unwilling to file a complaint. Following an investigation of approximately three weeks, the three patrolmen were given thirty-day suspensions from the force.

The function of the Internal Affairs Bureau is to investigate complaints against police officers. Upon concluding an investigation, the bureau provides information about the case to the policeman's commanding officers, who decide the appropriate punishment. The bureau makes no recommendations as to what action should be taken. Cases are reviewed by division heads, who consult with the accused officer's immediate commanders before making any recommendations to Deputy Chief Crumby. In cases that may involve possible prosecution, the final say is with Chief Price. It is he who decides whether to take the case to the Shelby County attorney general's office, take disciplinary action, or a combination of both.

A renewed call for an investigation of the police force occurred when the press reported irregularities in the department in the course of Internal Affairs Bureau investigations of police malpractices. These irregularities first received public attention in July 1972, with the disclosure by the press that Detective J.P. Bomprezzi, an investigator in the Internal Affairs Bureau, was the subject of harassment because of his job of investigating accusations made against fellow officers. The harassment consisted of ambulances, hearses, moving vans, cabs, and other vehicles being sent to his house as a result of anonymous telephone requests.

Shortly thereafter, another incident involving the Internal Affairs Bureau came into the news. Several uniformed policemen were reported to have disrupted a police bribery investigation. While the Internal Affairs officers were in the unmarked surveillance van, several police patrol cars drove up to the van and the officers got out of their cars, shook the Internal Affairs vehicle, and pulled their guns on the men inside. The incident was said to have taken place while Detective Bomprezzi and other officers of the bureau were waiting in a van seeking to observe whether policemen on patrol were taking bribes from the owners of a cocktail lounge. The investigation was initiated by the accusation of one of the owners of the lounge that he had to provide patrolmen in the area with money on a weekly basis in order to get them to stay away and so that vending machines, which had been disconnected because the lounge had no city license, could be used.

Controversy also centered around the issue of how the uniformed patrolmen were led to the surveillance truck. Detective Bomprezzi said that the only officers who knew about the surveillance were Chief Price and men in the Internal Affairs and Intelligence Bureaus. But another officer in the bureau said he was "convinced" that there was a leak in the case, but added, "I can't prove it."

In a press conference, Chief Price replied to the charges of police interference with the Internal Affairs Bureau by saying that the incidents had been "blown out of proportion in the newspapers." Price admitted that there was a surveillance van with four Internal Affairs men in it, but said that the uniformed police officers who drove up to the vehicle learned who was inside it and then left the scene.

"At no time were any guns drawn," Chief Price told the press conference. Price also stated that he was removing Detective Bomprezzi from the Internal Affairs Bureau because, he said, Bomprezzi "has a knack for making people mad. Officers aren't refusing to make a statement except to Bomprezzi."

Contacted after the press conference, Detective Bomprezzi commented that he was removed from the bureau just as he was "about to uncover something." He added, "Chief Price is a good man, but he has not backed Internal Affairs like it should be backed."[6]

In September 1972, Chief Price instituted a personnel shakeup in the bureau. Three officers, in addition to Bomprezzi, were transferred to other functions. Chief Inspector Graydon P. Tines, the bureau commander and a "favorite" during Lux's regime, on learning that Chief Price was planning to transfer him in the near future, announced his retirement from the department.

The disclosure of the irregularities in the police department prompted several city councilmen to support an investigation into the matter, but they suggested that the attorney general should perform it. One city councilman stated, "I think there's a great similarity between what's happening in New York and what is happening here and perhaps in other metropolitan areas."[7] It was now felt that the irregularities in the department no longer made possible an internal investigation of the wrongdoings of police officers. The viability of the Internal Affairs Bureau had become doubtful.

Civil and External Controls

The attorney general's office of Shelby County, in which Memphis is located, responded to the allegations of wrongdoings on the Memphis police force by opening a grand jury investigation that centered around the charges of bribery and corruption within the city's police department, including the charge by Internal Security detectives that fellow officers interfered with their investigations. The attorney general announced that two members of his staff were assigned "full time" to the police case and that he hoped a case would be presented to the grand jury. Although some members of the city council had earlier expressed a desire for a city council investigation of police wrongdoings, on August 11, 1972 the consensus of the council, reached in a secret meeting, was that they would support the attorney general's investigation of police bribery charges and would take no independent action.

On the following day, August 12, 1972, Mayor Chandler picked Robert G. Jensen, former agent in charge of the Memphis FBI office and now corporate security director of Holiday Inns, Inc., to conduct a special study of police Internal Affairs and Intelligence Bureau operations. The mayor said that Mr. Jensen's role was to improve the Internal Affairs Bureau and not to investigate the personnel of the department. Jensen was made available by Holiday Inns for thirty to forty-five days for the special study of the police department.

A survey conducted by *The Commercial Appeal* of some of the city's top civic and business leaders revealed that most of them favored an outside investigation of the Memphis police department and the hiring of a police director who "should be filled by somebody from outside the department ranks."[8] Editorials in *The Commercial Appeal* also called for answers to "questions concerning the police department." One editorial said: "The answers are needed from an unbiased source, which means investigation by a body unrelated to the police."[9] Another editorial in the same paper was highly critical of the city council's decision to "step back from the problems in the police department and leave investigation to the Attorney General." The newspaper accused the legislative branch of the city government of "taking the easy way out." It was especially disappointed that the decision reached by the council was made in a secret meeting, which, the editorial pointed out, was "a clear violation of the city charter."[10]

In a reversal of the previous stand against mounting an investigation of police malpractices in the city's police department, Chairman Fred Davis, a black legislator, announced to the press that he had appointed five councilmen to look into charges of police misconduct. Davis said that he was making the appointments on the basis of his prerogative as council chairman and added in his August 15, 1972 statement: "This is a matter of great public concern. I feel strongly that some kind of investigation should be conducted. It is a matter for the Council."[11] On the following day, however, the city council refused to authorize the council-directed investigation of police affairs in a six to six tie vote. One councilman justified his negative vote by saying that he considered it "laughable, really, for us to be on the trail of the wrongdoers. I never imagined myself as a sleuth."

Mayor Chandler now injected himself into the council debate by stating his opposition to a proposed city council investigation of police affairs. In an appearance at a meeting of the Memphis Chapter of the American Society for Industrial Security, Mayor Chandler said, "The two avenues being traveled," of having the attorney general's office investigate specific allegations of police wrongdoings and appointing former FBI agent Robert G. Jensen to study the police Internal Affairs Bureau, "are the proper avenues." The mayor expressed his criticism of the news media's printing of allegations against police officers and told a questioner in the audience that "to print that sort of thing is irresponsible journalism—yellow journalism."[12]

For another week the council continued behind closed doors to argue the merits of a council-appointed investigation of police matters. Compromise resolutions in lieu of Council Chairman Davis's original proposal calling for a five-member committee were offered. One compromise resolution proposed a seven-man investigatory committee, and another had the entire council on the committee. After several more secret meetings, the council was still deadlocked on the method and makeup of an investigation committee. The council could only agree that the investigation would not have the participation of a citizen advisory body, and that the committee would hire attorneys or investigators to do the legwork in the investigation. Near the end of one session, a councilman said, "I think we have lowered the dignity of our office by one of the unfunniest comedy hours." He went on to say: "It seems ridiculous that thirteen grown, adult people can't agree on a proposal that would insure the chairman's prerogative to appoint a committee, yet represent all factions of the council."[13] At this point, Mayor Wyeth Chandler changed his mind about his earlier opposition to a council investigation and said that he had "absolutely no objection" to an investigation that would not involve an outside citizen body and that would use attorneys or investigators to funnel information to the council.[14]

On August 24, 1972, with the city council still bogged down in its efforts to begin an investigation, the mayor announced that he would name an attorney to collect and investigate information about police misconduct. The mayor went on to attack charges made anonymously against city police officers and again criticized the news media for printing accusations against the police without naming their sources. The mayor said that he hoped that the city council would accept his appointment and "let him report to both of us." He added that if he did not name an investigator, the council would "end up with a committee which will go storming off in any direction hiring people willy-nilly." Finally, he voiced doubt about the ability of his own investigator to receive much reputable information. "I don't think many people will go to this man. I believe people who believe in law and order will already have gone to the police department or to the attorney general," Chandler said.[15] The attorney subsequently designated by Chandler to head an investigation of complaints against policemen declined the position, and the mayor was not able to find anyone to head the study.

The stalemate on the investigation was finally broken when the city council, in a near-unanimous vote, turned to its existing three-man police committee to function as a "committee of inquiry" into charges against policemen. Fred Davis, who as the council chairman had earlier designated an investigatory committee that was aborted by the council, cast the only vote against the resolution. Davis explained his objection: "That will not be the chairman's committee. That will be the council's committee."[16] The council's police committee subsequently recommended an investigation of the police department covering possible corruption as well as "other areas of irregularities." The police committee chairman said that charges of brutality by policemen "will be one area that will be touched on." The committee then chose three attorneys practicing in the city of Memphis to head the inquiry, and the full council allotted $50,000 for conducting the investigation. Among the investigators selected to work for the city council's investigating committee was Detective Bomprezzi.

Meanwhile, Robert Jensen completed his two-week special study of Internal Affairs Bureau operations. Among his conclusions was that "there is apparent friction within the Internal Affairs Bureau." The bureau, he said, "was divided into what can be defined as two groups. This they admitted openly. The result is a feeling among the men that this is a punishment detail."[17] Mayor Chandler acknowledged the friction and stated that the police were planning to shift personnel out of the bureau on a piecemeal basis. The mayor also took the opportunity to announce that a search was underway for an individual to fill the position of police director. The new position—a non-civil service rank—had been previously approved by voters in a referendum.

At the end of August the West Tennessee chapter of the American Civil Liberties Union proclaimed that it would conduct its own investigation of charges of corruption in the police department. The local ACLU chairman said that the investigation would be pursued "in the spirit of cooperation" with local officials and that governmental agencies would be supplied with the results. "It's our aim to serve the public, the Memphis Police Department and public officials to insure basic rights and effective law enforcement," the chairman stated. He added that between 100 and 200 ACLU members would be involved in the investigation, and that individual charges of police misconduct would be studied and compiled in a full report by an ACLU committee.[18]

Mayor Wyeth Chandler and Councilman Philip Perel, chairman of the council's police committee, questioned the motives of the ACLU in conducting their own investigation of police matters. "The ACLU are a left-wing organization which seems to want to inject themselves into any matter that will get them publicity," Chandler said. "I can't see any assistance they can render." Perel said that the proposed ACLU investigation "sounds like something of an organized witch hunt to me.[19] Nothing further was heard about the ACLU study.

On September 15, 1972, the month-old investigation by the Shelby County attorney general's office was concluded. The investigation led to indictments against four Memphis policemen, a former policeman, and two civilians by the Shelby County grand jury on bribery and extortion charges. The action was taken after the grand jury heard testimony from ten other policemen, two investigators with the attorney general's staff, and eight owners and employees of Memphis nightspots. The attorney general noted that the cases acted on did not represent the entire scope of the police investigation. He indicated that other cases would be turned over to the grand jury for action at a later time. Following the action of the grand jury, Police Chief Bill Price fired the four officers indicted for extortion and bribery. Mayor Chandler said of the indictments: "This is the way it has always worked and the way, in my judgment, it should continue to work." The mayor added that the indictments returned "have nothing to do with accusations made against policemen generally."[20]

That night, following the grand jury action, approximately 340 Memphis police officers held a grievance session. In attendance were Mayor Wyeth Chandler, Chief Bill Price, and City Councilman Robert Love. It was reported that the officers voiced their displeasure at the dismissal of the indicted policemen and also questioned the validity of the evidence used against the indicted men. Another grievance articulated by the policemen concerned the news media coverage of the controversy. They reportedly claimed that morale was low because of suspicion cast on all policemen.

The following day, amid rumors of threatened job action by police —there was an abnormal delay in changing uniform patrol car shifts —Mayor Chandler rescinded the previous day's firing of the four police officers indicted by the grand jury and ordered them rehired and placed on ten-day suspensions with pay. The mayor added that after the ten-day suspension, Chief Price would determine whether the men should be continued on suspension, fired, or rehired. In reply to a request by police officers urging the city to pay the defense costs of the indicted officers,

Chandler stated that the city could not finance legal defense for policemen involved in crimes or accused of crimes outside their duty. However, he added that he had asked the "100 Club," an organization that assists families of officers killed in the line of duty, to aid in the officers' defense.[21] Previously the policy in Memphis had been to automatically fire a police officer who was under indictment. However, the mayor and the city attorney said that after reviewing city ordinances and civil service regulations they saw no basis for automatic dismissal.

A query was made of police departments in seven cities by *The Commercial Appeal* to learn what their policy was in regard to officers under indictment on criminal charges. The general response from the departments queried was that in view of the nature of the charges, they were certain that in their cities the men would have been fired or, at the least, received indefinite suspensions without pay pending the outcome of their cases in court. A spokesman for the New York department said: "When it comes to a policeman being charged with making shakedowns, there's no doubt he would be suspended without pay." An official of the Atlanta police department's Internal Affairs Bureau stated that the police chief had discretionary authority, but in a case like the one in Memphis, suspension without pay would be "automatic." Similar responses were obtained from department spokesmen in St. Louis, New Orleans, Tulsa, and Jackson, Mississippi. Spokesmen for other departments explained that "although a police officer, like any other citizen, is considered innocent until proven guilty, he lives under the additional burden of relying on public trust to properly perform his duty."[22]

After reviewing the case against the four indicted police officers, Chief Price returned three of the men to the department in civilian capacities while a fourth was placed on indefinite suspension without pay pending the disposition of his indictment. The fourth police officer, a twenty-two-year veteran of the police department, was subsequently acquitted by a criminal court jury of charges of accepting a $100 bribe from a former lounge operator. The officer's attorney stated in his final argument at the trial that his client was "picked out" for prosecution on a police corruption charge "to satisfy publicity from newspapers running down the police department."[23]

In an appearance at Memphis State University, Mayor Wyeth Chandler cast doubt on the testimony against the police officers named in bribery and extortion indictments. He said: "Now we got into a situation where they took one or two allegations—and that's all they are at this point—by some tavern owners who had been in trouble with the police and had been brought before the beer board, I think, seventy-four times. They wanted the police off their backs, and so they said that these people were taking bribes. As a result, they appeared before the grand jury and these police-men were indicted." The mayor also questioned the need for the city council's police investigative committee, adding" "We can find evidence better than anyone else. . . . We do and will continue to do it. I think probably out of this whole thing, you are going to have three or four trials and I'm dubious as to whether you'll have more than one, or two, at the most, guilty verdicts."[24]

Shortly after the indictments were issued against the police officers charged with wrongdoing, Claude Armour—a figure from the past—now state commissioner of public safety, addressed a graduating class at the Police Academy. Armour told the twenty-three graduates of the academy that some of them might decide that they would "not fit" in the Depart-ment. "There is nothing wrong with this because all of us cannot succeed with everything we try to do. . . . The best thing to do is to seek other employment." He said that officers will realize that they do not belong on the force when they "begin to tell other people what is wrong with law enforcement and the police department." Armour advised the rookie policemen to support the present leadership of the police department because "they will get the job done and straighten out the mess that we have had that accumulated over the past few years."[25]

The mayor also spoke to the new policemen and told them that new improvements for the department were on their way in the form of better equipment and more police officers.

Meanwhile, the committee of attorneys selected by the city council to head their police investigating committee were hard at work on the inquiry, details of which were unknown even to the councilmen who had commis-sioned them. On December 8, 1972, the committee presented one case to the Shelby County attorney general with the promise of more cases as well as the presentation of an in-depth report to the council, the mayor, and the attorney general. On January 10, 1973, the committee issued its long-awaited report. The report was based on 179 complaints received by the committee. It stated that more than forty policemen might be involved in some kind of improper activity. The files on the 179 complaints received by the committee were made available to the council. "Evidence of a wide variety of unprofessional and criminal acts involving present officers of the police department appears in the files. Efforts should be made to establish the fitness or unfitness of these officers for service on the Memphis Police Department," the committee report read. The complaints covered a period beginning in 1967 and ending at the time the report was issued.

The committee also criticized "an attitude of defensiveness on the part of higher officers of the Memphis Police Department, including a tendency to look to other sources and institutions as the main cause of police problems." The committee recommended indoctrination of "all police officers against the use of excessive and unnecessary force and brutality." The report went on to say:

The key to a top-caliber and successful police department is intelligent, capable, professional and above all, respected leadership. It is the strong feeling of a large segment of the police department and many members of the public that the police department does not have this kind of leadership. The best attention of local government should be directed to encouraging the development and employment of highly qualified officers in positions of leadership.

The report also suggested better supervision of officers, the formation of a crime commission made up of private citizens, reexamination of policies concerning promotions—particularly as they relate to black officers—more efficient deployment of personnel, and improved procedures in the Internal Affairs Bureau. Finally, the report singled out Detective J.P. Bomprezzi for praise, "It should be stated that Detective J.P. Bomprezzi has been of great assistance in the conduct of the investigation." The report said, "In the judgment of members of the committee, Lt. Bomprezzi is a courageous, capable and dedicated police officer with high personal and professional standards and is the kind of officer who serves the citizens of Memphis well. He is deserving of commendation."[26]

Reaction to the report from city councilmen was favorable. The report was described as "hard-hitting" by one councilman, and another councilman stated that he was "very much impressed with the way the assignment was completed." The attorney general said, "It was a very full report."

But within the department, a different outlook was articulated by Deputy Chief W.O. Crumby: "As it stands right now, the report is another slap in the face for the police department," he said. "They have not come up with any definite cases. They are not stating any facts at all. As far as I'm concerned, the report is a $20,000 piece of garbage."[27]

The mayor declined to comment on the report's contents, saying that he needed time to study it. He added, however, that any punitive action against policemen implicated by the report would be undertaken by his office and not by the city council. The next day, Mayor Chandler issued a statement questioning the motives of two officers who helped the special committee investigate the police department. Chandler expressly mentioned Detective J.P. Bomprezzi and another former police inspector who was forced to retire the previous year.

"Since the inception of this investigation, this committee has surrounded themselves with police officers with strong personal feelings against the present police leadership," the mayor was quoted as saying. "Can we expect a fair and impartial investigation from such men?" He then went on to praise the present leadership in the police department, citing what he called "a tremendous increase in morale and efficiency" since Chief Price had taken office, and said the department had "honest, capable, professional and respected leadership." The mayor said that the committee had no proof refuting his assessment of the police leadership, and if no proof were forthcoming, "I would waive, and I hope the public would waive such charges aside as utterly meaningless and closely akin to libel." He added that he was troubled because the committee used "uncorroborated" and "unsubstantiated opinion" in their report and because "no accused officer has yet had the opportunity to speak in his own defense." Finally, the mayor ended the press conference by stating his intention to review the committee's files of the 179 complaints of police wrongdoing and to "do whatever is necessary to keep Memphis with the finest police department in the nation."[28]

By the middle of February Mayor Chandler had reviewed the files. He then attended an executive session of the city council to state that only a "handful of men" were involved in the 179 cases, saying there is "very little hope" of any indictments being filed or of policemen being relieved of duty as a result of the committee's work because it would be difficult to corroborate evidence. This brought criticism from two black members of the city council. Councilman Fred Davis said he feared results of the investigation might be "swept under" by the Chandler administration, adding, "From my study I think there's much, much more that can be delved into. . . much more substance" than the mayor's public statements had suggested.

Councilman J.O. Patterson, Jr., a member of the police and fire committee, said: "There are some cases that should warrant investigation by a grand jury. Mayor Chandler will probably never admit that there is any truth to it. The mayor, from the very beginning, was opposed to the investigation and opposed it every step of the way."[29]

On April 4, 1973, Mayor Wyeth Chandler announced that he lacked sufficient evidence to take action against the twelve "most accused" policemen. Chandler said that the investigation of charges against twelve of sixty-one officers accused of wrongdoing was almost completed and "pending the outcome of polygraphs [lie detector tests] there is no administrative action planned by the administration and no criminal prosecution to be brought." He justified his statement by saying that the evidence accumulated against the accused officers was mainly obtained from a former policeman now serving a prison sentence. "In most cases it boils down to [the policeman in prison] against them. Now if you or your attorneys feel that you should go to court on that basis, you can do it. We're just not going to do it," the mayor told the city council.

A number of councilmen immediately attacked the mayor's assertion that administrative or criminal action was not warranted. One councilman said the mayor might "be refusing to face facts."

Another councilman stated: "The Mayor has always taken a position when it comes to the police department that you have to have complete, unadulterated, unmitigated proof—before he would favor any disciplinary action."

Two of the three attorneys who headed the council's investigation of alleged police misconduct voiced their disappointment with the mayor's decision against taking action. "I regret the mayor's action very much. It is this type action that strikes at the heart of police credibility," said one attorney. "We went on the investigation in complete good faith and with open-mindedness. Even though there was some feeling that this might happen, we hoped for the best. . . . It is action such as this that does not indicate good leadership in Memphis."

The other attorney stated that he was not surprised by the mayor's decision. "It's unlikely that anyone who was hostile of the whole concept of the investigation from the beginning would change his view," he said. The third committee member declined comment.[30]

On May 19, 1973, police officials announced that a city policeman was dismissed from the force when he refused to cooperate in an investigation of police misconduct. The policeman, a seven-year veteran of the department, was dismissed following a hearing by police officials. A police official said that the officer was "named in a number of the . . . files and failed to provide satisfactory responses to investigation. He simply denied all the allegations." On July 17, 1973, Mayor Chandler announced that fifteen policemen named in the city council probe of the police department would be reprimanded and placed on probation. The reprimanded officers were not identified. Philip Perel, chairman of the council's police committee, said: "I'm glad to have [the affair] brought to a conclusion."[31] Thus were closed the council's files on the most serious allegations of police malpractice "ranging all the way from incidents of brutality through actual burglary or theft and also allegations of asking bribes."[32]

Management and Police Union

In August of 1972, Mayor Wyeth Chandler announced that he would name a civilian director of the police department, a man outside of the present force, while, at the same time he praised the service of Chief Bill Price. "I think the administration and leadership in the police department is as fine as we have ever had," he said. Shortly thereafter it was reported that City Councilman Robert Love, head of the police reserve and with close ties in the department, was the mayor's favorite for the post established in a city charter change approved by voters. However, a majority of city council members stated that they probably would not back the mayor's apparent first choice for police director because they felt that the city needed someone with no connections to the present police administration.[33] *The Commercial Appeal*, in writing about the upcoming appointment, said: "This will be one of Mayor Chandler's key appointments. We hope he makes the choice from outside the ranks of the police department. What is needed is a strong, independent leader, free from any ties with the department. He does not necessarily have to be a Memphian. He doesn't even have to have been in police work before."[34]

Mayor Chandler picked Marine Brigadier General Jay W. Hubbard to be Memphis's new police director. Hubbard's appointment was approved by the city council in October 1972. "He may be the man to straighten things out," said a councilman. "I hope so."

Mayor Chandler said that he belived General Hubbard was "the type of man who can bring about a great change for the better."[35] Among General Hubbard's assignments in the Marine Corps was that of Assistant Secretary of the General Staff and Director of Information at Marine Headquarters. His last military command was of the Marine Air Reserve Training Detachment at Glenview, Illinois.

Hubbard retired from the Marine Corps and assumed his new duties on December 1, 1972. In his first public speech in the city, the new police director predicted that Memphis could have "the elite force in the United States within two years." He said that this goal was achievable through "better management techniques" and by putting more men in the field, providing career opportunities for young police officers, improving in-service training, and improving benefits. He ended his speech by saying that he would not have accepted a similar position in New York City or Chicago because police departments there are "almost hopeless." In Memphis, Hubbard stated, "we have a coordinated, sensitive community that is used to orderly processes, that is ready to stand up for what it believes in and thinks, in an orderly manner."[36]

In his first two months in office Hubbard continually expounded his ideas for changes in the department on the banquet circuit. At one meeting he asked a group of Memphis businessmen, "How the hell did you let it get this bad?" after telling them that the department "has lived in benign neglect." He told them that he had asked the city council for a $5 million budget increase to about $22 million for fiscal year 1974. "I don't know how y'all let it get this bad, but we'd better fix it."[37]

He met with police officials for a discussion of the report provided by the city council's special investigating committee. "I've read over this and there's a lot here," he told the officials. "I can only come to one of three conclusions: either you were involved with it; you knew about it and turned your head; or you were so stupid you didn't know about it."[38]

In a press interview, Hubbard outlined his philosophy aimed at improving police efficiency and performance:

We need to increase the sense of professionalism. We need to establish more professionally-oriented incentives in the department, hoping that the results will be an end to this management vacuum which is being filled by the mayor and City Hall. We need to get merit promotions and advancement so set in concrete that there's no way we can step backwards into politics. We need to develop better supervisory leadership, men who are managers and not "supercops," men who are fair when they check on their people, making sure that they do right, then patting the men on the back or getting on their back—whichever step is justified.[39]

To accomplish his aims Hubbard reactivated the Planning and Research Bureau, promoted two new deputy chiefs—one of whom was Jack Wallace, who had been languishing in obscurity—and lifted the freeze on general promotions.

Another innovation instituted by Hubbard was the redesigning of the department's training class for new officers. Inspector W.W. Wannamaker, a holder of a master's degree in education, was named director of training, and the training academy was returned to a twelve-week training schedule instead of the nine-week program that had been in effect. The training program was to have more community relations education and less physical fitness instruction. "That's the trend all over the country," said Inspector Wannamaker. "What is the largest part of a policeman's job? It is dealing with people and trying to understand what factors come into play and what causes crime."[40]

On February 28, 1973, Police Director Jay Hubbard and Mayor Wyeth Chandler announced that a new decentralized police management structure with new ranks, greater opportunity for promotion, and use of more civilian personnel was going to be implemented. The plan included having uniformed patrol officers and detectives placed under the same command structure in decentralized precinct headquarters. It also called for civilians to perform most of the specialized technical functions, tasks that were being performed by commissioned police officers. Mayor Chandler said that civilians would be utilized in functions "such as photography lab, radio maintenance, data processing, accounting, graphic arts, headquarters jail, radio dispatchers and records."[41] Other changes consisted of the creation of an inspection group within the Internal Affairs Bureau, a planning research and analysis group, and a reorganized recruiting, community and media relations, speakers' bureau and information services bureau directly under Hubbard. Finally, the mayor and Hubbard announced that promotions to sergeant, lieutenant, captain and inspector would be forthcoming.

Subsequently, problems arose over the scoring of the tests taken by police lieutenants for promotion to captain. Originally, only eleven of the 145 lieutenants tested passed with qualifying scores. Since there were twenty-nine vacancies for captain, the tests were rescored in order to make more lieutenants eligible for promotion. Charges of favoritism emerged when it was learned that the tests were rescored twice, in some cases leaving off men who had made a passing score after the first time the tests were rescored and who now found themselves ineligible following the second rescoring. Criticism of this action was voiced by some police officers who felt the scores were adjusted to "accommodate certain 'favorites' of the police brass who failed the original test."[42] Mayor Wyeth Chandler and Henry R. Evans, city personnel director, took exception to the accusations and published a memorandum that said, "The grading and test security were consistent with the Civil Service rules and regulations and offered no favoritism to any officer or group of officers."[43] The adjusted test scores were left unchanged, and officers made eligible by the second rescoring were advanced to the higher rank.

Hubbard lobbied hard for more funds for the police department, both in public and in budget sessions with the chief administrative officer and the mayor. He gained favor with Clay Huddleston, the chief administrative officer, who stated: "Hubbard is a fresh new face, and he's asking the kinds of questions that have never been asked before. [The police] have got a sense of direction they never had before." The new police director was saying, Huddleston continued, "'Look, you're going to get what you pay for. If you want a really fine police force, one that's going to have an impact on crime, then you're going to have to pay for it.'"[44]

Hubbard got his budget. The mayor asked the City Council for a budget that established law enforcement as the city's top priority, with 24 percent of the fiscal year 1974 budget going to the police department. This meant that the police would receive an increase of 23.4 percent over the 1973 funds. The $21.8 million earmarked for the police force included funds for the addition of 115 policemen to the force, a standard 5.5 percent pay increase for all city employees, the replacement of 234 squad and detective cars and the purchase of 63 additional cars, and the creation of a Memphis-Shelby County criminal justice information system to computerize many record-keeping and information functions of the police and sheriff's departments and other law enforcement agencies in the area.[45] The council subsequently approved the mayor's budget request for the police and increased it by approximately $500,000 for purposes of continuing downtown walking patrols and stakeouts of robbery-prone businesses.[46]

On February 8, 1973, a group of Memphis policemen held a meeting to discuss the formation of a police association with the intent of "eventually" seeking recognition from the city as bargaining agent for lower-ranking patrolmen. A spokesman for the group said that they represented the views and sentiments of more than half the policemen on the force. He also announced that the association was not being established as adversary to the police or the city, but rather to establish communication representing the sentiment of the average police officer. The spokesman said, "The main benefits to the men will be to try to prevent where possible any type of job discrimination, unfair practices or reprimands, and to provide fair and equal promotional opportunities and generally fair treatment from superior officers." When Police Director Jay Hubbard was informed about the association meeting, he said, "I thought we were dealing with professionals . . . I'm disappointed."[47]

The reaction of the mayor to the proposed police association was critical. Chandler praised the leadership within the police department —both the director and the higher-ranking officers in the department—and described the efforts to form a police association as "incredible." Chandler said, "I would be very disappointed if what I consider a very professional organization should suddenly find itself in a collective bargaining position or a position to talk about collective bargaining. The door to this office is open to any member or group of police officers who feel they have a legitimate grievance as are the offices of Chief (Bill) Price at all times."[48] Shock and dismay at the possibility of the formation of a police association characterized the reported reactions of some city council members and top-level police officials. *The Commercial Appeal* published an editorial that stated that the creation of a police association "can only be interpreted as unpleasant news for Memphis."[49]

Two weeks later, in a meeting that was dominated by complaints about Director Hubbard, approximately 130 city policemen voted to create an association and to adopt a constitution. The constitution that was approved scrupulously avoided mention of strikes or work stoppages. "Hubbard has never been a policeman, he never will be one and he shouldn't be running the department now," an officer shouted during the meeting. "The police department should be run by the police."

Another patrolman said Hubbard had some good ideas, "but he still thinks he's in the Marines. He's called in some men and talked to them like dogs. Hell, I'm nearly thirty years old and he's not going to talk to me like that. I'm not an eighteen-year-old kid caught up in the service. He needs to be waked up." Another patrolman stated that there was a rumor going around that Hubbard promised to resign if an association was formed. This announcement was greeted with generous applause. The officers present at the meeting spoke highly of Police Chief Bill Price, Deputy Chief W.O. Crumby, and Inspector George W. Hutchinson. There was a discussion about allowing them to join the association. Another rumor that circulated during the meeting was that these three men were secretly encouraging the formation of the association because Director Hubbard had minimized their authority and selected other officers to make the major decisions in the department.[50]

Police Director Hubbard's response to the formation of the association was to say that he had no plans to recognize the organization as a bargaining agent for police officers. He voiced his disappointment with some "arrogant" officers in the department who had abused their "professional standing." Hubbard informed the press that one of the policemen who addressed the meeting had been reprimanded by him "just a little while ago" for misconduct. The unnamed officer had verbally abused a woman driver who had been "pulled over" for a traffic violation. Hubbard said, "My message to this type men is simply this: If you're abusing the public trust, or if you have been used to thinking you have some special privilege because you wear a badge, then you had better change now."[51]

Patrolman David E. Baker, newly elected president of the Memphis Police Association, in an address to the Democratic Women of Shelby County, articulated the aims of the association. He said that the association was formed to protect the constitutional rights of police officers and to upgrade the force's public image. He was very critical of policemen being forcibly ordered to take polygraph tests. Also, Baker said that one of his goals as president of the association would be to demonstrate that "police officers are not thieves and thugs" as much of the public had been led to believe. "About 99 percent of the men on the force deserve the respect of the city," he said. According to Baker, some of the priorities of the association included the establishment of a line of communication for the men with the police chief and the director, and to seek better salaries to help attract higher quality recruits.[52]

On April 28 about three hundred members of the Memphis Police Association voted unanimously to affiliate with the International Conference of Police Associations. Edward Kiernan, ICPA president, was present at the meeting and attacked the Memphis police department's new rule requiring police officers accused of wrongdoing to take the polygraph test. He told the men at the meeting that this rule should be fought in court and prevented in contracts. There was general concern about the use of polygraph tests for policemen at the meeting. The men also expressed their unhappiness about the recent firing of two patrolmen who were made to take a polygraph test even though charges of rape and crime against nature against them were dismissed in city court. David Baker, the association president, told the men that the association was going to fight the dismissal. The men were also unhappy about the promotion tests given the previous month. Complaints about discrepancies in administering and scoring the tests were aired during the meeting. One of the members of the association asked how the union could remove Hubbard from his position as police director. "Help us throw eight hundred dues check-off forms on his desk, and I'll show you how to start getting rid of him," was Edward Kirenan's reply.[53]

In a press conference, Director Hubbard discussed what he believed were the reasons for the growing union sentiment in the department. "It could very well be me," he said. "The fact that I'm taking a firm position in disciplinary matters; the fact that I've been handed a bag of worms to investigate and I don't intend to shirk my responsibilities; the fact that I've criticized management and have done something about it so it can articulate its needs better." Hubbard ended the session by saying that he would "grudgingly" accept the union as a bargaining agent when the city was "forced" to recognize it. "I don't intend to be hostile," he added. "I think they're making a mistake, but that's their business. I believe in unions."[54]

Mayor Chandler expressed his support of Hubbard and blamed police union sentiment on a "tremendous lack of understanding." He then called a meeting with a dozen top police commanders and asked them to publicly announce their support of the director. A press conference was then called, in which Chief Bill Price and Deputy Chiefs W. O. Crumby, George Hutchinson, and Jack Wallace voiced "100 percent" backing of Hubbard. Chief Price also said that he and his staff would handle most of the disciplinary actions against city policemen. However, Director Hubbard told the press that he would continue to review severe disciplinary actions.

The mayor said he was "very much elated" to learn that the high-ranking police officers supported Director Hubbard. The police leadership, he stated, "has been somewhat remiss in not letting their support be known to the men—a situation they intend to correct."[55] Chandler also said that the city would recognize the police union, however regretfully. "If they bring over enough signed cards we will appoint a negotiating team," Chandler said. He gave the impression, however, that he was not looking forward to naming the team.[56]

Russell X. Thompson, the Memphis Police Association attorney, felt that "a whole lot of the men" thought that there has been no rapport between them and the director. "There has been a lack of communication. He hasn't been read correctly by the men and I don't think he has read the men correctly. He has misread them insofar as his general attitude toward the job. He came in with the idea that he was going to whip them into shape without due consideration for their likes or dislikes," Thompson said.[57]

In a compromise reached by Director Hubbard and the Memphis Police Association, the two city policemen who were earlier dismissed from the department for "not cooperating" with an Internal Affairs Bureau investigation of rape charges brought against the officers were reinstated. Instead of being dismissed, the men were suspended for forty-five working days without pay. The case of the two discharged officers had served as the basis for rank and file disaffection with the police hierarchy, and especially with Hubbard. Reportedly, police officials agreed to the compromise in the hope that union sentiment in the department would be vitiated. Rape charges against the police officers were dismissed by a city court judge in a preliminary hearing. But the judge, at the time, stated that there was probable cause to seek warrants against the men for assault to commit a felony.[58]

On May 4 a spokesman for the Police Association said that over 50 percent of the eligible policemen in the department had signed dues check-off forms enabling the association to represent the men as a collective bargaining agent. "We have about five hundred plus cards signed and we will probably end up with about six hundred men. We will certify the number [of cards signed] ourselves and then take it to City Hall for approval by the mayor or a designate."[59] A month later Patrolman David E. Baker, Association president, and Henry Evans, city personnel director, announced that city officials had formally recognized the Memphis Police Association. For the present, both sides agreed to temporarily eliminate lieutenants and all first-year officers from the bargaining unit. Both sides agreed to initiate "full scale" negotiations dealing with the language of a no-strike clause and the deduction of dues from the paychecks of policemen. Baker said that in future meetings the union expected to bring up for negotiation such considerations as grievance procedures, wages, pensions, insurance, overtime pay and policies, equipment, and one-man squad cars.[60]

On July 18, sixty-five black officers in the Memphis department formed the Afro-American Police Association, Inc., in order to "deal with the problems of black officers." The police department has a total of ninety-seven black policemen. A spokesman for the group said that the association was not seeking to rival the seven-hundred-member Memphis Police Association, but to deal with such concerns as the "maltreatment of black women by white officers and the 'systematic littering of the files of black officers with slanderous letters designed to destroy their credibility.'" David Baker, president of the Memphis Police Association, stated that he was "surprised" to learn that the black officers had formed their own association.[61]

Director Hubbard voiced his disappointment with the formation of a black officers' group. "If there are black grievances in this department, then [the black officers] sure as hell have been slow in coming forward," he said. "They know that my door is open and so is my mind."

The reply from the group's spokesman, a black patrolman who is president of the organization, was: "I don't doubt that [Hubbard's] door is open. Sometimes you have to go through a chain of command to get to him, though. It isn't an easy process."[62]

The Police and The Press

In Memphis, the press had served as a "watchdog" over police affairs. The two newspapers, *The Memphis Press-Scimitar* and and *The Commercial Appeal*, and some television newsmen, have closely followed and reported on the activities of the police department during the past year. It was the news media that brought the irregularities and malpractices of the police to the attention of the public. From time to time, editorials appeared criticizing various government officials, including the mayor, city councilmen, and senior police officers, for their lack of responsibility in correcting the problems on the police force. There were editorial comments, too, in praise of officials who, by word or by deed, had asked for action to correct existing conditions in the police. The police received extensive news coverage after the disclosures of the harassment of personnel in the Internal Affairs Bureau by fellow officers in the department. For the zealous coverage of the events tied to the problems in the police department, the local press was attacked by the mayor, members of the police hierarchy, and the police rank and file. This had not, however, deterred the press from continuing to push for meaningful inquiries conducted by responsible outside parties into the operations of the police department.

Along with their routine coverage of the news related to the Memphis police, several newspapermen had done investigative reporting of police practices. Two exposés are especially noteworthy for their coverage and incisive research. The first was a series of articles written by Dale Enoch of *The Commercial Appeal,* which brought to light questionable practices by the police department in their selection process for police recruits. Writing in September 1972, Enoch reported that the department's selection process fell short of acquiring the best possible men because of irregularities. Although the police department had announced that a thirty-eight-member police recruit class consisted of the cream of those who had applied for a position, a check of the records indicated that several of the men had not received high scores in the rankings done during screening. The response by Police Chief Bill Price to this information was: "If we picked some bad ones, then we just did." He acknowledged, however, that subjective factors such as interviews by the police selection board may have had more importance than was intended.[63]

The applicants were supposed to have been judged by a total score derived from a civil service test, an agility test, and an interview with a biracial committee of policemen. There was also a second interview, one that apparently had an inordinate amount of importance in a selection process. This interview, the final step in the process resulting in the final selections, was with the Police Selection Board of high-ranking police officials. Based on the total scores of 150 applicants for the recruit class studied, *The Commercial Appeal* found that only five of the top ten on the list and only sixteen of the top fifty were picked for the recruit class. Ten members of the class were selected from the second fifty, and five came from the bottom thirty-seven who were ranked. Two recruits were chosen from a group of thirteen that could not be ranked because they did not possess an interview score and five others were not listed at all. Despite the rhetoric calling for college education among police recruits, twenty-five of the twenty-eight recruits had only a high school education.

The Commercial Appeal was not able to obtain a satisfactory explanation from police officials why thirty-four of the top fifty applicants, based on their scores, were passed over in favor of much lower ranking applicants with lower scores in all of the screening categories. However, some city and police officials suggested off the record that there had been "considerable pressure to get friends and relatives of police officers in the present class because of plans to require future recruits to have at least two years of college."[64] Twelve members of the recruit class had relatives on the Memphis police force.

In response to the stories in *The Commercial Appeal* about the questionable selection practices, Mayor Chandler announced his support for an upgrading of police selection, training, and reevaluation programs. Chandler said that the articles had "presented a fair assessment of the situation as it exists."[65] He added that the selection program should be reevaluated to "be absolutely sure that the recruits who enter each class are the best available."[66] However, the mayor stated that he was not ruling out that a man might be eliminated from consideration by a background investigation or by the police selection board even if he scored high on the civil service and agility tests and on the interview with a biracial committee of policemen. But reasons for rejecting an applicant who was ranked high in all categories must now be given. Interestingly, in the following class of police recruits fifteen of the thirty-seven members had relatives who were present members of the police force or served as police employees.[67]

Later noteworthy investigatory reporting was done by Barney DuBois and Menno Duerksen, *Memphis Press-Scimitar* reporters who wrote a series of five articles in May 1973, detailing the operations, practices, and performance of the Memphis police department. The articles were prompted by an alarming increase in the city's crime rate coupled with the reporting by the police department that fewer total arrests were made in 1972 than in any year since 1967. According to FBI figures, Memphis experienced a 22.8 percent increase in major crimes in 1972. In the first three months of 1973 the rate went up an additional 34 percent over the figure reported for the same period the previous year. No other city in the nation equaled these figures.

DuBois and Duerksen make the assertion that in Memphis the law enforcement problem is the fault of the police department and not of social conditions. While upholding the theory that urban poverty is a major cause of urban crime—as supported by the FBI Uniform Crime Reports yearly analysis of the patterns in city crime and by the myriad studies detailing the correlation of crime and urban blight—they discounted it as a primary cause for the crime rise in Memphis. First, they pointed out that according to a 1969 study by West Virginia University, the poverty rate in Memphis was the second highest in the nation, and this level was probably just as low throughout the 1960s. Why then, they asked, "has the city waited so long to begin reflecting this reality in its crime statistics." Second, if poverty and "oppressive social conditions" are the sole criteria for increases in the crime rate, then other cities with similar urban blight should also be suffering from rising crime rates. For example, San Antonio was judged the city with the highest poverty rate by the West Virginia study in 1969. But the crime rate in San Antonio only increased by 2.9 percent in 1972. Cleveland, whose poverty rate is approximately equal to that of Memphis, reported a reduction of 11.3 percent in its crime rate for 1972. St. Louis, with a large urban population, had a drop of 4.1 percent in its crime rate for that year. To this list could be added Washington (26.9 percent decrease), San Francisco (19 percent drop), Boston (8.8 percent drop), New Orleans (15.2 percent drop), and Pittsburgh (11 percent drop). In fact, of the twenty-eight American cities with populations from 400,000 to one million, only eight reported crime increases during 1972, and Memphis led the field.

Rejecting social conditions as the major reason for Memphis's "crime explosion," the authors also dispelled the argument that a population increase is to blame. Memphis's growth had been at a rate of approximately 2 percent a year, except for annexation years. This is a substantially lower growth rate than those of other cities that have shown a decrease in their crime rate. Instead, they blamed the increase in crime in Memphis to the operations of the police department and provided statistical evidence in support of their contention. The Memphis police department had the lowest clearance rate—crime solved by arrest—in the nation, with 15 percent for major crimes. A clearance rate of approximately 23 percent was the national average for large cities in 1972, with several cities boasting clearance rates of over 30 percent. Arrests per patrolman declined from sixty-four in 1971 to fifty-eight in 1972, a decrease of six for each patrolman on the street. Meanwhile, the number of major crimes committed per police officer increased from 22.3 in 1971 to 28.3 in 1972, an increase of six.

Table 7-1
Major Crime Rate Change in 1972

1.	MEMPHIS	up	22.8%	15.	Fort Worth	down	5.6%
2.	San Jose	up	11.6%	16.	Baltimore	down	6.5%
3.	Atlanta	up	10.5%	17.	Buffalo	down	6.7%
4.	San Diego	up	9.0%	18.	Boston	down	8.8%
5.	Phoenix	up	8.5%	19.	Columbus	down	9.5%
6.	Denver	up	3.2%	20.	Pittsburgh	down	11.0%
7.	San Antonio	up	2.9%	21.	Cleveland	down	11.3%
8.	Minneapolis	up	1.4%	22.	Kansas City	down	13.2%
9.	Dallas	down	2.6%	23.	New Orleans	down	15.2%
10.	Seattle	down	3.8%	24.	Honolulu	down	15.3%
11.	Milwaukee	down	3.9%	25.	Indianapolis	down	16.0%
12.	St. Louis	down	4.1%	26.	Nashville	down	18.0%
13.	Jacksonville	down	4.9%	27.	San Francisco	down	19.0%
14.	Cincinnati	down	5.0%	28.	Washington	down	26.9%

(All U.S. cities, 400,000 to 1,000,000 in population)

Source: *Memphis Press-Scimitar*, May 1973.[a]

[a]The source of the statistics in Tables 7-1 and 7-2 is Barney DuBois and Menno Duerksen's series of articles on the Memphis police department, published by the *Memphis Press-Scimitar* on May 15 through May 19, 1973. The data were compiled from the information provided by the Memphis police department; the FBI Uniform Crime Reports; the 1971 and 1972 General Administrative Survey of Police Departments in cities from 300,000 to 1,000,000 population which was done by the Kansas City Police Department; and from contact with the cities mentioned in the statistics, as the need arose, in order to clarify questionable information.

The poor performance by the Memphis police department has long been attributed to the lack of police officers by police leaders and City Hall. In this regard, Deputy Chief W.O. Crumby said: "You give me a policeman to stand on every corner and I'll do something about the crime rate." It is true that in 1972, Memphis placed in the lower one-third of cities in the number of police per 1000 population, with 1.69 officers per thousand. The median for all cities in that population range was 2.18 officers per 1000 population, ranging from 1.29 in San Jose, California, to 6.66 in Washington, D.C. However, four of the nine cities having the lowest number of policemen per 1000 reported crime-rate decreases for 1972. Another four had increases in their crime rate, but these were not significant when compared with their population growths. The ninth city in that group, Memphis, showed the only significant crime increase in 1972.

A dubious relationship between the direct addition of more policemen and a decrease in the crime rate was indicated by a study of several cities. In 1972, Phoenix increased its force by 131 patrolmen, but its crime rate increased by 8.5 percent. Atlanta added 129 men, but its crime rate went up to 10.5 percent. Conversely, New Orleans lost 48 men and its crime rate decreased by 15.2 percent, and Pittsburgh lost 74 men, but its crime rate went down 11 percent. An argument could be made, however, that cities with large numbers of police per 1000 population—those in the upper third in such statistics—uniformly reported decreases in their crime rates for 1972. The statistics for 1972 in table 7-2 show that in cities with more than three police per 1000, decreases occurred. But the cost factor is critical in maintaining large police forces. In Memphis, the expenditure on the police is $28.47 for each person in the city, compared to the median of $34.20 for cities of comparable population. In Washington, D.C., where there are 6.6 police per 1000 population, the per capita police expenditure is $124.85. In cities where there is a high ratio of police to population the median expenditure is approximately $50 for each citizen.

A more meaningful statistic than a comparison of police numbers was found to be the number of patrolmen actually on the streets, excluding all officers in nonpatrol capacities. Memphis had the second-lowest number of patrolmen on the streets, with 0.95 for each 1000 people during 1972. San Jose, California was the lowest, with 0.74. Significantly, the eight cities that showed crime rate increases in 1972 utilized less than the median 1.51 actual patrolmen on the street per 1000 population. The utilization of patrolmen was seen to have a stronger correlation with crime rate increases than indices of department size. Cities with fewer front-line patrolmen had an increase in major crimes per patrolman and subsequent increase in the crime rate.

A study of the utilization of the manpower of the Memphis police department indicated that it was "top-heavy with brass." The department had only 1.3 patrolmen for each nonpatrolman in the department, whereas the ratio among all cities in a comparable population group was a median of 3 patrolmen per nonpatrolmen. In 1972 the Memphis police department listed 577 patrolmen and 452 nonpatrolmen, including detectives, officers, administrators, and special details. The detective division, consisting of 273 men, had the largest number of nonpatrolmen in the department. The division had 48 of its members in Traffic and 26 on the Crime Scene Squad, with the remaining 199 men performing "traditional" detective functions. Memphis's complement of 199 functional detectives is larger than the median size of 166 for detective divisions in cities of comparable size.

The issue of pay is frequently raised by the police rank and file. The Memphis department pay scale compares favorably with the median scale for all cities of comparable size. Officers in Memphis with five to ten years service are paid $844 a month, which is only $3 less than the median of $847 a month. Pay for police officers in that longevity category ranges from $598 in New Orleans to $1161 in San Francisco.

Another significant factor for comparison was the method of patrolling used by the cities surveyed. Of the twenty-seven cities studied, only seven—including Memphis—employed only two-man patrol cars in 1972.

Table 7-2
Memphis Police Department Comparisons with Other Major Cities

Police Budget Per Capita		Major Crimes Per Patrolman		Base Pay for 5-10 Years Service		Police Per 1000 Population		Patrolmen Per 1000 Population	
1. Washington	$124.85	1. Denver*	55.6	1. San Francisco	$1161	1. Washington	6.66	1. Washington	5.55
2. Baltimore	$ 75.11	2. San Jose*	52.6	2. San Jose*	$1105	2. Boston	4.20	2. Boston	3.11
3. San Francisco	$ 68.98	3. Memphis*	50.3	3. San Diego*	$1078	3. Baltimore	3.80	3. St. Louis	3.05
4. Boston	$ 63.93	4. Jacksonville	40.9	4. Cleveland	$1020	4. St. Louis	3.59	4. Baltimore	2.79
5. St. Louis	$ 54.70	5. Minneapolis*	39.4	5. Minneapolis*	$ 996	5. Pittsburgh	3.14	5. Cleveland	2.67
6. Kansas City	$ 47.24	6. Atlanta*	37.9	6. Seattle	$ 980	6. Cleveland	3.13	6. Pittsburgh	2.37
7. Seattle	$ 46.59	7. San Antonio*	37.4	7. Denver*	$ 937	7. Buffalo	2.96	7. San Francisco	2.08
8. Buffalo	$ 44.63	8. Phoenix*	33.7	8. Buffalo	$ 923	8. San Francisco	2.73	8. Kansas City	2.00
9. Cleveland	$ 43.90	9. San Diego*	33.6	9. Kansas City	$ 909	9. Kansas City	2.55	9. Seattle	1.83
10. Pittsburgh	$ 40.83	10. Dallas	33.0	10. Pittsburgh	$ 875	10. Denver*	2.36	New Orleans	1.83
11. Denver*	$ 39.00	11. Cincinnati	32.6	11. Columbus	$ 866	11. New Orleans	2.35	11. Buffalo	1.64
12. Honolulu	$ 34.99	12. San Francisco	32.0	12. Washington	$ 864	12. Indianapolis	2.29	12. Dallas	1.56
13. Phoenix*	$ 34.39	13. Nashville	29.5	13. Boston	$ 858	13. Seattle	2.24	13. Columbus	1.54
14. Indianapolis	$ 34.20	14. Indianapolis	29.2	14. St. Louis	$ 847	14. Honolulu	2.18	14. Honolulu	1.51
15. Dallas	$ 31.64	15. Fort Worth	28.1	15. Atlanta*	$ 845	15. Cincinnati	2.16	15. Phoenix*	1.47
16. Minneapolis*	$ 30.23	16. New Orleans	27.8	16. Memphis*	$ 844	16. Dallas	2.12	16. Atlanta*	1.46
17. Cincinnati	$ 28.75	17. Seattle	27.5	17. Phoenix*	$ 844	17. Atlanta*	2.04	17. Cincinnati	1.42
18. Memphis*	$ 28.47	18. Columbus	27.3	18. Baltimore	$ 837	18. Minneapolis*	1.88	Minneapolis*	1.42
19. New Orleans	$ 28.12	19. Buffalo	24.9	19. Cincinnati	$ 830	19. Columbus	1.86	19. Denver*	1.33
20. Atlanta*	$ 26.54	20. Kansas City	23.9	20. Honolulu	$ 827	20. Phoenix*	1.74	20. Indianapolis	1.29
21. Columbus	$ 25.16	21. St. Louis	22.7	21. Indianapolis	$ 781	21. Memphis*	1.69	21. Nashville	1.28
22. San Jose*	$ 23.24	22. Honolulu	21.3	22. Dallas	$ 780	22. Fort Worth	1.59	22. Fort Worth	1.15
23. Fort Worth	$ 22.72	23. Cleveland	20.8	23. Jacksonville	$ 753	23. Nashville	1.50	23. San Diego*	1.11
24. Jacksonville	$ 22.00	24. Baltimore	20.2	24. San Antonio*	$ 752	24. Jacksonville	1.46	24. San Antonio*	1.05
25. San Diego*	$ 21.79	25. Boston	19.5	25. Nashville	$ 681	25. San Antonio*	1.40	25. Jacksonville	1.03
26. Nashville	$ 20.37	Pittsburgh	19.5	26. Fort Worth	$ 645	26. San Diego*	1.36	26. **Memphis***	**0.92**
27. San Antonio*	$ 20.31	27. Washington	8.9	27. New Orleans	$ 598	27. San Jose*	1.29	27. San Jose*	0.74

*Cities with crime rate increases during 1972.

Source: *Memphis Press-Scimitar*, May 1973.

In Memphis, thirty-one patrol cars are on the street during a basic shift. Each car holds two officers for a total of sixty-two men patrolling the streets. On the other hand, Kansas City, which reported a 13.2 percent decrease in its crime rate in 1972, uses sixty-five patrol cars on the street during a basic shift, each with one officer, for a total of sixty-five men. Kansas City thus has twice the number of cars on the street as Memphis, while utilizing the same number of policemen.

Poor morale and political considerations in the department are also blamed for the uninspired performance by the Memphis police. "All of the men interviewed, with the department now or who had left, other than those in the Price-Crumby faction, agreed that morale is the chief factor for the poor performance by police officers in Memphis. Politics and arbitrary management procedures at the top police echelon, they say, are the reason for low morale, and, for the city's booming crime rate," DuBois and Duerksen wrote. The exposé of the Memphis department concluded with the summarization of the department's problems as being caused by "management inefficiency [in the civil service ranks], manpower utilization, lack of new ideas on the management level [again applying only to officers holding civil service rank], factionalism within the department, political considerations, and the resulting low morale and performance by otherwise capable officers."

Shortly after the DuBois and Duerksen series of articles on the Memphis police department was written, Mayor Wyeth Chandler addressed a graduation class at the police training academy. He told the graduates that he was "satisfied with the city's police leadership 'from top to bottom.'" Of the police leadership, Chandler said, "It is the greatest it has ever been." Then he lashed at the *Press-Scimitar's* series on crime in Memphis. "If a monkey was given a typewriter he could eventually write a novel if given enough time," Chandler stated. "But if you give two monkeys a typewriter, they can come up with a five-part series in the *Press-Scimitar*." He concluded his address by urging the graduates "not to read too much, but to work real hard."

Later that summer, Director Hubbard, who had attacked the Memphis Police Association on its formation earlier in the year, paid tribute to the police union and its leadership for being attentive to increasing professional standards and the elimination of police corruption. He also stated that "there was a great deal of corruption" in the department before he assumed his job of police director. Then, he admitted it was "probable" that some corrupt practices may still be going on in the department because it is easier for officers "who want to operate outside the law . . . than it is for the normal citizen."[68]

Police and Democracy: Bridging the Gap

For an occupation to be regarded as a true "profession" requires that it have more than just status or a monopoly over a certain skill in a particular kind of work. Fundamentally, the concept of professionalism involves the ascendancy of moral values in the work organization and, crucially, the use of controls to assure the preservation of these moral values. The application of this concept to the police bureaucracy means that the police must be infused with the moral values of a democratic society and that they must be accountable to the rule of law. Furthermore, the organization should serve to reinforce these moral standards to the extent of employing sanctions when they are disregarded.[1]

Police officials are all too often given to claims of professionalism in the police. However, the term *professionalism,* as used by the police, generally implies a self-regulating guild seeking insulation from civilian control. In reality, the police are nowhere near achieving the essential criteria that could establish them as a professional group. Police discretion, the source of great power, is often "hidden" from view and offers the policeman an opportunity to obscure the legal process by behavior inimical to the rule of law. Internal control mechanisms in the police bureaucracy do little to uphold such democratic values as civil liberty and justice. Internal controls over police officials are tempered by institutional goals of efficiency and are likely to be guided by these instead of by moral standards. For example, the emphasis on arrest productivity and the clearance rate as measures of departmental and individual achievement are internal control processes that reinforce the institutional bias in favor of efficiency.

The failure of internal controls to support moral values has made necessary the availability of viable external controls. Evidence of a scarcity of external controls is an indictment of the indifference of the political system at the local level—and, in some cases, at all levels of government——to the practice of democracy. There is also evidence that police standards of efficiency are reinforced by the general public and by elected officials.

The public concern about order and safety has, in many cases, led the political system to opt for "efficient" law enforcement even when this does violence to civil liberties and the rule of law. There are also examples of public officials supporting a local police force even when it has proved to be "inefficient." This deplorable condition of local government occurs espe-

155

cially where elected officials tamper with public institutions for political and personal reasons. Parenthetically, this is done either with the concurrence or the indifference of the majority of the public who have allowed, by their apathy or recklessness at the ballot box, the public good to be ordered by those who seek private gain. Meanwhile, some opportunistic police officials have been able to exploit the failings of the political system by colluding with public officials for personal benefit.

The emergence of the phenomenon of police unions has caused not only a challenge to the existing control mechanisms over police practices and behavior, such as they are, but has also given the police political power in support of their autonomy and freedom. The growth of police unionization has been the product of policemen viewing themselves as "craftsmen" or "workers" demanding freedom from infringement on their group autonomy.

The discretionary authority of the individual policeman is seen institutionally as intrinsic to the principles of worker initiative in the police bureaucracy. Conversely, the ideal of bureaucratic practice precludes discretionary innovation by individuals in the organization. In the police context, bureaucratic controls and the rule of law are designed to constrain the behavior of police officials and are, therefore, antagonistic to the principle of worker initiative. The growth of their political power, through collective action, has enabled the police rank and file to fend off restraints on their individual initiative, as well as to challenge all other actors, either within the bureaucracy or in the political system, who are sympathetic to the needs for constraint and review of police practices. Significantly, the growth of the political power of the police comes at a time when there are scant countervailing checks on their operations.

The potential for aggrandizement has been made possible by the aggregating and articulating of police rank and file interests through their national unions at all levels of government in the political system. In effect, the police have become a powerful interest group capable of influencing policy outputs at the local level and are earnestly striving to duplicate this feat on a wider political scale by escalating their demands to the state and national levels. The recognition of the police as a potent interest group by public officials, coupled with the prevailing support of the police by large segments of the general public, has influenced accommodation of the police through deed and rhetoric on the part of political actors. While the police are developing the capability for making unitary demands on the national political system, local political units continue to guard zealously the practice of home rule for the police and local law enforcement. Parochial control of local law enforcement agencies may have become impractical with the ability of the workers in these agencies to wield political "muscle" on a far broader political scale than their atomized parental bodies. It is not too difficult to foresee a future when the local political masters of the police bureaucracy find themselves unable to control an institution with transnational occupational linkages and access to a political arena that transcends the boundaries of the locality charged with its control. When this happens, "home rule" over law enforcement will become totally meaningless. And yet, it is, at present, unrealistic to expect—or to urge—a national police organization as an alternative for improved law enforcement or as a countervailing control over a "nationalizing" craft in view of the American paranoia about a "national" police. The question then is: When and where will control over the police emerge?

The panaceas of earlier reformers whose hope for the improvement of the police was in their professionalization and in improved public relations are no longer valid.[2] It is now apparent that essential improvements in police departments are necessary in order to preserve the rule of law in many cities. Even though the unlikelihood of inducing changes in the conduct of law enforcement invites pessimism, innovations in the police bureaucracy must be pursued in order to attain order and safety without subverting justice and civil liberty. Innovations must occur for democratic values to be upheld in law enforcement as well as for law enforcement agencies to become more effective in the performance of their tasks.

Specifically, these innovations concern changes in *how the law is enforced* and in *how the agencies of law enforcement are controlled. How the law is enforced* is ultimately resolved at the discretion of the individual policeman. Police discretion—the initiative of the worker in the police bureaucracy—is the product of individual *gestalt* as influenced by the values of the institution and the craft, and the society that supports them. Changes in the discretionary behavior of police officials can occur only when craft and institutional values and goals, and the expectations of the community serviced by them, are reordered. This requires some drastic innovations in the present system of selection and training of police officers, their occupational environment, and the conditions and attitudes that prevail in the external environment. Any fundamental restructuring of the values of the police bureaucracy must begin with the dispelling of the police monolith. So long as the police remain a solidly homogeneous group, existing norms and values cannot help but be perpetuated, and the vicious circle of incumbent policemen selecting and indoctrinating like personalities will endure.

Madison's argument in *Federalist No. 10* regarding the advantages of a multiplicity of interests in society for the preservation of the rights of citizens can be appropriately applied to the police bureaucracy operating in society. A multiplicity of interests, according to Madison, necessitates compromises in the forming of ruling majorities, and this brings the actors participating in the process to moderation and accommodation. To be successful, the application of the multiplicity of interests theory requires a diversity of social representation in a group or in society.[3] By promoting social complexity in the police bureaucracy with the infusion of members of groups holding varying value structures, the police would be less likely to form a monolithic political force threatening the well-being of the community. A socially diverse police bureaucracy would safeguard the public from abuses of authority that are presently made possible by the solid homogeneity of the value structure of the members of the craft. Also important, the development of social complexity in the police would enable the craft to become more effective in its law enforcement tasks as well as in its service responsibilities to the general public. This would result from the enlistment of segments of society that have not, until now, been either readily accepted in the police bureaucracy nor voluntarily sought to join it.

Making the police socially complex means "civilizing" the craft. The integration of new civilians into the police bureaucracy must begin at the selection stage. In order to attract the best available personnel in the community, the selection process must include the means for lateral entry. Lateral entry has been successfully practiced by most public agencies and by the private sector. Unlike the police, where recruitment is only for the lowest levels and where recruits are expected to work their way up the hierarchy, it is common American practice to produce management talent by hiring college graduates and starting them out in lower managerial ranks, or by locating and attracting the most capable personnel from other agencies and putting them in positions of responsibility commensurate with their proven abilities. Major American corporations do not start all their employees as production-line workers with the expectation that a management cadre will be realized from among the most efficient of the workers. In the military, too, managers, with rare exceptions, do not rise from the enlisted ranks. They come from the service academies or from civilian colleges and universities, and it is from these young men and women that an officer corps is derived. In the police, however, the entire organizational hierarchy is generally made up of one social class, one standard value structure, and one way of getting to the top—"reading the system." The recruit enters the organization as a patrolman and after twenty years or so—with the right breaks and the right connections—he may be a twenty-year patrolman who becomes chief of police. This practice is equivalent to having an army commanded by noncommissioned officers.

To prevent having twenty-year patrolmen running police departments, lateral entry is indispensable. There is no reason why police departments should not pursue a dual-level selection process such as is done in the military services in the recruitment of officers and enlisted men. The police would not only benefit from obtaining talented resources directly for management by lateral entry, but they would also be able to attract qualified personnel for specialized and technical positions such as ballistics experts and laboratory technicians.

The European experience with lateral entry in their police departments serves as an example for the American police to follow. Civilians literally run most police departments in Europe. In Sweden, where over 20 percent of the police department personnel is made up of civilians, most of the high-level positions, including that of police chief in the larger cities, are held by attorneys. Three hundred of the top police positions in Sweden are reserved for lawyers, who are selected directly for the upper ranks. Furthermore, the director of the entire police operation in the country is a former judge, and the head of the main police academy in Stockholm is a former teacher of French. The German police have police commissioners and division heads who are mainly made up of civilians, and this includes the heads of the criminal police or detective forces. In that country, the police commissioners, as well as a great number of their division heads, generally possess doctorates in law. Ten percent of the German detective forces are recruited from the legal profession. In France, civilians hold half of the executive posts, and the director of the national police—the most important police position in France—was formerly chief of staff at the Ministry of Education. Furthermore, half of the lieutenant candidates selected in the French police are civilians holding a baccalaureate degree, and half of the candidates for the rank of inspector are law school graduates.[4]

The most serious impediment to lateral entry in American police departments is the civil service system. In most cities all jobs in the police department, including the position of chief of police, are protected by civil service regulations, forcing departments to select a chief, and other high-ranking officers from no source other than their own ranks. Police chiefs and police directors seeking to improve the management of their departments have had to work around the restrictions of the civil service system. This has been done by bypassing incapable high-ranking officials protected by civil service regulations and giving them unimportant assignments. Cities seeking to make bureaucratic innovations in their police departments, by attempting to get the best applicants for the top-echelon jobs, have done away with a civil service program altogether. Kansas City, for example, dispensed with its civil service program when the present head of the FBI, Clarence Kelley—then a former FBI agent—was hired as chief of police.

"The civil service provides a protective haven for incompetents," was the comment made by a police officer who has endured inefficient leadership in a police department.[5] The loss of the protective aspects of civil service regulations for workers can be readily replaced by the trade union activities already displayed by police unions. In effect, the existence of these employee groups and their demonstrated power capabilities has made civil service superfluous. If lateral entry were established, a clear demarcation between management and workers would exist and the workers' unions would act out their power leverage in the hierarchy by the traditional bargaining role on behalf of salaries, working conditions, and fringe benefits. In this situation, the maintenance of a civil service system that is identically applied to workers and managers makes no sense. The emergence of police unions is an accomplished fact; to preserve civil service concurrently with the unions is redundant. Even now, civil service does little more than protect the incompetent and provide a major obstacle to reform in police management. Furthermore, civil service, created to replace patronage and spoils in public bureaucracies, has been unable to curtail these practices in the police. The principle of spoils is institutionalized within police forces despite the presence of civil service.

The dual-level recruitment of police officers would mean that the majority of police recruits would be selected for the "enlisted men's" duties of patrol. However, the current prevailing requirements of most police departments of a high school diploma and, at most, three months of police training for commissioned officers is insufficient background for the responsibilities and decisions that a policeman faces daily in his work. Henry Lux is correct when he says that in the space of one to two minutes upon arriving at the scene of a crime a policeman must determine what happened, "glean these facts, take these facts and apply them to one of thirty thousand laws we ask him to enforce, and then make a decision."[6] Because of this awesome responsibility, a two-year college requirement for officers should be universally adhered to in police departments. But most important, an on-going training program should be intrinsic to the development of a police official, with as much training as possible to be done in a civilian environment. Although arrest techniques and weapons training are most appropriately performed in a police setting, instruction in community relations, urban problems, management techniques, and psychology and sociology for policemen should be conducted within a general college and university system.

The in-service training program undertaken by the Birmingham police department is an instructive model for the utilization of civilian resources. The Birmingham department participates in the Region Three Police Training Center, which employs the services of the University of Alabama in Birmingham. The Region Three Police Training Center includes the city of Birmingham and Jefferson County, in which the city is located, and the six surrounding counties of Chilton, Saint Clair, Walker, Winston, Blount, and Shelby. The training center is funded by the State Law Enforcement Planning Agency. The funds are provided the university for the employment of instructors to conduct training classes in the seven counties and for a criminal justice expert who serves as a consultant to the Region Three Police Training Center.

Dr. George Felkenes, a professor of Criminal Justice and coordinator of the Criminal Justice Program at the University of Alabama in Birmingham, and consultant to the Region Three Police Training Center, is the administrator of the program. He employs the members of the professional staff who conduct the training of police officers, and he provides consultant services to the training center and the participating police departments. Felkenes consults on all training matters and performs a task-analysis survey of rookie academy training to determine if the training appropriately coincides with actual job requirements. In addition, he spends time with the police departments in the seven-county region and gives them the benefit of his counsel. Finally, Felkenes attends staff meetings of the Birmingham police department and participates in a capacity similar to that of a deputy chief. He makes contributions regarding all aspects of law enforcement including patrol operations, investigations, training, community relations, and police corruption.

There are approximately 1500 police officers in the seven-county Region Three Police Training Center, and they are all included in the training program. The training is offered at the rookie academy and in service. There are approximately four hundred hours of training in the rookie academy and one-fourth of the instruction hours are provided by University of Alabama professors and other professionals employed under the grant for the program. Examples of courses given at the academy under the grant are Adult Psychology, Adolescent Psychology, Abnormal Psychology, Federal Courts, Police Community-Relations, Sociology for Policemen, and Introduction to Street Encounters. Some in-service courses offered by the training center are The Law and The Policeman, Handling Juvenile Offenders, Crowd Psychology, a drug identification institute, a teacher-training institute, and Minority Group Relations. As an indication of the value of the in-service training program, Felkenes received a letter of appreciation from an elderly policeman in one of the outlying counties who wrote that this was the first training that he had undergone in seventeen years with the police department.

The grant for the program was written so that every police officer in the region would receive forty hours of training a year. Felkenes stated that on almost any night in the week there are from seventy-five to one hundred police officers from the seven-county region attending a training course somewhere in the region.

Professor Felkenes believes that the relationship between the police departments and the university, through the training center, is good, and that the input the university can provide police departments cannot help but improve police operations. Most important, he feels that the superior officers of the police departments, and especially those of the Birmingham police department, are committed to the concept of the training center and the tie-in with the university. Finally, he believes that most rank and file police officers appreciate the training.

The dual-level selection process would recruit distinctly for separate levels of entry in the hierarchy, but initial entry at the lower level should not foreclose possible advancement to a managerial position. The rewards to be gained should encourage promising patrolmen to pursue advanced education beyond an associate of arts degree with the incentive of attaining a management rank if they demonstrate promise in their job and intellectual capabilities. Additionally, selection for the police rank and file should also strive for social heterogeneity, with every effort made to attract members of minority groups into the organization. Finally, the discretionary authority of the patrolman on the streets should be minimized by having first-line supervisors and lower-ranking police managers at close hand to provide continuous supervision.

Another innovative method of police selection concerns the recruitment of high school graduates desiring a career in law enforcement, but postpones their entry in the police department until they have completed two years of college study financed by the department. This selection method is attractive because it earmarks future resources in the eighteen to twenty-one age bracket and retains their interest in law enforcement, as well as prepares them for their chosen occupation, by subsidizing their academic preparation. With this kind of a "police cadet" program, police departments need not continue losing a valuable source of recruits who may have found other career opportunities, despite a primary preference for police work, by the time they reach the normal age minimum (twenty or twenty-one years of age) required by most departments for the entry level.

Inspector W.W. Wannamaker, who retired as head of the Memphis Police Training Academy in August 1973 to become the director of the Shelby State Community College criminology program, announced to the press that the Memphis police department had initiated a "police cadet" program with the help of city and Law Enforcement Assistance Administration funding.[7] The Memphis program calls for having thirty-five cadets selected from among applicants who recently graduated from high school. The cadets, screened by a biracial, multirank board of police officers, would receive two years free tuition to college for studies in criminology, a twenty-hour-a-week job paying $300 a month with the police department while attending school, and an opportunity to enter the police training academy at the end of the two years.

The cadets would be required to maintain a passing average while in school and would then be committed to serving three years with the department if they successfully complete their police training. Their education would consist of standard college courses—and courses deemed helpful in police work, like psychology and sociology. They would complete approximately eighteen credit hours in criminology. To round out their education, the cadets, while working in the department, would be circulated through the various police functions, such as communications and uniformed patrol, so that they could obtain an overall view of police operations.

The Memphis department is using the cadet program on an experimental basis. If the cadets prove to make "good officers," the program will be considered "successful" and renewed on a yearly basis. "It is all part of an effort to make the police life more attractive," Wannamaker stated. "This should be a big help in drawing the kinds of people we want."

The involvement of the states in police selection and training would be of great benefit in standardizing qualifications for policemen. At present local departments lack agreement on minimum standards of education and mental and emotional qualifications for recruits. A state police council, such as that urged earlier by the President's Commission on Law Enforcement and the Administration of Justice, could facilitate dual-level recruitment and lateral entry into police departments. The state agency could become the logical instrument for the implementation of a statewide selection program for policemen, set minimum standards for policemen along with minimum training standards, and coordinate the shifting of available personnel resources among police departments within the state in conformance with the dual-level entry process.[8]

Innovations in the occupational environment should include provision for having maximum police manpower involved in the conspicuous police field services: beat patrol, criminal investigation, and traffic control. Too often, commissioned police personnel have been used for inappropriate tasks, with the result that the police force actually performing field services has been far below the complement of men in the department. To optimize the utilization of manpower in conspicuous law enforcement tasks would require having the nonline functions that provide technical, special, or supportive services—i.e., communications, records, lab services, research and planning, and data processing—performed by personnel other than commissioned officers, such as civilian employees in the department or by contracted private firms.

The traffic function, albeit a part of police field services, does not require the same set of qualifications necessary for the "awesome responsibilities" of beat patrol and criminal investigation. Consequently, officers recruited for this function need not have the same high mental and physical qualifications, or level of completed education, as required of personnel selected for beat patrol and criminal investigation. High school graduates could well be utilized for this less demanding role and receive a commensurately lower salary. However, access to duty in the beat patrol and criminal investigation should be provided to traffic officers who better themselves educationally by completing the required college and in-service training in addition to having demonstrated a capacity for service in the more sensitive areas of law enforcement. The effect of these innovations is to use commissioned officer resources most effectively by streamlining the role of the policeman so that the best resources are used in the major police tasks of patrol and investigation.

A further institutional refinement concerns the separation of investigation from patrol in the department. One of the advantages of this innovation is that by making distinction between preliminary and continuing investigative work, the quality of criminal investigation in a metropolitan region could be improved. The organizational format would have local police agencies in a metropolitan area conducting all preliminary investigative work; if further investigation is required, then this would become the responsibility of a larger police agency, either the county or a special police district—with its boundaries corresponding with the most logical area for providing police service—for the continuing investigative tasks. This method would allow local police agencies to concentrate their manpower resources on the prime enforcement task of patrol. The efficiency of criminal investigation would be improved by using the integrated resources of a larger governmental agency with the ability to disregard local governmental boundaries in its law enforcement responsibility.

The efficiency made possible by specialization of tasks would also be gained by having technical and special services integrated on a metropolitan-wide basis. Functions that could reasonably benefit from integration include records, laboratory services, data research and planning, processing, and communications. Another advantage of the separation of patrol and investigation is the potential it affords for greater control over police misbehavior. Separation of the two distinct functions, by assigning them to different governmental jurisdictions, would tend to weaken craft solidarity and make it possible for the separate police entities to watch each other.[9]

The police, by themselves, are somewhat helpless to change the conditions and attitudes in the external environment affecting law enforcement. There is little the police can do about the social conditions that breed crime. A recent study conducted by the Council on Municipal Performance (COMP), a nonprofit research organization in Manhattan, found that hiring more police or paying them more will not "buy better crime protection." An analysis of the country's thirty-three largest cities revealed that the cities with more police per capita had higher FBI-reported crime rates than cities with lower police per capita. Furthermore, poverty was not significantly associated with the crime rates. "Instead, what seems to affect inter-city crime rate differences," said Arthur Carol, research director, "is the degree of income inequality in a city. Cities with the greatest income inequality have the most reported crime." Additionally, while income inequality was associated significantly with violent and nonviolent crime rates, the racial composition of cities was related only to the violent crime rates.[10]

Although the police are, in the main, unable to affect the determining causes of crime, the priorities for federal grant funds to law enforcement agencies have come under criticism. The Law Enforcement Assistance Administration's five-year 2.4-billion-dollar grant program has been taken to task for spending too much on equipment and consultants and not enough in high-crime areas.[11] Realistically, it is hard to imagine how the funds from a grant program such as the LEAA's can redress the debilitating social conditions found in many urban areas of the nation. Improvements in urban social conditions would require the mobilization of far greater resources and the enlistment of the myriad public agencies that are more appropriately designed to service urban problems. It is simplistic to remand serious social problems to the care of the police.

One of the most damaging activities to police morale and integrity is vice suppression. This function not only has contributed to the corruption and disillusioning of police; it also has impaired public support for law enforcement. If vice were removed from the crime category, the rate would probably be reduced drastically, for much urban crime, such as robbery and burglary, is perpetrated to support drug habits. Undoubtedly, removing vice from police control would necessitate an unparalleled maturity and open-mindedness on the part of much of the general public. The police have little influence over the social mores and norms of the community; they only reflect them.

Much police business with criminals is with recidivists, whose skills in criminality were improved in prison. Other criminals walk the streets preying on new victims while awaiting trial in overburdened courts for crimes they have already committed. And this occurs because the police receive the lion's share of the law enforcement dollar, while the courts, jails, and rehabilitation programs go neglected. The interrelatedness of criminal justice functions requires an integrated approach to the problem of crime. The police alone are unable to clear the streets of all criminals, and they are further overburdened by a geometric growth in the criminal force because of the incapacities of the courts, jails, and rehabilitation programs. Statistics show that the police solve approximately 20 percent of reported crimes. For every ten criminals apprehended, seven will commit more crimes within three or four years after the original conviction.[12] If this condition is to be changed, the public must be compassionate and intelligent enough to spend tax money not only on the police but on the courts, jails, and rehabilitation as well. To do otherwise is to abdicate society's responsibility in stopping crime and unrealistically to consign the problem to an already overtasked police.[13]

There is one area where the police can help themselves in improving attitudes toward law enforcement in the external environment. Police, through the conduct of individual officers, can earn the respect and support of the entire community by an equal treatment to all citizens, civility to the public, and helpful and courteous service to those who request it. A police force that is more reflective of the broader base of values found in the civilian population is more likely to establish rapport with the various elements in the community. A better educated, better trained, better supervised, and better managed police force encouraged to "do the right thing" as well as the "efficient" thing can do much to improve the image of the police. When all police officials practice good community relations the entire law-abiding community will be more inclined to view the police as its guardians and champions.

Even if all police departments undergo institutional innovations that lead to positive changes in how the law is enforced, it would still be necessary for the police to be strictly accountable for their practices and behavior. This is especially crucial at a time when the police exercise great autonomy in their discretion, making accountability—*how the law enforcement agencies are controlled*—a test of the American commitment to the democratic process.

Present-day control mechanisms have been for the most part ineffective. Civil accountability as exercised by local government has been impeded, on the one hand, by a vacuum in political power, allowing an excessive number of competing public officials to fragment the control over bureaucratic agencies or, on the other hand, by instances of reluctance by public officials to force police accountability even when the departments badly need to be made accountable for their practices. Judicial controls often are hampered by an overdependence on maintaining the good will of the police bureaucracy for the sake of the symbiotic interrelatedness of the criminal justice system. The press, which in many communities has served as a "watch dog" over police activities and practices, has not always been allowed free expression. Additionally, the press suffers from a credibility gap with some members of the public. The internal investigatory arms of police departments, as presently constituted, have been pretty much useless as internal controls over police malpractice. Finally, many citizens, either by their indifference or because they support the "men in blue" no matter what, have not demanded police accountability.

Despite many obstacles to imposing adequate control upon the police, and in view of the inadequacies of existing channels, the need for police accountability is crucial in a democracy, and the absence of effective controls means that new institutional innovations must be created. Internally, bureaucratic "checks and balances" would be gained by separating patrol and investigation. Also, the infusion of civilians in the top levels of management in the hierarchy would, undoubtedly, serve to energize the internal affairs bureaus of the departments to act as agencies of control, a function for which they were designed. Managers reflecting the democratic values of society, as well as dedicated to making the police more effective, would see to the maintenance of realistic internal controls.

Even if civilians achieved control of the bureaucracy and were able to promulgate institutional reforms, there would still be no guarantee that police malpractice would never occur. Consequently, "someone must watch the watcher,"[14] and this requires effective external controls with the general public having access to police affairs, especially as they relate to internal investigations of complaints and disciplinary action against officers resulting from the complaints. Obviously, there is a need for either civilian review boards or an ombudsman, a person or office, originally created in Scandinavian countries, empowered to obtain redress against administrative abuse. Civilian review boards can only be viable so long as they possess an adequate investigative staff and are representative of the community. The current practice of having the members of the board made up of city hall political appointees should be replaced by a method of appointment that would allow broad representation to include the intelligent and concerned citizens of the community. The ombudsman, an alternative to the civilian review board, must also have an adequate investigative staff. He must, under no circumstances, be a political appointee. Furthermore, his professional qualifications for the position should be certified by such institutions as the local bar association and/or the university in the area. He should be empowered with the capability to not only investigate citizen complaints against the police, but also to initiate investigations in his own right. While the civilian review board or the ombudsman would act in an advisory capacity to the police department, in the investigation of police malpractice and disciplinary action, their counsel should have a bearing upon the disposition of those cases by police officials.

The civilianizing of the police bureaucracy would provide a democratic administrative structure based upon formal and standardized rules and procedures. The democratization of the police should also allow policemen to take part in the decision making. Police unions, in addition to their legitimate trade union concerns about wages, working conditions, and fringe benefits, could also play a role in professionalizing the occupation. The application of European examples is appropriate in this matter. In Sweden, there are joint management boards with craft union representation; the German police use employee councils; in Great Britain there are police representatives on a police council that advises and negotiates with the Home Secretary; and policemen in France choose almost half of the membership of police promotion and disciplinary boards.[15] Some of these practices could well be adopted in this country.

Furthermore, some aspects of the "Police Bill of Rights" presently pursued by national police associations have merit and should be implemented by police departments. Such features as the requirement that policemen under investigation be represented by lawyers and receive adequate notice of disciplinary actions, and the allowing of police representation on complaint review boards are justifiable. However, the fight against the use of polygraph tests (lie detector tests) for policemen under accusation and the protection of officers "from having to disclose their finances to department authorities," promoted under the guise of restoring to policemen "the full rights of judicial due process and the safeguards inherent in the Constitution to all free citizens," do little to promote integrity among the ranks of police officials.[16] The integrity of a police officer, as the enforcer of law in society must be beyond reproach. The provisions asked for by police associations, although consistent with freedoms guaranteed by the Constitution, would make police accountability difficult. After all, when a man dons a blue uniform and a gun and a badge he becomes more than a mere citizen; he carries far greater authority than his civilian counterpart. In order to protect the civil rights of the civilian, it may be necessary to restrict some civil rights of the policeman. There is, ultimately, no constitutional right for a police officer to hold the job on his own terms.

Clearly, the major problem with the police today is political, and not technical. Police departments in the nation are badly in need of reform. So long as the police bureaucracy remains closed to outside influences and is made up of officials who cling to the status quo, little change can be expected in contemporary practices. If change is to occur, it must come from outside the bureaucracy. The responsibility for this transpiration resides with the political system and the myriad actors that make it up. Political power has to be mobilized in order to bring about a democratic police. The quest is not directed at destroying the agency of law enforcement; it is to revitalize and reform it so that it can best serve the community. There is no questioning the necessity of the police in society, but there is a need for society to examine the role of the police, and to insure its conformance with democratic practice. Police must always be made to act as servants of society, not as masters.

Realistically, prescriptions for structural innovations within the police bureaucracy and in the institutions that may hold the police accountable face a dubious future in the prevailing urban political climate. Urban politics occur within the framework of group theory that holds that problems are settled through a process of accommodation made possible by working out compromises among competing groups. Additionally, urban political organizations respond most readily to interest groups that best articulate demands and can mobilize political strength on their behalf.[17] Normally, in this political environment the initiative is with the groups or coalitions, and their accommodation takes precedence over the public interest.

The police, as a cohesive interest group, have an advantage in this milieu by virtue of their political strength and especially by an absence of an equally cohesive and compelling countervailing group. Unless reform is instigated in the bureaucracy itself—and few indications justify optimism—the prospects for innovation are dim, because political institutions have shown little capacity to induce changes in police practices and accountability.

Additionally, the characteristically decentralized nature of political authority found in a great many urban municipalities allows interest groups to bargain with public officials on the basis of reciprocating support. This has provided the police bureaucracy with a leverage in its relationship with political institutions and actors that need to rely on the police for support.

Police autonomy is also aided by the prevailing political culture that assumes that fundamental political problems can be treated administratively and turns these over to technical "experts" for solution.[18] Once the police have been acknowledged as "expert" in all matters of law enforcement, the public and political institutions have avoided involvement by deferring judgment on these questions to the police. The supposition is that the treatment of related problems in a technical and impersonal way by a designated bureaucracy will result in having public policy administered fairly and efficiently. In practice, this belief has little validity. Public agencies are far more devoted to insuring their own interest, often at the expense of any larger, public interest. The police are by no means innocent of this practice.

In view of the realities of urban politics, it is clear that the maintenance of the status quo in the police decidedly has the upper hand. This tendency can only be redressed if the issues of *how the law is enforced* and *how the agencies of law enforcement are made accountable* become subjects of public interest and essential policy considerations. Most significantly, responsible citizens groups and political actors must join to articulate their concern about law enforcement issues and vie for the attention and "favors" of the political system. The press—all of the communications media—can play an important role by alerting the public, and public officials, to the need for reform in police forces. Change in the police bureaucracy will only occur when the political influence of the police as an interest group can be equaled—or bettered—by a challenging group or coalition.

Admittedly, groups have arisen to challenge police autonomy. This has especially occurred with some frequency in minority communities and among counterculture groups, where dissatisfaction with the police is greatest. However, much of their activity—their goals and their tactics of political "confrontation"—have been counterproductive and have alienated the majority of the public. The fallacy of most of these efforts to date at achieving so-called "community control" of the police is that they intend, either implicitly or explicitly, the dismemberment of the police to the detriment of effective law enforcement. American society cannot afford to have its police emasculated. Instead, what is needed is a police capable of maintaining order and safety, while responsive to democratic principles. To abuse the police is to invite anarchy; to reform the police is to seek the public interest.

The political influence of minority groups, especially of black citizen groups gains in importance not only in proportion to their coercive acts, but also because of demographic trends in many American cities. Blacks have already become the majority in several cities—Washington, Newark, Atlanta, and Gary, Indiana—and it is projected that they will attain an ethnic plurality in a number of other major cities—New Orleans, Richmond, Chicago, Oakland, Baltimore, Cleveland, Detroit, Philadelphia, and St. Louis—by the 1980s.[19] Furthermore, their power base, anchored in their large numbers, is made real by the practices of racial-bloc voting and racial interest organization. Public officials, including the police, are fast becoming aware of the political influence of minority groups, and such innovations as community relations programs were initiated in response to pressure mounted from the black community. Urban police officials can anticipate more demands on them from the black community, especially if they remain fixed against further needed bureaucratic innovations. Whether police forces can be improved and made to serve the public interest better will depend on the willingness of public officials to plan and implement needed reforms, and on groups growing in political power to act responsibly if, or when, they gain control over the police.

At present, efforts directed at controlling the police—civilian review boards and community controlled police forces—have, in most communities, become identified as minority group interests. As a result, the police have been able to muster the support of a great many white citizens to defeat proposals for institutional controls by exploiting the tensions of racial politics and stressing that public safety would be threatened by the implementation of these proposals.

A case in point was the November 8, 1966 referendum in New York City, which had at issue an amendment to the city charter that would have made illegal a civilian-controlled complaint review board. The Patrolmen's Benevolent Association, which had been the driving force behind the collection of signatures on a petition calling for the referendum, led the opposition against the review board. Aligned with the PBA were the Conservative Party, American Legion posts, parents' and taxpayers' groups, and the Brooklyn Bar Association. The coalition formed in support of the board included the New York City Civil Liberties Union and a number of labor, civil rights, civic, and religious organizations.

The surface justification for the removal of the board, as articulated by the PBA, was that the board threatened police efficiency and morale. On the other side, the pro-board coalition maintained that the civilian review agency was needed to "restore" public confidence in the police.

But underneath the surface of official statements was one issue that dominated all the others—race. Because it was generally regarded by the public and the press as a means to satisfy Black and Puerto Rican demands, a civilian review board became identified as a civil rights issue. The result of this identification was to make the referendum a measure of the degree of "white backlash," that is, resentment by white voters against Blacks and rights for Blacks.[20]

The vote in the referendum was 1,313,161 to abolish civilian review and 765,468 to retain the board. The vote pretty much went along racial lines, with blacks overwhelmingly favoring civilian review, and whites voting against it.[21]

From this example it is evident that the politics of race has an important bearing on public policy and voting behavior regarding law enforcement in urban areas. The exacerbation of the white-black racial dichotomy has been a useful device enabling the police and their allies to preserve police autonomy. So long as police reform and accountability can be labeled as solely beneficial to minority groups, to the detriment of public order, the maintenance of the status quo in police service is likely to obtain the support of a majority of the white citizenry. And so long as innovations in police practice and accountability are sought only by minority groups and their allies, the labeled association is confirmed.

Even without the support of whites in urban areas, the emerging phenomenon of the "blackening" of our cities has the potential for tipping the electoral scales in favor of the developing black majorities in a number of large municipalities. How prudently the black majority and its allies exercise their growing political power will have a direct consequence on the nature and style of law enforcement in some urban areas in the near future. A vendetta directed at police forces, or a style of law enforcement that gives comfort to lawbreakers, as urged by some irresponsible groups, would make life in these cities untenable. Decent people of all colors would then urgently try to seek refuge elsewhere, if they can. Those who are blocked from moving away from the city because of race, or income limitations would be forced to endure a hazardous existence, a condition far beyond the scope of present physical dangers found in contemporary urban life.

But to allow police forces to act on their own terms, and in their own interest, is to tempt oppression and an urban reality that is a mockery of democratic principles and human decency. To be subject to an unethical and unprincipled police has no greater virtue than being at the mercy of criminal elements. Then there is also the vicious practice of a partnership between a corrupt police and their underworld counterparts that systematically victimizes a community with impunity. And the two, a corrupt police and flourishing criminality, go hand in hand. Alas for decency, civil liberties, and the democratic process if they are willingly sacrificed for the sake of "public order" at all costs.

The lack of integrity in police forces is symptomatic of, and abetted by, a general degeneration of integrity in government. Corrupt police are the instruments of a corrupt political regime. Unhappily, the prevalence of this kind of relationship bares some of the rottenness in the American political system. A summary report on "integrity in government" was released on August 9, 1973 by the National Advisory Commission on Criminal Justice, which felt compelled to discuss this issue because "the American public believes there is 'widespread corruption' among public officials at all levels of government."[22] The commission established by the Nixon administration to design a national program against street crime charged that government corruption "stands as a serious impediment to the task of reducing criminality in America." The commission stated that corruption in government is a serious concern not only because it results "in a staggering cost to the American taxpayer," but, crucially, it breeds further crime by providing a model of lawlessness "that undermines an acceptable rule of law." The committee's conclusion was that as long as official corruption flourished, "the war against crime will be perceived by many as a war of the powerful against the powerless; 'law and order' will be a hypocritical rallying cry and 'equal justice under law' will be an empty phrase."

Appendix
The Police-Civilian
Opinion Poll

Sample questions used in the survey described in Chapter 5:[a]

001. What is your age? (*Check One*)

a. Under 25 ☐   f. 45-49 ☐
b. 25-29 ☐   g. 50-54 ☐
c. 30-34 ☐   h. 55-59 ☐
d. 35-39 ☐   i. 60 & over ☐
e. 40-44 ☐

002. Are you married now and living with your husband or wife—or are you single, divorced, separated, or what? (*Check One*)

a. ☐ Married   d. ☐ Separated
b. ☐ Widowed   e. ☐ Single
c. ☐ Divorced   f. ☐ Common-law

003. What is your ethnic origin? (*Check One*)

a. ☐ White   d. ☐ Indian
b. ☐ Black   e. ☐ Oriental
c. ☐ Puerto Rican   f. ☐ Mexican-American

004. How many years of education did your father complete? (*Check One*)

a. None ☐
b. Grade school only ☐
c. Some high school ☐
d. Completed high school ☐
e. Completed high school, plus other noncollege study ☐
f. Some college, but no degree ☐
g. College bachelor's (4-year) degree ☐
h. College bachelor's degree, plus master's degree ☐
i. College bachelor's degree, plus Ph.D. or other professional degree ☐

005. How many years of education did your mother complete? (*Check One*)

a. None ☐

---

[a]Only the questions that are germane to the study in chapter 5 are included here. The original questionnaire was somewhat lengthier. Some of the questions originated in Nelson A. Watson and James W. Sterling, *Police and their Opinions*, (Washington, D.C.: International Association of Chiefs of Police, 1969).

b. Grade school only ☐
c. Some high school ☐
d. Completed high school ☐
e. Completed high school, plus other noncollege study ☐
f. Some college, but no degree ☐
g. College bachelor's (4-year) degree ☐
h. College bachelor's plus master's degree ☐
i. College bachelor's plus Ph.D. or other professional degree ☐

006. About what do you think your total family income (before taxes) was for yourself and your immediate family for last year. If you are dependent upon your parents for most of your support, indicate your parents' income. (*Check the blank space that corresponds to the correct income category.*)

a. ☐ Under $1,000
b. ☐ $1,000-1,999
c. ☐ $2,000-2,999
d. ☐ $3,000-3,999
e. ☐ $4,000-4,999
f. ☐ $5,000-5,999
g. ☐ $6,000-6,999
h. ☐ $7,000-7,999
i. ☐ $8,000-8,999
j. ☐ $9,000-9,999
k. ☐ $10,000-11,999
l. ☐ $12,000-14,999
m. ☐ $15,000-19,999
n. ☐ $20,000-24,999
o. ☐ $25,000-49,000
p. ☐ $50,000 and over

007. How many years of education have you completed? (*Check One*)

a. ☐ None
b. ☐ Grade school only
c. ☐ Some high school
d. ☐ Completed high school
e. ☐ Completed high school, plus some other *noncollege* study
f. ☐ Some college, but no degree
g. ☐ College bachelor's (4-year) degree
h. ☐ College bachelor's plus master's degree
i. ☐ College bachelor's plus Ph.D. or other professional degree

008. Please indicate below the answer that most closely reflects your church attendance, or your position with respect to religion. (*Check One*)

a. Catholic ☐
b. Jewish ☐
c. No organized church ☐
d. No church ☐
e. Baptist ☐
f. Methodist ☐
g. Presbyterian ☐
h. Episcopalian ☐
i. Church of Christ ☐
j. Other Protestant ☐

009. Would you say you go to church regularly, often, seldom, never?

    a. ☐ Regularly   c. ☐ Seldom
    b. ☐ Often   d. ☐ Never

010. Please indicate below your sex:

    a. ☐ Female   b. ☐ Male

011. American social scientists have made studies that indicate that there are several major social classes in our society. In which of the following social classes would you say that *your* family belongs? (*Just check one*).

    a. ☐ Upper   d. ☐ Lower-Middle
    b. ☐ Upper-Middle   e. ☐ Working
    c. ☐ Middle-Middle   f. ☐ Lower

012. In which of the following occupational areas are you employed? (*Check One*)

    a. ☐ Professional, technical, or the like.
    b. ☐ Manager, official, proprietor (except farm), retail trade.
    c. ☐ Clerical, clerk, secretarial, salesman, sales worker.
    d. ☐ Craftsman, foreman, mechanic, or the like.
    e. ☐ Machinery operator, driver, or the like.
    f. ☐ Private household worker, service worker, military, police, etc.
    g. ☐ Laborer (except farm or mine), teamster, warehouseman, or the like.
    h. ☐ Farmer, farm manager, farm foremen or worker, or the like.
    i. ☐ Other:

013. Which of the following best describes you? (*Check One*)

    a. ☐ Employed
    b. ☐ Unemployed, laid off, or sick
    c. ☐ Retired
    d. ☐ Permanently disabled (under 65)
    e. ☐ Housewife
    f. ☐ Student
    g. ☐ Other (specify)

014. Generally speaking, which of the following would you say is the best way to describe your own identification with one of the political

parties in the country at the present time? Do you consider yourself to be: (*Check One*)

a. ☐ Strong Democrat
b. ☐ Not very strong Democrat
c. ☐ Independent, closer to the Democratic Party
d. ☐ Independent
e. ☐ Independent, closer to the Republican Party
f. ☐ Not very strong Republican
g. ☐ Strong Republican
h. ☐ American Party
i. ☐ Other minority party: (Please name)

015. Suppose you had to classify yourself as either a conservative, liberal, or moderate. Which would you say you are? (*Check One*)

a. ☐ Conservative
b. ☐ Liberal
c. ☐ Moderate
d. ☐ Other (please specify)

Policemen Only: Answer the Following Questions:

016. Which of the following categories best describes your present position with the Memphis Police Department?

a. ☐ New to the Memphis police force.
b. ☐ Reservist.

017. If you answered "a" to question 016, in which of the following occupational areas were you formerly employed? (*Check One*)

a. ☐ Professional, technical, or the like.
b. ☐ Clerical, clerk, secretarial, salesman, salesworker.
c. ☐ Manager, official, proprietor (except farm, retail trade.
d. ☐ Craftsman, foreman, mechanic, or the like.
e. ☐ Machinery operator, driver, or the like.
f. ☐ Private household worker, service worker, military, etc.
g. ☐ Laborer (except farm or mine), teamster, warehouseman, or the like.
h. ☐ Farmer, farm manager, farm foreman, or the like.
i. ☐ Other:

018. How many years did you spend in the above mentioned occupation?

a. ☐ Less than one year   e. ☐ 11-15
b. ☐ 1-3   f. ☐ 16-20
c. ☐ 4-6   g. ☐ 21-25
d. ☐ 7-10   h. ☐ 26 or more

019. Do you have any relatives in the Memphis Police Department?

a. ☐ No
b. ☐ My husband/wife
c. ☐ My child
d. ☐ My brother/sister
e. ☐ Parent
f. ☐ Specify other:

020. Total years of police experience, if any?

a. ☐ less than one year   e. ☐ 11-15
b. ☐ 1-3   f. ☐ 16-20
c. ☐ 4-6   g. ☐ 21-25
d. ☐ 7-10   h. ☐ 26 or more

021. In what aspect of police service would you prefer to work? (*Check One*)

a. ☐ Patrol
b. ☐ Detective
c. ☐ Juvenile
d. ☐ Training
e. ☐ Communications
f. ☐ Highway Patrol
g. ☐ Traffic
h. ☐ Lock-up/Detention
i. ☐ Administration
j. ☐ Other (Please specify)

Now we would like you to read (in the statements below) some of the different things that have been widely used in a large number of attitude and opinion surveys by others in this country and to tell us whether you agree or disagree with them. Just read each of the following statements one at a time, and *check the answer that's closest to how you feel.* By that we mean when you read each of the statements, just check the one of the four boxes that indicates whether you *"agree a lot," "agree a little," "disagree a little,"* or *"disagree a lot."*

	Agree A Lot	Agree A Little	Disagree A Little	Disagree A Lot
022. Good police work requires that officers concern themselves with the consequences of crime and not its roots or causes.				
023. Court decisions on interrogating suspects will undoubtedly result in fewer solutions of criminal cases.				
024. The good policeman is one who gives his commanding officer unquestioning obedience.				
025. In sections of the city, physical combat skills are more important to the policeman on the beat than book learning and a courteous manner.				
026. Since ours is a government "of the people, by the people, and for the people," the public has a right to pass judgment on the way police are doing their jobs.				
027. The trouble with psychology and sociology is that they are not related to the everyday realities of the policeman's job.				
028. It is absolutely essential for police officers to learn how to do their work in compliance with court decisions.				
029. The way a police officer handles an arrest has a great effect on the image of a police department in the community.				
030. All citizens encountered by the police should be treated with the same degree of courtesy and respect.				

	Agree A Lot	Agree A Little	Disagree A Little	Disagree A Lot
031. We should use the death penalty for felonies where the victim loses his life.				
032. If a protestor calls policemen pigs, the police have every right to use physical retaliation.				
033. The people who say they are intellectuals would be better off using common sense.				
034. Being poor does not provide any sort of explanation for the high incidence of crimes committed by the poor.				
035. The most effective measure of police professionalism is a reduction in the crime rate.				
036. Police operations should be the concern of police professionals and not be subject to pressure from politicians and citizens.				
037. Civilian police boards are more effective than police internal affairs bureaus in controlling police malpractice.				
038. Because of the nature of his work, a policeman should have a better than average understanding of values such as justice, freedom and dignity.				
039. The most effective way to improve police professionalism is to introduce new technical innovations, modern management systems, and effective allocation of police manpower.				

Included with this questionnaire on the next sheet of instructions is a device that has been used in a large number of surveys.

If you have a *warm* feeling toward a group, or feel favorably toward it, you would give it a score somewhere between 6 and 9.

If you don't feel very favorable toward some of these groups, you would place them somewhere between 1 and 4 on the "thermometer."

We would like you to use the scale to indicate your feeling toward the groups and people listed on the next page. For each group, just *write in the blank space the number that corresponds to your feelings* about that particular group. If you just don't know or feel anything at all about that group or person, just check 5.

"Feeling Thermometer" Used to Measure Direction and Intensity of Feeling:

9 = Very warm or favorable feeling about group.
8 = Good warm or favorable feeling about the group.
7 = Fairly warm or favorable feeling about the group.
6 = A bit more warm or favorable than cold feeling.
5 = No feeling at all about group. Don't know much about them.
4 = A bit more cold or unfavorable feeling.
3 = Fairly cold or unfavorable feeling.
2 = Quite cold or unfavorable feeling.
1 = Very cold or unfavorable feeling.

040. Our first group is the American Legion. Where would you place them on the "feeling thermometer?" Just write in the blank space beside the group the number of "degrees" that best indicates your feelings toward this group. Then repeat this procedure for all the other groups, writing in the blank space beside each group the number of degrees that best indicates your feelings toward each separate group.

a. ☐ American Legion
b. ☐ Labor unions
c. ☐ Black Panthers
d. ☐ College professors
e. ☐ National Guard
f. ☐ Jews
g. ☐ Conservatives
h. ☐ Democrats
i. ☐ Republicans
j. ☐ Liberals
k. ☐ John Birch Society
l. ☐ Women's Liberation
m. ☐ Government workers
n. ☐ Blue collar workers
o. ☐ Policemen
p. ☐ Blacks
q. ☐ Schoolteachers
r. ☐ Ku Klux Klan
s. ☐ Whites
t. ☐ The military

041. Rank the following occupations according to which you think is most prestigious. (Number 1 to 14)

a. ☐ Detective   h. ☐ Insurance Salesman
b. ☐ Soldier   i. ☐ College Professor
c. ☐ Policeman   j. ☐ Doctor
d. ☐ Minister   k. ☐ Lawyer
e. ☐ Student   l. ☐ Judge
f. ☐ Sales Clerk   m. ☐ Politician
g. ☐ Electrician   n. ☐ Teacher

The sample for the survey in chapter 5 consisted of four groups:

1. A group derived from a sample of white neighborhoods in Memphis, Tennessee. Neighborhoods were chosen for their reputed socioeconomic and class representation so that the sample afforded a broad cross-section of the city's white community. The sample was randomly chosen in such differentiated neighborhoods as East Memphis, Fox Meadows, Whitehaven, Raleigh, and Frayser among other. (N=231)

2. A representative group of the black community in Memphis. As with the sample of white citizens, this sample was obtained by a random survey of black citizens residing in various black neighborhoods that cut across class and income cleavages. Neighborhoods sampled include the black residential areas of north and south Memphis, and the "Orange Mound" area. (N=83)

3. A group of undergraduate and graduate students sampled from Political Science and Public Administration classes at Memphis State University. (N=56) While the undergraduates were regular, full-time students, a large number of the graduates were part-time students whose principal occupation was something other than "student." This latter group (N=20) was broadly representative of the civilian community by their variety of backgrounds adding to the sample's offering of class and income groups.

4. A group representing the officers of the Memphis police department. The sample was obtained from all three work-shifts and included a broad distribution of ranks and functional assignments. (N=164)

The demographic characteristics of the civilian and police samples were portrayed in chapter 5. Table A-1 provides an occupational description of the police sample.

The total sample (N=534) was tested by means of the questionnaire, and responses from the questionnaire were converted into "order-stability"/"democratic-active" scales. The scales were intercorrelated for independence using the chi-square statistic. Tables were then constructed using the scales as dependent variables, and age, race, income,

Table A-1

Description of Police Sample by Experience, Rank, and Assignment

Descriptions	Police Sample	Percent
Police Experience		
Less than one year	7	4.52
1-3 years	28	18.06
4-6 years	47	30.32
7-10 years	48	30.97
11-15 years	13	8.39
16-20 years	7	4.52
21-25 years	4	2.58
26 years or more	1	.65
Totals	155	100.00
Present Rank		
Patrolman	124	79.49
Acting Sergeant	8	5.13
Sergeant	2	1.28
Detective	4	2.56
Warrant Officer	3	1.92
Lieutenant	10	6.41
Captain	4	2.56
Chief Inspector	0	0
Deputy Chief	0	0
Assistant Chief	0	0
Chief	0	0
Other	0	0
Totals	156	100.00
Assignment		
Patrol	129	82.69
Detective	8	5.13
Juvenile	1	.64
Training	7	4.49
Communications	1	.64
Highway Patrol	4	2.56
Traffic	1	.64
Lock Up	1	.64
Administration	2	1.28
Other	2	1.28
Totals	156	100.00

education level, religion, sex, political party identification, and political ideology as the demographic variables. The data was analyzed at the Memphis State University Computer Center using the SLAP program[b] on a Xerox Sigma 9 computer. Alpha levels of .05 or higher were used as the significance level, and only tables showing significance were reported.

[b]Sarah Miravalle, Jerry L. Jennings, and William R. Pierce, Statistical Language Processor (SLAP), Memphis State University Computer Center, Memphis, Tennessee.

The response range from the survey questions used to construct the "order-stability"/"democratic-active" scale was from ten through forty. The questions used were Likert questions with responses limited to "agree a lot," "agree a little," "disagree a little," or "disagree a lot." The grouping factors for classification into three categories was obtained by using a summated scale:

   a. Low response sums=31-40
   b. Medium response sums=21-30
   c. High response sums=10-20.

The high categories (10-20) represent the "order-stability" group, while the low categories (31-40) represent the "democratic-actives." The moderate category (21-30) was not significant for analysis of the hypothesis, but was included on the appropriate chi-square tables.

   The civilian sample's significant demographic associations with values about law enforcement, and supporting data, were presented in Chapter 5. Evidence of the police sample's values about law enforcement is depicted in table A-2. The data clearly shows the absence of "democratic-active" values in the police sample.[c]

Table A-2
Police Values About Law Enforcement

Race and "Order-Stability"/"Democratic-Active"			
	Low	Medium	High	Total
White	47	92	0	139
Black	8	1	0	9
Totals:	55	93	0	148

$\alpha^2 = 10.980$, p = .0046, df = 2

Education Completed and "Order-Stability"/"Democratic Active"			
	Low	Medium	High	Total
None, grade school, some high school, and high school.	19	51	0	70
High school noncollege study.	6	2	0	8
Some college	29	39	0	68
College, and college degree plus postgraduate study	2	1	0	3
Totals:	56	93	0	149

$\alpha^2 = 9.852$, p = .6299, df = 4

Note: Low scales indicate "order-stability" values, while high scales are "democratic-active."

---

[c] Although the police sample tables describing values about law enforcement (table A-2) are not valid per chi-square computation, the frequency counts are used to illustrate that none of the policemen sampled were in the "democratic-active" category.

Table A-3 details the total sample's responses to each question. The responses are broken down by "democratic-active" and "order-stability" groups in the civilian sample, and the police sample group. Additionally, the table shows how each group responded to each question. The categories for the responses are according to the following Likert scale:

1=agree a lot.
2=agree a little.
3=disagree a little.
4=disagree a lot.

Table A-3
Responses to Questions by Groups

Question Number	DEMOCRATIC-ACTIVE Frequency Count (Likert Scale)				Question Number	ORDER-STABILITY Frequency Count (Likert Scale)				Question Number	POLICE Frequency Count (Likert Scale)			
	1	2	3	4		1	2	3	4		1	2	3	4
022	4	1	6	23	022	50	37	50	70	022	24	23	38	76
023	1	5	9	19	023	108	66	19	11	023	81	33	27	18
024	0	0	6	28	024	59	78	52	20	024	31	45	62	24
025	1	1	5	28	025	88	70	28	21	025	55	55	31	21
026	22	6	3	1	026	68	84	24	34	026	26	68	28	40
027	0	1	6	27	027	70	71	44	21	027	55	47	36	24
028	27	5	2	0	028	128	60	9	12	028	104	40	8	10
029	32	2	0	0	029	162	37	6	6	029	119	34	5	5
030	30	2	2	0	030	123	45	24	19	030	84	34	24	21
031	7	4	5	18	031	141	30	11	26	031	139	14	4	6
032	0	0	1	33	032	30	26	51	103	032	24	13	48	77
033	1	3	6	23	033	139	60	7	1	033	88	55	13	4
034	3	0	10	21	034	88	36	42	42	034	60	27	47	27
035	2	6	7	19	035	96	69	27	17	035	56	52	26	27
036	2	1	5	26	036	126	36	32	17	036	118	27	13	4
037	20	9	3	2	037	22	38	43	104	037	6	5	24	128
038	28	4	2	0	038	162	38	5	5	038	115	36	4	8
039	10	10	4	10	039	116	71	9	10	039	101	45	10	7

Notes

Chapter 1
Police: The Extraordinary Bureaucracy

1. David C. Perry and Paula A. Sornoff, "Politics at the Street Level: The Select Case of Police Administration and the Community" (paper prepared for delivery at the 1972 annual meeting of the American Political Science Association, Washington, D.C., 1972).

2. Eli B. Silverman and Jae T. Kim, "Social Values in Administrative Innovation and Change: An Approach to Police Bureaucracies" (paper prepared for delivery at the National Conference on Public Administration, New York, 1972).

3. Perry and Sornoff, p. 2.

4. *Ibid.*, p. 3.

5. Murray S. Stedman, Jr., *Urban Politics* (Cambridge, Mass.: Winthrop Publishers, Inc., 1972), pp. 257-58.

6. See O.W. Wilson and Roy Clinton McLaren, *Police Administration* (New York: McGraw-Hill Book Company, 1972), p.5; John H. Baker, *Urban Politics in America* (New York: Charles Scribner's Sons, 1971), pp. 242-43; David L. Norrgard, *Regional Law Enforcement: A Study of Intergovernmental Cooperation and Coordination* (Chicago: Public Administration Service, 1969), p. 2.

7. See Silverman and Kim, p. 6; Baker, p. 343; see William A. Westley, *Violence and the Police: A Sociological Study of Law, Custom, and Morality* (Cambridge, Mass.: The M.I.T. Press, 1970).

8. Ramsey Clark, *Crime in America: Observations on Its Nature, Causes, Prevention and Control* (New York: Simon and Schuster, A Touchstone Book, 1971), p. 139.

9. Abraham S. Blumberg, *Criminal Justice* (Chicago: Quadrangle Books, 1970), p. xxiii.

10. Perry and Sornoff, p. 13.

11. Baker, p. 345.

12. Bruce Smith, *Police Systems in the United States* (New York: Harper & Brothers, 1960), p. 19.

13. Silverman and Kim, p. 7.

14. Jerome H. Skolnick, *Justice Without Trial: Law Enforcement in Democratic Society* (New York: John Wiley & Sons, Inc., 1966), p. 235.

15. Ronald Kahn, "Conflict Theory and Bureaucratic Change in Urban

Politics: The Case of Police Accountability in New York City, 1953-1970,'' (paper prepared for delivery at the annual meeting of the American Political Science Association, Washington, D.C., 1972), p. 43.

16. Nicos P. Mouzelis, *Organization and Bureaucracy* (Chicago: Aldine Publishing Co., 1968), p. 10.

17. Perry and Sornoff, p. 3.

18. Emmette S. Redford, *Democracy in the Administrative State* (New York: Oxford University Press, 1969).

19. The rationale concerning a democratic police force is provided in the Royal Commission Report on the Police Command, 1728 (London: Her Majesty's Stationery Office, 1962), p. 45.

20. This argument was expressed during interviews with a number of police officials in various police departments.

21. Skolnick, pp. 3-4.

22. *Ibid.*

23. Pete Hamill, "Patrick V. Murphy: The Future of a Law-and-Order Liberal," *New York,* October 4, 1971, p. 35.

24. Skolnick and Ernest Jerome Hopkins, *Our Lawless Police* (New York: The Viking Press, 1931).

25. Rodney Stark, *Police Riots: Collective Violence and Law Enforcement* (Belmont, Calif.: Focus Books, published by Wadsworth Publishing Company, 1972), p. 55.

26. *Ibid.,* p. 61.

27. Fred J. Cook, "The Pusher Cop: The Institutionalizing of Police Corruption," *New York,* August 16, 1971, p. 22.

28. *Ibid.*

29. *Ibid.,* p. 30.

30. *Ibid.,* p. 26.

31. Hamill, p. 34.

32. Cook, p. 30.

33. *The Commercial Appeal,* Memphis, Tennessee, April 2, 1973, p. 3.

34. Captain James C. Parsons, "Police Community Relations: A Candid Analysis of the Problem" (unpublished paper, Birmingham, Alabama, 1972), p. 4. In 1972, when he wrote this paper, Chief Parsons held the rank of police captain.

35. *Memphis Press-Scimitar,* August 7, 1972. The subsequent dialogue attributed to the police officer was obtained from this article.

36. Cook, p. 30.

37. *Ibid.*

38. Silverman and Kim, p. 21.

39. *Ibid.,* p. 23, quoting George Berkley, "The European Police: Challenge and Change," *Public Administration Review,* 28:5 (September-October 1968), p. 427.

40. *Ibid.,* p. 424.

41. Silverman and Kim, p. 25.

Chapter 2
Everything You Wanted To Ask About the Police But Were
Afraid to Know

1. A.Didrick Castberg, "The Exercise of Discretion in the Administration of Justice," (paper prepared for delivery at the 1972 annual meeting of the American Political Science Association, Washington, D.C., September 5-9, 1972), p. 2.

2. *Ibid,* pp. 5-6. The physical requirements referred to serve to exclude Orientals and Mexican-Americans from police departments.

3. James F. Ahern, *Police in Trouble: Our Frightening Crisis in Law Enforcement* (New York: Hawthorn Books, Inc., 1972), pp. 4-5.

4. William A. Westley, *Violence and the Police: A Sociological Study of Law, Custom, and Morality* (Cambridge, Mass.: The M.I.T. Press, 1970), p. 189.

5. Castberg, p. 8.

6. Westley, p. 35.

7. *Ibid.,* p. 42.

8. Harold K. Becker, *Issues in Police Administration* (Metuchen, N.J.: The Scarecrow Press, Inc., 1970), p. 27.

9. Ahern, pp. 28-29.

10. Jerome H. Skolnick, *Justice Without Trial: Law Enforcement in a Democratic Society* (New York: John Wiley & Sons, Inc., 1966), p. 236.

11. Murray S. Stedman, Jr., *Urban Politics* (Cambridge, Mass.: Winthrop Publishers, Inc., 1972), p. 263; William A. Westley, p. xvi-xvii.

12. Richard A. Compton, "The Need for Higher Education in the Improvement of the Police Officer's Status," in Charles H. Newton and Arthur J. Crowns, Jr., (eds.) "Mutual Responsibility in Community Relations," *Proceedings of the Third Annual Law Enforcement Institute,* May 22-25, 1968. (Published by the Department of Sociology and Anthropology at Memphis State University, 1968), p. 156.

13. Becker, pp. 26-27.

14. Sally Grimes, "Foot Patrolmen Losing Out to Red Cars," *Philadelphia Bulletin,* Feb. 4, 1971, p. 3, in Eli B. Silverman and Jae T. Kim, "Social Values in Administrative Innovation and Change: An Approach to Police Bureaucracies," (paper prepared for delivery at the 1972 National Conference on Public Administration, New York, March 22-25, 1972), p. 24.

15. Skolnick, p. 180.

16. Robin Moore, "Why They Got Popeye," *New York,* January 31, 1972, pp. 31-32.

17. Ahern, p. 27; and as obtained from personal contact and observation of various police departments and the practices of police officers and detectives of those departments.

18. Pete Hamill, "Patrick V. Murphy: The Future of a Law-and-Order Liberal," *New York,* October 4, 1971, p. 32.

19. *Ibid.*

20. *Ibid.,* p. 34.

21. *The Commercial Appeal,* Memphis, Tennessee, April 3, 1973, p. 9.

22. *Ibid.,* April 2, 1973, p. 3.

23. James Q. Wilson, "What Makes a Better Policeman." *Atlantic Monthly,* March 1969, pp. 129-35.

24. Rodney Stark, *Police Riots: Collective Violence and Law Enforcement,* (Belmont, Calif.: Focus Books, published by Wadsworth Publishing Co., 1972), p. 116.

25. *The Commercial Appeal,* December 7, 1972, p. 77.

26. *The New York Times,* March 29, 1972.

27. Gary T. Marx and Dane Archer, "The Urban Vigilante," *Psychology Today,* January, 1973, 6:8, pp. 45-50, quotation from pp. 45-46; *The Commercial Appeal,* January 14, 1973, p. 18.

28. *The New York Times,* April 30, 1972, section I, p. 33. © 1972 by The New York Times Company. Reprinted by permission.

29. *Ibid.,* March 13, 1972, section II, p. 37. Shortly after the transfer of the original resident policemen, the New York City police department introduced six new residential policemen volunteers to the press. The publicity surrounding the designation of new resident policemen was criticized by the volunteers because they felt that it would invite the same treatment that befell the original police volunteers.

30. David C. Perry and Paula A. Sornoff, "Politics at the Street-Level: The Select Case of Police Administration and the Community" (paper prepared for delivery at the 1972 annual meeting of the American Political Science Association, Washington, D.C., September 5-9, 1972, p. 36.

31. *The New York Times,* April 14, 1972, Section 5, p. 40 © 1972 by The New York Times Company. Reprinted by permission.

32. *Ibid.,* March 11, 1972, section 3, p. 14 © 1972 The New York Times Company. Reprinted by permission.

33. *Ibid.,* March 18, 1972, p. 28 © 1972 by The New York Times Company. Reprinted by permission.

34. Castberg, p. 9.

35. Stark, p. 181.

36. Julie Baumgold, "Cop Couples: Till Death Do Them Part," *New York,* June 19, 1972, p. 31.

37. *Ibid.*

38. *Ibid.*

39. Julie Baumgold, "Batman and Robin: Jumping Into Fame," *New York,* June 26, 1972, p. 30.

40. *Ibid.,* p. 32.

Chapter 3
Street-Level Politics: Police-Community Relations

1. David C. Perry and Paula A. Sornoff, "Politics at the Street-Level: The Select Case of Police Administration and the Community," (a paper prepared for delivery at the annual meeting of the American Political Science Association, Washington, D.C., September 5-9, 1972), p. 37.

2. Joseph F. Zimmerman, *The Federated City: Community Control in Large Cities* (New York: St. Martin's Press, 1972), pp. 42-48.

3. Perry and Sornoff, p. 36.

4. James Baldwin, *Nobody Knows My Name* (New York: Dell Publishing Company, 1962), pp. 65-67.

5. "Minority Police Officers Recommend 22-Point Plan to Improve Relationship With Minority Community," *Urban Affairs Today,* Michigan State University Center for Urban Affairs, 3:2 (Spring, 1972), p. 1.

6. For a thorough investigation of police-community relations techniques and programs, see Betty Bertothy, *Police-Community Relations: A Practical Guide for Texas Police Officers,* (Austin, Texas: Texas Commission on Law Enforcement Officers Standards and Education, 1970).

7. Data for the case studies presented in this chapter first appeared in Alan Edward Bent, "Toward Improving the Police Image: Survey of Urban Police-Community Relations Programs," Institute of Governmental

Studies and Research, Memphis State University, June 1972. The original data was revised and updated for this chapter.

8. "No Bull," *Newsweek,* April 16, 1973, p. 78. Copyright Newsweek, Inc. 1973, reprinted by permission.

Chapter 4
Police Accountability: Dilemmas of Democratic Control

1. V.A. Leonard and Harry W. More, *Police Organization and Management,* Police Science Series (Mineola, N.Y.: The Foundation Press, Inc., 3rd ed. 1971), p. 12.

2. William O. Winter, *The Urban Polity* (New York: Dodd-Mead and Co., 1969), p. 386.

3. *Ibid.*

4. O.W. Wilson and Roy Clinton McLaren, *Police Administration* (New York: McGraw-Hill Book Co., 3rd ed., 1972), p. 28.

5. *Ibid.,* p. 15.

6. The discussion about the influences of various local government types on our police service is largely derived from Leonard and More, pp. 14-21.

7. *Ibid.,* p. 16.

8. *Ibid.,* p. 18.

9. *Ibid.,* p. 21.

10. Ramsey Clark, *Crime in America: Observations On Its Nature, Causes, Prevention and Control* (New York: Simon and Schuster, A Touchstone Book, 1971), p. 128.

11. *The New York Times,* March 29, 1972, section 2. p. 29. © 1972 by The New York Times Company. Reprinted by permission.

12. Winter, p. 385.

13. Leonard and More, pp. 13-14.

14. *Ibid.,* pp. 11-12.

15. *New York Times News Service* in *The Commercial Appeal,* Memphis, Tennessee, May 3, 1973, p. 13.

16. "Ellsberg: Case Dismissed," *Newsweek,* May 21, 1973, p. 25. Copyright Newsweek, Inc. 1973, reprinted by permission.

17. *The Commercial Appeal,* April 30, 1973, p. 4.

18. *Ibid.,* May 2, 1973, p. 14.

19. *Ibid.,* June 25, 1973, pp. 1 and 3.

20. *Ibid.*

21. *The New York Times,* March 20, 1972, section 3, p. 16. © 1972 by The New York Times Company. Reprinted by permission.

22. *Ibid.,* April 29, 1972, section 1, p. 36.

23. Stephen Halpern, "The Role of Police Employee Organizations in the Determination of Police Accountability Procedures in Baltimore, Philadelphia and Buffalo," (a paper prepared for delivery at the 1972 annual meeting of the American Political Science Association, Washington, D.C., September 5-9, 1972), p. 2.

24. Rodney Stark, *Police Riots: Collective Violence and Law Enforcement* (Belmont, Calif.: Focus Books, published by Wadsworth Publishing Co., Inc., 1972), p. 199.

25. Nat Hentoff, "If You Liked '1984,' You'll Love 1973," *Playboy,* May 1973, p. 147. Copyright © 1973 by Playboy.

26. Stark, p. 220.

27. Hentoff, p. 156.

28. Eli B. Silverman and Jae T. Kim, "Social Values in Administrative Innovation and Change: An Approach to Police Bureaucracies," (a paper prepared for delivery at the 1972 National Conference on Public Administration, New York City, March 22-25, 1972), pp. 14-17.

29. Pete Hamill, "Patrick V. Murphy: The Future of a Law-and-Order Liberal," *New York,* October 4, 1971, p. 38.

30. Silverman and Kim, pp. 15-16.

31. Hamill, p. 38.

32. Ronald Kahn, "Conflict Theory and Bureaucratic Change in Urban Politics: The Case of Police Accountability in New York City, 1953-1970," (a paper prepared for delivery at the 1972 annual meeting of the American Political Science Association, Washington, D.C., September 4-9, 1972), pp. 47-48.

33. Ed Cray, *The Enemy in the Streets* (Garden City, N.Y.: Anchor Books, 1972), p. 302.

34. *Ibid.,* p. 263.

35. Stark, p. 193.

36. Silverman and Kim, p. 19.

37. Carl E. Heustis, "Police Unions," *Journal of Criminal Law, Criminology and Police Science,* vol. 48 (November 1958), p. 643, quoted in M.W. Aussieker, Jr., *Police Collective Bargaining* (Chicago, Ill.: Public Employee Relations Library, 1969), p. 1.

38. *Ibid.*

39. *The New York Times,* October 24, 1968, p. 59, quoted in Aussieker,

pp. 8-9. © 1968 by The New York Times Company. Reprinted by permission.

40. Seymour Martin Lipset, "Why Police Hate Liberals and Vice Versa," *Atlantic Monthly,* March 1969, p. 79.

41. *The New York Times,* December 19, 1968, p. 55, in Aussieker, p. 9. ©1968 by The New York Times Company. Reprinted by permission.

42. Lipset.

43. Aussieker, p. 12.

44. *The Commercial Appeal,* May 3, 1973, p. 43.

45. *Ibid.*

46. The information about events surrounding police opposition to a civilian review board in Philadelphia was obtained from Stephen C. Halpern, "The Role of Police Employee Organizations in the Determination of Police Accountability Procedures in Baltimore, Philadelphia and Buffalo" (a paper prepared for delivery at the 1972 annual meeting of the American Political Science Association, Washington, D.C., September 5-9, 1972), pp. 3-7.

47. William Turner, *The Police Establishment,* (New York: Putnam, 1968), p. 214, quoted in Halpern, p. 5.

48. *Ibid.,* pp. 5-6.

49. *Ibid.,* p. 6.

50. *The New York Times,* March 7, 1972. © 1972 by The New York Times Company. Reprinted by permission.

51. *Ibid.*

52. *Ibid.,* March 1, 1972 b p.43. © 1972 by the The New York Times Company. Reprinted by permission.

53. *Ibid.,* March 7, 1972.

54. *Ibid.,* March 14, 1972, p. 47. © 1972 by The New York Times Company. Reprinted by permission.

55. *Ibid.*

56. James P. Gifford, "Professionalizing Police Labor Relations: The New York City Police Department's Response to Unionization" (a paper prepared for delivery at the annual meeting of the American Society for Public Administration, Los Angeles, April 1973), p. 20.

57. Stark.

Chapter 5
Police and Society: Reflections in a Silver Shield

1. For a complete biography of "Boss" Crump, see W.D. Miller, *Mr.*

Crump of Memphis, (Baton Rouge: Louisiana State University Press, 1964).

2. These descriptions of Memphis were selected among interviews conducted for this study with a number of local residents about their views of the city.

3. See Appendix.

4. The examination of "order-stability" and "democratic-active" values for their impact on police bureaucratic behavior and innovation is a test of the hypothesis formulated by Silverman and Kim about the relationship of these social values to the police. See Eli B. Silverman and Jae T. Kim, "Social Values in Administrative Innovation and Change: An Approach to Police Bureaucracies" (a paper prepared for delivery at the National Conference on Public Administration, New York City, March 22-25, 1972).

5. James Q. Wilson, "Dilemmas of Police Administration," *Public Administration Review,* 28:5 (September-October, 1968), p. 415.

6. See Appendix.

7. The phenomenon of the association of respondents in the sample holding postgraduate degrees and "order-stability" values corresponds somewhat to an earlier study of socioeconomic variables and voting preference among the white population in Memphis. Wei and Mahood found that in the 1968 presidential election, white respondents in their population sample were evenly divided for Nixon and Wallace, with no one in that sample group showing a preference for Humphrey. The results provided by the two Memphis studies seem to indicate a preference for conservative sociopolitical values on the part of the best educated in the white population in the city of Memphis. For the earlier study of socioeconomic variables and voting preference among whites, see Yung Wei and H.R. Mahood, "Racial Attitudes and the Wallace Vote: A Study of the 1968 Election in Memphis," *Polity,* vol. 3 (Summer 1971), pp. 532-49.

8. It must be noted that in Tennessee there is no political party registration for primaries and general elections. The identification with a political party by the population sample is for the most part purely attitudinal.

9. "Order-stability" and "democratic-active" sample groups were derived by classifying tested individuals according to summated scores for their responses to associated questions. Individuals in the total sample who scored in similar ranges—high scores on the significant questions meant "order-stability" values; low scores equaled "democratic-active"—were placed in the appropriate "value" group. The classification scheme used for the grouping drew on those subjects who responded strongly on both ends of the summated scale. Those who scored in between "strongly agree" or "strongly disagree" were placed in the moderate, or indifferent,

classification and excluded from subsequent statistical consideration. The modal group of subjects for the total survey was neither "order-stability" nor "democratic-active" (N=262), but 211 respondents were "order-stability," while only 34 were "democratic-active." None of the police respondents were "democratic-active," and 36 were in the "order-stability" group. As with the civilian sample, the largest number of policemen (N=124) were not committed to either value.

Chapter 6
"Making It" in the Police System

1. The break in Crump's reign as "Boss" of Memphis was in the period 1916 to 1927. In 1916, Crump was forced to resign during his third term as mayor by the state supreme court for not upholding prohibition in Memphis. He returned to power in 1927 when he succeeded in having his personally backed candidate, Watkins Overton, win the city's mayor office with the help of the Crump machine. For a complete history of Ed Crump and the Crump machine, see: William D. Miller, *Mr. Crump of Memphis,* (Baton Rouge: Louisiana State University Press, 1964); Alfred Steinberg, *The Bosses,* (New York: The Macmillan Company, 1972), and especially the chapter entitled "Ed Crump, Plan Your Work and Work Your Plan"; and the chapter "Tennessee: The Civil War and Mr. Crump," in V.O. Key, Jr., *Southern Politics in State and Nation,* (New York: Vintage Books, 1949).

2. Steinberg, p. 110.

3. Dialogue attributed to police officers came as a result of a number of interviews with various members of the Memphis police department in January through March 1973. The men quoted in this section chose to remain anonymous.

4. *Memphis Press-Scimitar,* May 18, 1973.

5. *Ibid.*

6. *Ibid.,* May 17, 1973.

7. This quote and other related quotes used to describe the attitude of the police officers of the Memphis police department toward Lux's management innovations were obtained from the third of five investigatory articles written by Barney DuBois and Menno Duerksen for the *Memphis Press-Scimitar,* May 15, 1973, through May 19, 1973.

Chapter 7
A Year in the Political Life of a Police Department

1. *The Commercial Appeal,* Memphis, August 6, 1972, p. 1.
2. *Ibid.*
3. *Ibid.,* August 7, 1972, p. 1.
4. *Ibid.,* August 6, 1972, p. 1.
5. *Ibid.,* August 13, 1972, section 1, p. 21.
6. *Ibid.,* August 3, 1972, p. 1.
7. *Ibid.,* August 11, 1972, p. 1.
8. *Ibid.,* p. 33.
9. *Ibid.,* August 10, 1972, p. 6.
10. *Ibid.,* August 12, 1972, p. 6.
11. *Memphis Press-Scimitar,* August 15, 1972, p. 1.
12. *The Commercial Appeal,* Memphis, August 17, 1972.
13. *Ibid.,* August 23, 1972, pp. 1 and 4.
14. *Ibid.,* p. 4.
15. *Ibid.,* August 24, 1972, p. 1.
16. *Ibid.,* August 30, 1972, p. 1.
17. On November 22, 1972, the city council approved an additional $15,000 appropriation to keep the committee investigating the police alive through January 11, 1973. This was done at a time when only $5000 of the original $50,000 appropriation had been spent (*ibid.,* November 22, 1972, p. 13).
18. *Ibid.,* August 31, 1972, p. 35.
19. *Ibid.,* September 1, 1972, p. 19.
20. *Ibid.,* September 15, 1972, pp. 1, 4.
21. *Ibid.,* September 16, 1972, p. 1.
22. *Ibid.,* September 19, 1972, p. 11.
23. *Ibid.,* September 30, 1972, p. 1; *ibid.,* March 29, 1973.
24. *Ibid.,* October 5, 1972, p. 35.
25. *Ibid.,* October 12, 1972, p. 1.
26. *Ibid.,* January 10, 1973, pp. 1 and 11; *ibid.,* January 10, 1973, pp. 1 and 13.
27. *Ibid.,* January 10, 1973, p. 13.
28. *Ibid.,* January 11, 1973, p. 1.
29. *Ibid.,* February 21, 1973, p. 13.

30. *Ibid.*, April 4, 1973, p. 15.

31. *Ibid.*, July 18, 1973, p. 19.

32. *Ibid.*

33. *Ibid.*, August 8, 1972, p. 1; *ibid.*, August 10, 1972, p. 1.

34. *Ibid.*, August 8, 1972, p. 4.

35. *Ibid.*, September 30, 1972, p. 17.

36. *Ibid.*, December 10, 1972, section 2, p. 6.

37. *Ibid.*, January 19, 1973, p. 25; *ibid.*, February 5, 1973, p. 17.

38. *Ibid.*

39. *Memphis Press-Scimitar,* May 19, 1973.

40. *The Commercial Appeal,* Memphis, February 8, 1973, p. 88.

41. *Ibid.*, February 28, 1973, p. 1.

42. *Ibid.*, April 25, 1973, p. 17.

43. *Ibid.*, May 1, 1973, p. 17.

44. *Ibid.*, April 8, 1973, section 2, p. 7.

45. *Ibid.*, April 11, 1973, p. 5.

46. *Ibid.*, April 29, 1973, p. 1.

47. *Ibid.*, February 9, 1973, p. 1.

48. *Ibid.*, February 10, 1973, p. 1.

49. *Ibid.*, p. 6.

50. *Ibid.*, February 25, 1973, p. 1.

51. *Ibid.*, February 27, 1973, p. 15.

52. *Ibid.*, April 16, 1973, p. 21.

53. *Ibid.*, April 29, 1973, p. 3.

54. *Ibid.*, May 1, 1973, p. 1.

55. *Ibid.*, May 2, 1973, p. 25.

56. *Ibid.*, May 1, 1973, p. 1.

57. *Ibid.*, p. 13.

58. *Ibid.*, May 4, 1973.

59. *Ibid.*, p. 25.

60. *Ibid.*, June 5, 1973, p. 19.

61. *Ibid.*, July 19, 1973, p. 3.

62. *Ibid.*

63. *Ibid.*, September 8, 1972, p. 1.

64. *Ibid.*, p. 6.

65. *Ibid.*, September 15, 1972, p. 27.

66. *Ibid.*

67. *Ibid.,* August 11, 1972, p. 33.

68. *Ibid.,* August 24, 1973, pp. 1 and 3.

Chapter 8
Police and Democracy: Bridging the Gap

1. Emile Durkheim, *Professional Ethics and Civic Morals,* translated by Cornelia Brookfield, (Glencoe, Ill.: The Free Press, 1958), p. 29.

2. William A. Westley, *Violence and the Police: A Sociological Study of Law, Custom, and Morality.* (Cambridge, Mass.: The M.I.T. Press, 1970), p. xiii.

3. The use of Madison's argument is made to prevent the police from being bound together by a single passion or interest. Necessary to the argument is the theory of extended territory which limits groups joined together by common passion or interest from engaging in schemes of oppression. To the extent that the extended territory argument is decisive, reliance on simply a multiplicity of interests, in this case, must be tentative. Nonetheless, society would benefit from an attempt to encourage the dispelling of a police monolith that is factious by nature and thereby inimical to the interests of the society it serves. See the argument in Federalist No. 10 in Alexander Hamilton, James Madison, and John Jay, *The Federalist.*

4. George Berkley, "Quality of Modern Law Enforcement," in Jon N. Sutherland and Michael S. Werthman, (eds.), *Comparative Concepts of Law and Order* (Glenview, Ill.: Scott, Foresman and Company, 1971), pp. 24, 33.

5. *Memphis Press-Scimitar,* May 19, 1973.

6. *The Commercial Appeal,* Memphis, Tennessee, October 6, 1972, p. 19.

7. *Ibid.,* August 6, 1973, p. 13.

8. The President's Commission on Law Enforcement and the Administration of Justice, *Task Force Report: The Police,* (Washington, D.C.: U.S. Government Printing Office, 1967), pp. 216-20.

9. Some of the arguments concerning this innovation are discussed in David L. Norrgard, *Regional Law Enforcement: A Study of Intergovernmental Cooperation and Coordination,* (Chicago: Public Administration Service, 1969); and Rodney Stark, *Police Riots: Collective Violence and Law Enforcement,* (Belmont, Calif.: Focus Books, published by Wadsworth Publishing Co., 1972), p. 237.

10. *The Commercial Appeal,* Memphis, May 15, 1973, p. 9.

11. *Ibid.,* June 21, 1973, p. 18.

12. *Ibid.,* October 6, 1972, p. 19.

13. *Ibid.*

14. Stark, p. 237.

15. George Berkley, "Quality of Modern Law Enforcement," in Sutherland and Werthman.

16. *The Law Officer,* 6:2 (April 1973), pp. 16-17.

17. Murray S. Stedman, Jr., *Urban Politics* (Cambridge, Mass.: Winthrop Publishers, Inc., 1972), p. 149; the model of interest group predominance in urban politics also takes effect in cases where there are active political parties competing in an environment of partisan politics. The party is a coalition of interest groups and its role is to ratify and articulate the demands that the interests have agreed upon. The essential difference between a partisan and a nonpartisan framework is the arena in which interests compete. Proponents of party government will argue that party responsibility is the key to holding administrators accountable to the electorate. While this may be appealing in theory, the dearth of *responsible* partisanship in large American cities makes the formula difficult to substantiate.

18. *Ibid.*

19. *Ibid.,* p. 30.

20. *Ibid.,* p. 276.

21. See Lucy S. Dawidowicz, *The 1966 Elections: A Political Patchwork,* (New York: The American Jewish Committee, April 1967); and David W. Abbott, Louis H. Gold, and Edward T. Rogowsky, *Police, Politics, and Race* (New York: The American Jewish Committee, 1969).

22. *The Commercial Appeal,* Memphis, August 19, 1973, section 1, p. 15.

Index

About the Author

Alan Edward Bent is associate director of the Institute of Governmental Studies and Research and assistant professor of political science at Memphis State University. A specialist in urban politics and public administration, he received the Ph.D. from the Claremont Graduate School. He is the author of a book, *Escape From Anarchy: A Strategy for Urban Survival,* a monograph on police-community relations, and several articles. One of his consultancies is with the Memphis Police Academy of the Memphis Police Department Training Division.